The CAST IRON Cookbook

CINNAMON COOPER

FALL RIVER PRESS

New York

*This book is dedicated to my mother and brothers who ate everything
I made and to Huffy for helping me make it better.*

FALL RIVER PRESS

New York

An Imprint of Sterling Publishing Co., Inc.
1166 Avenue of the Americas
New York, NY 10036

ISBN 978-1-4351-6699-8

For information about custom editions, special sales, and premium and corporate purchases,
please contact Sterling Special Sales at 800-805-5489 or specialsales@sterlingpublishing.com.

Manufactured in China

2 4 6 8 10 9 7 5 3 1

sterlingpublishing.com

Contents

Acknowledgments

I have to thank: my grandfather for teaching my mother to cook; Cecil for always wanting seconds; the readers and editors of GapersBlock.com and One Good Meal who push me to share more, try more, and learn more; Veronica, Tony, and Elizabeth who have been patient, loving, and supportive without end; my mother-in-law for always trying to make things better and my father-in-law for seeing value in the way it was; Jen who ate her way across the country with me; Naz who shared the flavors of his country and his plate with abandon; Amy Carlton who is full of great ideas; The Chicago Craft Mafia for rubbing out self-doubt and providing support; the Purvi family and my Ohio crew for feeding me for years; the Movie Dictators for feeding my heart and killing my soul softly; Sushi Mike who showed me the meaning of umami and blushed when I cried from delight; Michael Nagrant who asks great questions; the SeriousEats.com staff for making me hungry every day; Chef Efrain for sharing his soup recipe; the Minicucci family for showing me how to make a true gravy; Anthony Bourdain for being just as nice as he is adventurous; Megan Reardon for reminding me that it's okay to play with your food as an adult; Alison for leading my taste buds through Austin; Tom and Rosa who have shared their love and knowledge of food; our party attendees for liking tater tots as much as I do; Chicago for giving me too many options; New Orleans for better or worse; Hugh and Mary Ramsey for years of lagniappe; The Kitchen Witch for pounds of research material; Bruce Sherman for suggesting I study Alsatian cooking; Dan and Kathryn who love the Happy Food Dance; Amy Richard for being just as happy around food as I am; Carolyn for her discerning taste; Señora Garcia for sharing her tamales with a grateful guera; the Twitterverse, Flickrverse, and Blogosphere for encouraging me while offering advice; and everyone else, of whom there are far to many to thank individually, for sharing their love, knowledge, enjoyment and appreciation of food with me. I couldn't have done this without you all.

Introduction

THERE ARE AS MANY theories on the "right" way to cook as there are people who cook. This book contains one set of opinions related to cast iron. The tips, tricks, techniques, and recipes found here describe everything you'll need to know to begin using, or improve how you currently use, cast-iron cookware.

These glossy black pans provide benefits and challenges that other cookware doesn't provide. And they result in dishes that taste different (many say better) from what you'll create with other pans. Cast-iron cookware requires an investment in time and care not necessary with other types. But if you make the initial investment, you'll be pleased, and may ignore some of the other pieces you own in favor of cast iron. So whether you've found grandma's old skillet that held piles of pancakes on Saturday mornings, or you've just seen a cooking show and decided to follow a food-based whim and give these pans a try, you'll be challenged *and* satisfied. After you've used your pans for a while, you may even find yourself bragging about them to your friends and family.

Cooking in cast iron doesn't limit you to grandma's American classics like cornbread, pancakes, and bacon-fried everything. These dishes are very good and you'll find many of them in this book, but Americans aren't the only ones who use cast iron for cooking. German, French, British, Welsh, Japanese, African, Asian, and South American cuisines use cast-iron pans, and that doesn't cover all cultures. Cast iron's durability makes it a great choice, no matter what cuisine you're cooking.

Even if you've never been to any of these places, or met someone from these cultures, you can create food that is inspired by their cooking. Most Americans have never been to Mexico, but taco night is common across the country. Nothing can stop you from making a West African chicken stew, a pot of Belgian mussels, or even a sweet and tangy pork dish from Iceland.

The recipes you'll find here are inspired by these cuisines, and most of the ingredients needed are available at your local grocery store.

Eggs, for example, are eaten by people all over the world, and frying an egg is the simplest way to cook it. A fried egg is basic breakfast food in America, but in Korea it would be placed on top of a bowl of Bi Bim Bop (vegetables, rice, and light pickles that are mixed together and baked), or in France it would be part of a toasted ham and cheese sandwich to make a Croque Madame. Sauerkraut is a uniquely German dish and served as a plain side dish or on a sausage as a garnish. But when baked by the Alsatian French with bacon, sausage, and beer, it becomes Choucroute. The ingredient loses the sharp, pickled flavor, and becomes a heart-warming and hearty winter dish. And all of these dishes can, and should, be made in the cast-iron pans you're likely to find at your local department store, hardware store, or high-end cooking store. The iconic shiny, black skillet is the most commonly used pan you'll find, but Dutch ovens, griddles, grill pans, chicken fryers, and a wide variety of bakeware can be found easily as well. And as you'll discover, newer isn't necessarily better. So go through grandma's attic, visit flea markets and yard sales, or shop online to find the pan that may transform how you cook, think about cooking, and how you enjoy the world's cuisines.

Chapter 1

Getting Back to Basics
with Cast-Iron Cookware

Many people think of cast-iron cookware as retro, old fashioned, or simply outdated. With the prevalence of brightly colored and shiny cookware that boasts of recent advances in cooking technology, you might believe them. But the cook *in the know* realizes that cast-iron cookware, while far from glamorous, is truly superior and can be used for cooking almost any recipe.

Benefits of Cooking with Cast Iron

No matter how appealing the television star's face was on the box of cookware, if the shiny pan is hard to clean, gets scratched easily, and costs a lot of money, you'll find cooking to be less appealing. Cast-iron cookware has a low celebrity profile, but can help you make better recipes with fewer problems.

Low Cost, High Value

Most cast-iron cookware comes in non-enameled versions. These skillets, Dutch ovens, and sauté pans will seem like a deal after browsing the aisles looking at high-end cookware. But for $15–$20 for new skillets (and often less for those you may find at a yard sale or flea market), you'll come home with a pan that will gain value with each dish you make. New cast-iron skillets cost 10–50 percent less than skillets made from other materials.

Even though we call a deep pan with a tightly fitting lid a Dutch oven, it wasn't invented by the Dutch. Cast-iron pots with lids have been used for hundreds of years and on several continents. In the late 1600s, the Dutch system of creating these pans was seen as the most advanced, and they produced the nicest pans.

The Ability to Cook on High Heat

Many non-stick and other lightweight pans cannot be used over high heat. Because the metal is thin and conducts heat quickly, they can get too hot and then cool off easily. But with cast iron, you can place your pan over high heat. You can even place your pan directly over the hot coals on a grill or over a campfire.

It Will Become a Nonstick Pan

When you first get your skillet, you have to season it a few times before you can cook something without worrying about it sticking. But once you've got a healthy seasoning base on the skillet (page 4), you'll find yourself cooking with less oil than you would in other pans. When you have a skillet with at least several months of seasoning, you can cut the oil called for in the recipe by a third to a half.

It Has Health Benefits

When used over high heat, Teflon-coated pans have been shown to emit fumes that are dangerous to small birds. So even if you're lucky enough to have a non-stick pan that won't warp over high heat, it may release fumes that could be toxic to your family. Cast iron doesn't give off any fumes and it imparts iron into the food cooked in it, even after it is seasoned. If you tend to be anemic, you may be able to reduce your supplement intake by cooking most of your dishes in cast iron. Be sure to follow your doctor's orders and get tested before changing your prescribed health plan.

How to Choose a New or Used Pan

When it comes to cast iron, you can choose new or used, enameled or non-enameled pans. Used pans are likely to come from a yard sale, flea market, online auction, or as a gift. Enameled pans are cast-iron pans that have an enameled coating, usually on the inside and out. This coating is often white on the inside and comes in a variety of colors on the outside, depending on the manufacturer.

Brand New and Dull

When buying new cookware, look for pans that don't have any large pits, bumps, or cracks on the cooking surface. These imperfections can make it harder to cook with your pan. Ideally the pan has a similar texture to that of a piece of high-grit sandpaper. The pan should be dull gray and it shouldn't be smooth. As you cook with it, it will become blacker and smoother. And finally, you want to make sure that the thickness of the bottom and sides of the pan is even. Pans with bottoms and sides that get thinner around the edge are less likely to conduct heat evenly and more likely to break.

Cast-iron pans, if cared for properly, get better with age and use because they become more seasoned with each use. Even an old pan that is rusted or covered in bumpy residue can be salvaged, and will likely be better than a new one. You need to sand off rust with steel wool, large grit sandpaper, a rust eraser, a small steel brush, or even just scouring powder. Thick carbonized residue can be removed by placing your skillet in the oven during the self-cleaning cycle. You can also spray the pan with oven cleaner, place it in a plastic-bag, and let it sit for a few days. Wash the pan thoroughly using soap and water and scrub the affected areas with steel wool if necessary to get back to the bare metal.

> You can ruin a cast-iron pan beyond repair by changing the temperature of the skillet dramatically and quickly. If you pour ice water into a heated skillet, or if you have a skillet in the freezer and then place it over a high heat, the skillet may crack.

If your pan has had paint or any thick and sticky oil stored in it, you can use the techniques described earlier to clean it. Make sure your pan doesn't have cracks, even if they don't go all the way through. Look for black epoxy used to fill any pits or cracks. It can be hard to see epoxy-filled cracks, but if you see black paint, ask before you buy if you intend to cook with it. Epoxy is poisonous and will release toxins when heated.

How to Season (or Reseason) a Pan

The interior of a new pan has a roughly textured surface, but a fully seasoned skillet is smooth and black. Every time you use the skillet, as long as you clean it properly, you'll start to bond the oils and fats from the cooking into the surface. If you have a pan with an enameled coating on the inside, it will not season. The enameling process eliminates the need for seasoning.

Seasoning the Unseasoned Pan

The first step is to remove the paraffin-like or shellac coating on the pan that will prevent your skillet from seasoning properly. The best way to do this is by washing and scrubbing it in hot soapy water. Be sure to clean every edge, the handle, and the outside of the skillet thoroughly. Dry it completely before proceeding. Place the skillet over a medium burner and let the water evaporate. If you smell a strong, chemical smell, wash and dry the skillet again.

Now that you have a clean pan, you're ready to add the first seasoning layer. Preheat the oven to 350°F and place a layer of aluminum foil or a baking sheet on the bottom rack of the oven. Cut off a tablespoon-sized chunk of shortening and rub it over the entire surface of the skillet, inside and out. Place the pan upside down in the oven. Any excess will drip off the pan as it bakes. Set your timer for one hour.

You'll likely notice a slight burning smell and see some smoke. This is normal and should not be a cause for concern. The oil you applied is smoking and the pan is soaking up the oil and the carbonization that it creates. Once the hour is up, turn off the heat and leave the pan in the oven to cool overnight. The surface should be darker, but it won't be black and shiny yet. It will take several uses and proper cleaning to get the desired appearance.

If you have a glass top range, don't drag the pans across the range. This will scratch the surface. Because it takes a while for electric ranges to cool down, move your cast-iron pan off the burner if you want it to stop cooking. Alternately, if you're close to finishing a dish, you can turn off the burner but leave the pan in place so it finishes cooking slowly.

Cleaning and Prepping the Seasoned Pan

There is some disagreement about whether pre-seasoned skillets are worth their greater cost. For the occasional cook, not having to go through the steps described above for an unseasoned skillet may make the higher price worth it. You just need to wash a pre-seasoned pan without soap using hot water and a stiff-bristled brush. Dry the pan completely, pour some vegetable oil on a paper towel, and rub it over the surface of the pan until you're ready to use it.

Cleaning and Prepping a Healthy Older Skillet

If the inside of the skillet is smooth and shiny, all you should need to do is rinse it with hot water, dry it thoroughly, and wipe it with a fresh coating of oil. If you're concerned about latent bacteria, place an inch of water in the pan over high heat. Let the water boil for one minute. Hold the pan over a sink and swirl the pan around so the hot water coats the interior. Then simply dry it and coat it with oil before using.

Prepping a Needy Older Skillet

After you've stripped the rust or corrosion off the skillet you'll need to follow the same seasoning steps as you would for a new pan. If the skillet seems dry and not glossy after the initial seasoning, it may mean the oil used in the seasoning was soaked into the surface of the skillet. It may be beneficial to run it through a stovetop seasoning step before cooking in it. Pour some vegetable oil on a paper towel and rub it over the entire surface of the skillet. Place the skillet over medium heat and let it cook until the oil starts to smoke. Turn off the heat and let the skillet cool to the touch before using.

How to Clean and Store Cast Iron

Unless you're hanging your newly seasoned skillet for decoration, you're going to need to care for it slightly differently than you would your other cookware. Because it must be maintained differently, cast iron scares away many people, but if cared for correctly, you'll find clean up time is actually faster than with other pots and pans.

Cleaning is Easier Than You Think

The main rule of cleaning a cast-iron skillet is never to use soap with it. Using soap won't ruin it, but will remove some of the seasoning that you've worked to build up. Most messes can be cleaned with hot water, a stiff-bristled brush, some salt, and occasionally a potato. A hot pan is easier to clean than a cold skillet because the metal is expanded and more likely to release what is stuck to it. Place a hot pan under running water and scrub it with the brush to remove the stuck-on bits.

What is the best way to clean a dirty pan?
Make sure your pan is hot before you try to clean it. Pour in ½ tablespoon of water and a tablespoon of kosher salt. Wad up a paper towel, hold it with tongs, and rub it over the surface of the pan to loosen anything stuck to it. The salt will help grind it away. When the salt looks dirty, dump it out, wipe the surface clean, and your pan is sealed and ready for storage.

If you have a particularly stubborn mess or if your paper towel starts to fall apart, don't break out the heavy artillery until you've tried cleaning it with oil. Pour two tablespoons of salt (kosher or pickling salt works best) in the skillet and cut a potato in half. Hold the potato like a scrub brush and rub it firmly over the surface of the skillet. The salt should act like scouring powder to help you rub off the stuck-on food. Neither the potato nor the salt will damage the surface of the pan and the potato will protect your fingertips from abrasions.

If you still can't remove the mess, which is more likely to happen with a new skillet, try scraping it with a butter knife. This may result in spots that are lighter than the rest of the pan, but these will disappear after a few uses. And if nothing else seems to help, use some hot and soapy water. This should be a last resort since it does remove some of the seasoning.

Storage of Your Cast-Iron Pan

Since these pans don't scratch, you can stack them together. You can also hang them from a firmly attached pot rack. Or, you can leave them on the stove top or in the oven, like many cast-iron users do. If you rarely cook or have to store your pans for an extended period of time, it's best to coat them lightly in vegetable oil inside and out. It's a good idea to oil newer pans after each use and pans that you've had to clean with soapy water. The oil not only keeps the pan from rusting, it also keeps the oil on the rough surface of the pan from drying up and after time makes the pan easier to clean and cook with.

Special Care for Enameled Cast-Iron Cookware

Cast-iron cookware that has an enameled coating on the inside and/or the outside requires slightly different care than non-enameled cookware. The surfaces that are enameled won't rust and can't be seasoned. With a quick wash they're ready to use straight out of the box. Because they can't be seasoned, you may find yourself using more oil than a recipe calls for. But, because the iron isn't in touch with the food, you don't have to worry about cooking dishes high in acid in a new skillet.

> An added benefit of cooking in a non-enameled cast-iron pan is that you can use any cooking utensil you please. Wood, metal, plastic, and silicone are all perfectly fine in these pans. Because the surface doesn't scratch, you can even use a regular fork for turning meat or adjusting things in a pan.

Cleaning enameled cast-iron pans is relatively easy. You should wash them with hot, soapy water. Because the enameled surface can scratch, you should use only plastic scrub-brushes and sponges.

Day-to-day care for enameled cast-iron cookware is trickier than non-enameled cookware. Because the enameling can scratch, be sure to use only wooden, plastic, nylon, or silicone cooking tools. The lighter-colored surfaces can stain fairly easy, but soaking them for a few hours in a mild bleach solution will remove the stains. The enameled surface is also prone to chipping so you may not want to stack your enameled cookware when you store it. Dropping the pans can result in chips and cracks, as can using the pans over very high heat. Because high heat can damage the enameling, it's safest to not use these pans on a grill, over a campfire, or when cooking over high heat on a stove top.

Tips for Cooking with Cast Iron

Not only is cast iron healthier, indestructible, inexpensive, and improves with age, it also gives you flexibility in cooking that other pans don't provide. The recipes in this book provide you with many opportunities to make your cookware work for you.

Dense Metal Assists in Even Heating

Using cast iron makes it easier to cook a variety of dishes because the thick, dense metal absorbs and conducts heat slowly and evenly. Although a cast-iron pan takes longer to get hot after placing it on a burner, it's more likely to stay hot when you add cold foods. The even heating also makes it great for cooking sauces or things that may burn easily. If the pan is made properly, it will keep almost the same temperature on the edges as it does in the center. And since cast iron retains heat so well, you'll find that it makes a great serving vessel.

> When cooking with cast iron and using other cookbooks, always preheat your pan if you're going to be cooking on the stove or want a crispy crust on something you're baking in the oven. This preheating step takes a few more minutes, but gives much better results.

All-Metal Construction Provides Flexibility

Most cast-iron pans are manufactured from a single, solid piece of metal. Some enameled pans come with a tempered plastic handle, and some Dutch ovens have metal handles. But as long as your pan doesn't use wood or non-tempered plastic, you can begin the cooking process on the stovetop and finish in the oven or under a broiler.

Cast Iron Promotes Crisping

Not everything that comes out of a cast-iron pan is going to be crispy, but if you're cooking something that should have a crispy or even crunchy exterior and a soft interior, cast iron is the best choice. The surface of the pan encourages food to brown and crisp better than even the most expensive non-stick skillet on the market. Even a brand-new, freshly seasoned skillet can give food a crispy texture.

A Seasoned Skillet Leads to Healthier Cooking

Cook dishes with a high fat or oil content the first eight to ten times you use a new cast-iron skillet. As your skillet gets more seasoned, you'll need less fat and oil. And because the surface and metal used in your skillet will help you create a crust on foods, you won't miss that fat. With cast iron, your boneless, skinless chicken breasts will look like browned comfort food.

Precautions for Cast-Iron Pans

Even though you may find yourself wanting to use your cast-iron pans for everything, this type of cookware does have a few drawbacks. Cast iron is heavy and you'll most likely need two hands to pour from a skillet or to lift a full pan out of the oven.

Aside from the weight there are a few other things you should be careful about when using cast iron. Highly acidic foods can often end up tasting metallic if cooked in a less-than-seasoned pan. And the acid can cause a pan's seasoning to dissolve. Make sure to use an enameled or a well-seasoned pan when you're cooking with tomatoes or tomato sauce, wine, beer, citrus juices, or vinegars.

The recipes in this book provide cooking times for cast-iron pans. Because of the even-heating properties of cast-iron pans, when you're using other recipes for different types of cookware, you may find that you need to reduce cooking times by 5–10 percent.

Serving food in cast iron makes a great presentation and keeps the food warmer longer than if you transfer it to a bowl. But never store food in your skillet in the refrigerator or on a table for more than a few hours. The acids and liquids in the foods will start to break down the seasoning. Once the seasoning starts to break down, your food will begin to taste metallic. There is nothing carcinogenic or poisonous about this taste, but many people find it off-putting.

Hot liquids can also remove the seasoning from pans if you're not careful. If you've only used your Dutch oven a few times, boiling liquids may cause the seasoning to start to dissolve along the edges. If you notice that your seasoning is worse after cooking, wash the skillet normally, then dry it by placing it over a medium heat on your stovetop and rubbing some oil into the surface of the pan while it is hot. As the pan cools it will absorb the oil and will be ready for your next use.

Ready, Set, Cook

Now that you know the basics on how to choose a pan, how to season it, how to cook with it, and how to clean and store it, you're ready to begin cooking. But what to cook?

When most Americans think of cast-iron cooking, thoughts of soul-food classics and *Little House on the Prairie* dishes come to mind. But many people all over the world use cast-iron pans, and the advantages of cooking with cast iron are the same no matter where a dish is prepared. The recipes in this book may call for ingredients you don't normally stock and occasionally may be hard to find, but even with substitutions, you'll be able to prepare dishes that capture the spirit of cuisines from countries around the world.

Chapter 2

Recipes to Cook in a New Skillet

Basic Hamburger

This burger actually tastes better when you use ground beef with a fat content of 10–15%. Making the burgers thinner creates the crunchy edges that are popular at diners.

INGREDIENTS | SERVES 3–4

1 pound ground beef
Pinch garlic powder
Pinch salt
Pinch pepper
Dash Worcestershire sauce

Variations on a Theme

Adding cheese is an easy way to add flavor to the average burger. You could also add sautéed onion slices, fried bacon, or a grilled pineapple ring. Or sauté some chopped shallots, mushrooms, and garlic and mix it into the meat before cooking.

1. Place a skillet over medium-high heat.

2. Divide the ground beef into six equally sized portions. Shape them into balls.

3. Place a ball in the skillet. Press down on it with a spatula to flatten it. Sprinkle it with a pinch of garlic powder, salt, and pepper. Add a dash of Worcestershire sauce. Repeat with other meat balls.

4. Cook for 2 minutes then flip. Season the cooked side like the first side. Cook for 2 minutes.

5. Reduce the heat to medium. Cover and cook for 2 minutes. Serve while hot.

Oven-Fried Potatoes

Almost everyone likes crispy, fried potatoes, but deep-frying is messy and unhealthy. This method gets you the same texture with a fraction of the oil needed for deep-frying.

INGREDIENTS | SERVES 4

2 medium Yukon Gold potatoes
1 tablespoon olive oil
Salt to taste
Pepper to taste

1. Preheat oven to 400°F. Place a skillet in the middle of the oven.

2. Scrub the potatoes clean and pat dry with a lint-free towel. Cut each potato into ¼" or ⅜" slices. Cut the slices into strips the same width. Cut those strips into cubes. Place into a bowl and drizzle with olive oil. Sprinkle with salt and pepper and toss so they're evenly coated.

3. Pour potatoes into the warm skillet so there is one even layer on the bottom. Place the skillet in the middle of the oven and bake for 30 minutes. Stir once or twice. The potatoes should be soft in the middle with crispy edges. Serve while hot.

BLT Sandwich

This sandwich became popular after World War II when supermarkets started carrying fresh lettuce and tomatoes year round.

INGREDIENTS | **SERVES 2**

6 slices thick-cut bacon

4 slices sandwich bread

2–3 tablespoons mayonnaise

4 slices tomato

2 lettuce leaves

Variations on a Classic

Spread a clove of roasted garlic on the bread instead of mayo, use a flavored mayo instead of regular, add slices of avocado to the sandwich, use basil instead of lettuce, or add cheese to the sandwich.

1. Place a skillet over low heat and layer the bacon in the pan, being careful not to overlap the slices. Use tongs to flip them frequently as they cook for 5–7 minutes, or until some of the fat has rendered out of the slices. Increase the heat to medium-high and cook for another 5–7 minutes, or until the bacon is crisp. Place the slices on paper towels to drain.

2. Toast the bread and spread mayonnaise on one side of each slice.

3. Place the bacon on one slice of bread, add tomato and lettuce and top with the other slice of bread. Serve while warm.

Baked Onions

These onions make a great appetizer or side with grilled meats or fish. If you prefer, you can sprinkle them with tarragon, basil, or rosemary.

INGREDIENTS | **SERVES 4**

1 pound small sweet onions, peeled and stem trimmed

4 tablespoons butter, in wrapper

1 teaspoon salt

½ teaspoon ground black pepper

1 teaspoon dried thyme

1. Preheat the oven to 350°F and place a rack in the middle of the oven.

2. Rub the onions with the stick of butter until they're completely coated. Place them in the skillet and sprinkle with salt, pepper, and thyme.

3. Place the skillet in the middle of the oven and bake for 45 minutes. They should be very soft. Serve while hot.

Down-Home Classic Green Beans

This dish is great hot or warm and it can be made ahead of time and warmed later when ready to serve.

INGREDIENTS | SERVES 4–6

3 slices bacon, diced

1 small onion, diced

1 pound fresh green beans, trimmed

1 russet potato, diced

½ cup chicken broth

1 garlic clove, minced

1 teaspoon salt

¼ teaspoon pepper

1. Place a large skillet over medium heat. Once the skillet is warmed, add the bacon and the onion and cook until bacon is brown but not crispy, about 5 minutes.

2. Add the green beans, potato, chicken broth, garlic, salt, and pepper and cook for 3–4 minutes.

3. Reduce the heat to medium-low and cover. Cook for 5 minutes. The potatoes should be almost soft and the green beans should be bright green. Remove the lid and increase the heat to medium-high. Let the broth evaporate. Serve immediately.

Stir-Fried Asparagus

Asparagus is tasty, but often expensive, even during the spring when it's in season. If you can't get asparagus, substitute green beans. Choose smaller beans, remove the stem ends, and cook them whole.

INGREDIENTS | SERVES 4

2 tablespoons olive oil

1 pound thin asparagus

2 tablespoons water or chicken broth

Pinch salt

Pinch pepper

1. Wash the asparagus and snap off the bottoms. Cut them into 1" slices on an angle.

2. Place a skillet over medium heat. Once it has heated, add the oil and the asparagus. Sprinkle them with salt and pepper and stir continually for 2 minutes until they're coated.

3. Add 2 tablespoons of water or chicken broth and cover. Cook for 2 minutes.

4. Turn off the heat but keep the skillet covered for 3 minutes, or until tender. Serve while hot.

Ham and Red-Eye Gravy

It's legend that General Andrew Jackson told his cook, who had been drinking the night before, that for breakfast he wanted ham with gravy as red as his eyes. This gave ham gravy a new name.
Serve with biscuits, if you like.

INGREDIENTS | SERVES 4

4 slices country ham, ¼" thick
1 cup hot coffee
2 tablespoons brown sugar

1. Place a skillet over medium heat. Place one or two ham slices in the skillet and cook each side for 3–5 minutes, or until the ham is browned and the fat has rendered. Remove ham from the skillet and keep warm.

2. Add ½ cup of coffee to the skillet with the brown sugar. Stir until it is melted. Add the ham slices back to the skillet, cover, and cook 3 minutes. Remove the ham to a plate and keep it warm.

3. Discard any pieces of fat in the skillet. Add the rest of the coffee. Increase the heat to medium-high, and stir to remove any stuck-on bits. Simmer for 3 minutes.

4. Pour the gravy over the ham and serve while warm.

Fried Green Tomatoes

If you have any leftover batter, try dredging some pickle slices in it and frying them.
They'll cook in about 1½ minutes and are just as tasty as fried green tomatoes.

INGREDIENTS | **SERVES 6–8**

1½ cups all-purpose flour

½ cup cornmeal

½ teaspoon salt, plus 1 pinch

¼ teaspoon ground black pepper

¼–½ cup milk

3–4 large green tomatoes

¼ cup vegetable oil

¾ cup ranch dressing

1. Mix together the flour, cornmeal, ½ teaspoon salt, and pepper in a large bowl. Pour ¼ cup of milk into the bowl and stir to combine. If mixture looks dry, add more milk until you get a thick batter. Slice the tomatoes into ¼" slices. Pat dry with paper towels.

2. Place a skillet over medium heat and add the oil. Dip each tomato slice into the batter and let the excess drip off. Slide them into the skillet so they're not touching. Cook each side for 1½–2 minutes. Remove them and place on a rack over paper towels to keep them from getting soggy.

3. While they're still hot, sprinkle with a pinch of salt. Serve them with ranch dressing as a dipping sauce.

Juicy Turkey Burger

Turkey tends to dry out when it is ground and cooked. But the same trick that keeps the Moist Turkey Meatloaf (page 286) moist keeps these burgers juicy and nutritious.

INGREDIENTS | SERVES 4

2 teaspoons vegetable oil

½ cup shredded onion

¾ cup bread crumbs

1 teaspoon soy sauce

1 teaspoon Worcestershire sauce

½ teaspoon garlic powder

¼ teaspoon ground mustard

¼ teaspoon ground black pepper

1 teaspoon salt

¼ cup shredded zucchini

¼ cup mushrooms, minced

1 pound ground turkey

1. Place a skillet over medium heat. Once it is heated, add 1 teaspoon vegetable oil and the onion. Cook for 3–4 minutes, or until very soft. Remove the skillet from the heat, and put the onion in a large bowl. Combine all other ingredients, except for the turkey and other teaspoon of vegetable oil, and stir until well combined.

2. Break the turkey up over the surface of the bowl. Use your hands to gently massage the meat into the other ingredients. Combine the meat into four equally shaped balls.

3. Flatten balls into patties and then wrap them in plastic wrap. Place in the refrigerator to rest for at least 20 minutes.

4. Place a skillet over medium heat and add 1 teaspoon of vegetable oil. Place two patties into the skillet and cook for 4–5 minutes, or until well browned.

5. Flip patties, cover the skillet with a lid, and let cook for an additional 4–5 minutes. Check the center to make sure they're cooked through.

Ground Beef Tacos

You can use flour or corn tortillas in this recipe. Flour tortillas are soft and corn tortillas can be steamed lightly to soften them or fried to make them crunchy.

INGREDIENTS | **MAKES 16 TACOS**

1 tablespoon vegetable oil

1 medium onion, chopped

2 jalapeños, minced

3 garlic cloves, minced

1 tablespoon chili powder

1 tablespoon dried oregano

¼ teaspoon powdered cayenne pepper

1 teaspoon salt

¼ teaspoon pepper

2 pounds of ground beef

16 small tortillas or taco shells

Salsa for garnish

Shredded cheese for garnish

Chopped tomatoes for garnish

Shredded lettuce for garnish

Sour cream for garnish

2 limes cut into wedges

1. Place a skillet over medium heat. Once it is warm add the oil, onion, and jalapeños. Sauté 5–7 minutes. Add the garlic and stir frequently for 2–3 minutes. Add the chili powder, oregano, cayenne powder, salt, and pepper and toss to combine.

2. Reduce the heat to low. Crumble the ground beef over the skillet and stir to cook. Once the outside of the meat is brown, cover the skillet with a lid and cook for 10 minutes.

3. Drain off the grease and discard.

4. Serve with warmed tortillas and top with salsa, cheese, tomatoes, lettuce, sour cream, and limes, if desired.

Homemade Taco Shells

Place a skillet over medium-high heat and add 1" of corn oil. Once the oil is heated, hold 1 tortilla with a pair of tongs and place half of it in the skillet. Hold it in a taco shape. Cook until it is golden brown. Repeat with the other side. When cooked, place over paper towels like a tent to drain.

Bacon-Wrapped Pork Tenderloin

If you don't have a meat thermometer, cut into the center of the largest piece.
If no red liquid comes out, the meat is done.

INGREDIENTS | SERVES 4

1½ pounds pork tenderloin, trimmed
8–10 slices of bacon, 1 per pork slice
Pepper to taste
¼ cup maple syrup
2 garlic cloves
1 tablespoon balsamic vinegar
2 tablespoons Dijon mustard
Pinch salt

1. Cut the tenderloin into 1½" slices.

2. Place a skillet over medium-low heat. Once it is heated add one bacon slice per pork medallion to the skillet. Cook slowly for about 8–10 minutes. When it starts to brown (not crisp), place on paper towels to drain. Discard all but 2 tablespoons of the bacon fat from skillet.

3. Season the medallions with pepper. Wrap one piece of bacon around each medallion and use a toothpick to keep in place, or tie with kitchen twine.

4. Place the skillet over medium-high heat. Once it is heated place 3–4 medallions in the skillet so they're not touching. Cook for 5 minutes on each side. Then balance the medallions on their sides and cook in 1-minute increments, slowly rolling the medallions until the bacon is crispy on all sides and the center of the pork registers at 145°F. Transfer to a plate to keep them warm.

5. Add the remaining ingredients to the skillet, stirring until the browned bits are scraped off the bottom of the skillet. Let it simmer for 35 minutes. The contents should be thickened. Place the pork in the skillet and cook for 1 minute on each side to reheat. Serve with the sauce poured over the pork.

Croque Madame

This French sandwich contains hot ham and cheese with a fried egg on top.
If you leave off the egg, you have a Croque Monsieur. Croquer is French for "to crunch."

INGREDIENTS | SERVES 2

2 tablespoons butter, softened

4 slices sourdough or wheat bread

2 teaspoons Dijon mustard

4 ounces Gruyère or Emmentaler cheese, thinly sliced

5 ounces sliced smoked ham

2 eggs

Pinch salt

Pinch pepper

1. Butter one side of each slice of bread. Spread the other side of each bread slice with a thin smear of mustard. Assemble two sandwiches using half of the cheese and ham on each. Make sure the buttered sides are on the outside of the sandwich.

2. Place a skillet over medium heat. When heated, place the sandwiches in the skillet. Cook each side for 3–4 minutes, or until they're toasted and golden brown. Remove to a plate and keep warm.

3. Place the remainder of the butter in the skillet. Once it has stopped foaming, slowly pour 2 eggs into the skillet. Sprinkle each egg with salt and pepper. Cover and let the eggs cook for 3–5 minutes, depending on how firm you like the yolks.

4. Center an egg on top of each sandwich, or inside for easier eating, and serve while warm.

French Toast

You can use any flavoring extract in place of the vanilla. You can also grate citrus zest and whisk it into the eggs to make flavored French toast. This recipe can easily be doubled.

INGREDIENTS | **SERVES 2**

3 tablespoons vegetable oil

3 eggs

3 tablespoons milk

¼ teaspoon vanilla extract

6 slices bread

Butter, as needed for topping

Maple syrup, as needed for topping

Is French Toast Really French?

The short answer is that no one really knows. There were mentions of this dish in medieval times in England and France. And the *Oxford English Dictionary* has an eggless version listed in 1660. But the name French Toast came about in the late 1800s alongside Egg Toast, Spanish Toast, and German Toast.

1. Place a skillet over medium heat and add 1 tablespoon of vegetable oil.

2. While the skillet heats crack the eggs into a wide, shallow bowl and whisk in the milk and vanilla extract.

3. Once the skillet is heated and the egg mixture is thoroughly combined, dip the bread slices into the mixture so each side is coated. Swirl the oil in the skillet if necessary so the bottom is evenly coated. Place two slices of dipped bread in the skillet.

4. Let the bread cook for 2–3 minutes on each side, or until the bread is golden brown. Place on a plate and keep warm while repeating with the remaining slices of bread.

5. Serve warm with butter and maple syrup.

Blini

These thin, Russian-style pancakes are great served with sweet fruit jam, honey, or served with sour cream and caviar. They're traditionally made from a yeast-based mix, but this quick-rising batter makes for faster cooking.

INGREDIENTS | **MAKES 15 PANCAKES**

2 eggs, beaten
1 tablespoon sugar
¼ teaspoon salt
½ cup all-purpose flour
½ teaspoon baking powder
2½ cups milk
2 tablespoons vegetable oil
¼ cup soft butter for spreading

1. Whisk together the eggs, sugar, and salt in a large bowl. Sift the flour and baking powder over the bowl and pour the milk on top. Mix until blended.

2. Place a skillet over medium heat and brush the surface of the pan with a little of the oil.

3. Pour 2 tablespoons of batter onto the skillet surface and gently rotate the skillet on a slight angle to spread it out evenly.

4. When the edges start to crisp and the center looks dry, use a spatula to flip the pancake. Cook 1 minute, or until the other side is lightly browned and then move it to a plate.

5. Spread butter on the pancakes and keep them warm in a stack until ready to serve.

Pan-Roasted Turkey Wings

Chicken wings come in three parts. The tips are inedible but are great for creating stock and aren't needed for this dish.

INGREDIENTS | SERVES 4

8 turkey wings, tips removed and sections separated

1 teaspoon salt

2 tablespoons olive oil

3 cups ketchup

3 cups apple juice

2 teaspoons Tabasco sauce

1 large onion, chopped

8 garlic cloves, smashed

2 teaspoons fresh thyme leaves

1. Preheat the oven to 300°F. Place a rack in the middle of the oven.

2. Sprinkle the wing pieces lightly with salt. Place a skillet over medium heat. Once it is heated, add the oil and the wings to the skillet. Cook on each side for 3 minutes, or until they're lightly browned.

3. Whisk the ketchup, apple juice, Tabasco sauce, onion, garlic, and thyme in a small bowl. Pour the sauce over the wings, and place the pan in the middle of the oven.

4. Cook 30 minutes. Use tongs to turn them over and continue cooking them for another 15–20 minutes, or until the meat is tender and the sauce has thickened.

5. Serve the sauce in a small bowl alongside the wings.

Maryland Crab Cakes

The crab flavor and spices are dominant in these cakes.
Serve with tartar sauce, cocktail sauce, spicy mayonnaise, and lemon wedges.

INGREDIENTS | SERVES 4

½ cup mayonnaise

1 large egg

1 tablespoon mustard

1 tablespoon Old Bay® seasoning

1 pound jumbo lump crabmeat, shells and cartilage removed

1 tablespoon vegetable oil

Spicy Mayonnaise

If everyone eating crab cakes likes spicy food, you can add a ¼ teaspoon of cayenne pepper to the crab cake mixture. But if only some of your dinner guests like it spicy, you can mix ½ cup of mayonnaise with 2 tablespoons of chili sauce and juice from half of a lemon.

1. Preheat oven to 400°F and place a skillet on a rack in the middle.

2. Whisk together the mayonnaise, egg, mustard, and seasoning. Once the egg is completely incorporated, gently stir in the crabmeat. Be careful not to break up the lumps.

3. Divide the mixture into four even pieces. Form each piece into a patty.

4. Add the oil to the skillet and add the patties. Bake the patties for 12 minutes and flip. Bake for 5–8 minutes on the second side. Remove immediately from the skillet and let sit for 5 minutes before serving.

Sautéed Mushrooms

Even white button mushrooms can have a lot of flavor if they're cooked right.
Use this technique to make the Hearty Gourmet Mushroom Soup (page 272).
These mushrooms can also be served over steaks, with eggs, or with polenta.

INGREDIENTS | SERVES 4

3 tablespoons butter
3 tablespoons olive oil
1 pound mushrooms, sliced
4 large shallots, minced
Pinch salt
Pinch pepper

1. Place a large skillet over medium heat. Add 1 tablespoon of butter and 1 tablespoon of oil.

2. Once the butter has stopped foaming, add one large handful of mushrooms. Sprinkle them lightly with salt and pepper. Cook for several minutes on each side, or until they've shrunk in size and turned dark brown. Remove from skillet and keep them warm.

3. Repeat with the rest of the butter, oil, and mushrooms until all of the mushrooms are cooked.

4. If the skillet is dry, add a small amount of oil. Add the shallots and stir frequently for 5 minutes, or until they're soft and starting to brown.

5. Return the mushrooms to the skillet and stir occasionally for 3 minutes, or until the mushrooms are hot again. Serve hot.

Pan-Seared Scallops and Chorizo

Chorizo comes in many varieties. Spanish varieties are more like a firm, cured sausage while the Mexican varieties are soft with a texture more like that of breakfast sausage. Both varieties will work in this dish.

INGREDIENTS | **SERVES 4 AS AN APPETIZER OR 2 AS A MEAL**

6 ounces chorizo sausage
1 pound scallops, cut in half if large
Juice from 1 lemon
Fresh ground pepper to taste
¼ cup chopped fresh parsley

1. If using a firm sausage in casing, slice into ¼" rounds.

2. Place a skillet over medium heat. Once heated, add the chorizo. If cooking rounds of sausage, cook 3 minutes or until lightly crispy on each side. If using loose sausage, spread the sausage evenly over the bottom of the skillet and cook 5–7 minutes or until the sausage is cooked through. Break up the sausage into bite-sized chunks.

3. Remove the chorizo and place in a bowl. Drain off all but 1 tablespoon of oil from the skillet. Add the scallops to the skillet and cook for 1 minute on each side.

4. Return the chorizo to the skillet and pour the lemon juice and sprinkle with ground pepper while stirring to coat.

5. Remove the chorizo and scallops to plates and sprinkle fresh parsley on top.

Seared and Roasted Pork Belly

Pork belly is the cut of meat that is used to make bacon.
For this dish it is not cured or smoked.

INGREDIENTS | SERVES 4

1¼ pounds skinless, boneless pork belly

¼ cup salt

½ cup sugar

4½ cups water

2 cups ice

½ cup chicken broth

5 garlic cloves

10 peppercorns

Go Belly Up

You may not find pork belly in the butcher case, but your butcher should be able to get it for you. Ask for a piece that is equally fatty and meaty. It may be easier to locate pork belly at a Chinese butcher shop.

1. Rinse the pork belly and remove any loose pieces along the edges. Place the salt, sugar, and 4 cups of water into a small saucepan over medium heat. Stir frequently until the salt and sugar are dissolved. Place the pork belly into a sealable container that is deeper than the pork belly, but not much wider. Stir ice into the pan of water. Once the ice is melted, pour the mixture over the pork. Refrigerate for 12–24 hours.

2. Preheat oven to 300°F. Remove the pork from the brine and rinse it. Pat it dry and cut it into four even pieces. Place them in the bottom of a small Dutch oven. Pour in ½ cup of water and the broth. Sprinkle the garlic cloves and peppercorns around the pan. Cover with a lid, place in the middle of the oven, and cook for 2½ hours. The pork should be very tender.

3. Drain the liquid and peppercorns from the pan. Save the garlic cloves. Turn the pork over so it is fat-side down. Smear a garlic clove over the meaty side of each slice of pork. Place the Dutch oven over high heat and cook for about 3–5 minutes, or until the fat is crispy and golden brown. Serve immediately.

Braised and Pan-Seared Duck Legs

This dish is more commonly known as duck confit, but only if you plan on keeping the meat in the jar with the fat in your refrigerator.

INGREDIENTS | **SERVES 2**

2 duck legs with skin on
Salt to taste
Pepper to taste
2 bay leaves, crumbled
Thumb-sized bundle of fresh thyme
Skin from remainder of duck

The Glory of Duck Fat

Duck fat rivals bacon fat for flavor but its higher smoke point makes it perfect for frying. Duck fat can be substituted in any vegetable recipe that requires 1–3 tablespoons of oil. French fries cooked in duck fat are the most flavorful you'll come across. They're perfect when served with garlicky mayonnaise for dipping alongside the French or Belgian Steamed Mussels (page 119).

1. Sprinkle the duck legs with salt and pepper. Place in an airtight container with bay leaves and thyme and refrigerate for 12–24 hours.

2. Place a skillet over medium-low heat. Once it is heated, add the skin to the skillet and cook for 1 hour, stirring occasionally to keep the fat from sticking. Cool for 15 minutes.

3. Preheat the oven to 300°F. Carefully place the duck legs in the skillet with the bay leaves and thyme. Place in the middle of the oven and cook for 2 hours, or until the bone moves independently of the meat. The skin should be crispy.

4. Remove the pan from the oven and set it aside to cool. Let the oil cool and pour off the fat.

5. Duck fat will keep for up to 2 months in an airtight container in the refrigerator.

Japanese Pork Cutlets

Panko is a Japanese bread crumb used for breading and frying. It creates a much crunchier breading than American-style bread crumbs but doesn't usually have added flavors, so it can be used when frying almost any breaded dish.

INGREDIENTS | SERVES 4

2 teaspoons soy sauce

1 teaspoon yellow mustard

1 teaspoon honey

½ cup ketchup

2 teaspoons Worcestershire sauce

½ cup cornstarch

2 large eggs

1 cup vegetable oil

3 cups panko-style bread crumbs

4 boneless pork loin chops, ¼" thick

Salt to taste

Pepper to taste

Sizzling Schnitzel in Japan

This dish became popular after World War II when there were a number of Germans living in Japan. In Japan this dish is usually served with a bowl of shredded cabbage and rice along with a hot English-style mustard and Tonkatsu sauce. It's very similar in technique, if not flavor, to German Schnitzel.

1. Whisk the soy sauce, mustard, honey, ketchup, and Worcestershire sauce together. Set aside.

2. Preheat the oven to 200°F and place a baking pan in the middle of the oven.

3. Place the cornstarch in a wide, shallow bowl. Place the eggs in a second wide, shallow bowl and beat 1 tablespoon of vegetable oil into eggs. Place the panko in a third wide, shallow bowl.

4. Pat the pork dry with paper towels. Season with salt and pepper. Dip pork lightly in the cornstarch and shake to remove any excess. Dip pork in the egg and let the excess drain off. Lay the cutlet in the panko and make sure the meat is covered. Place on a wire rack and let dry for 5 minutes. Repeat with the other cutlets.

5. Once the pork breading has dried, place ½ cup of oil in a skillet over medium-high heat. The oil is hot enough for frying when a piece of breading dropped in the oil sizzles and floats. Place two cutlets in the oil and cook them until the bottom side is golden-brown, about 2–3 minutes. Turn them over and let them cook for another 2 minutes. Place them on the baking pan in the oven to stay warm. Drain the oil, wipe the skillet, and repeat with the remaining oil and pork.

6. Serve whole or sliced with the sauce.

Zucchini Pancakes

To preserve your zucchini bounty, you can freeze it. Follow the steps below to shred, salt, and squeeze them dry. Spread them onto a cookie sheet, freeze, and then break them into chunks to put in a freezer-safe container for up to 3 months.

INGREDIENTS | **MAKES 24–30 PANCAKES**

1½ pounds zucchini
(3 large zucchini), shredded

1 teaspoon plus 1 pinch salt

¼ Vidalia onion, thinly sliced
and separated

1 large egg

¾ cup fine bread crumbs

½ cup vegetable oil

Pinch pepper

1. Place the zucchini in a colander. Sprinkle with 1 teaspoon salt and toss to coat evenly. Let this sit in your sink for half an hour to 1 hour if it is humid.

2. Preheat oven to 200°F so you can keep cooked pancakes warm before serving.

3. Squeeze as much of the water out of the zucchini as you can. Place them in a bowl. Sprinkle the onion over the zucchini and mix in the egg and bread crumbs.

4. Place a skillet over medium-high heat and add the oil. If it starts to smoke, lower the temperature. Use your hands to scoop up a heaping tablespoon of the mixture and flatten it into a pancake. Place it in the skillet and fry 2–3 at a time. Cook on each side for about 3 minutes until they're light brown.

5. Remove them from the skillet and place on a rack over a cookie sheet in the middle of the oven. Sprinkle with salt and pepper. Repeat with the remaining mixture until they're all cooked. Serve while warm.

Sweet Potato Latkes

Latkes are traditionally served for Jewish holidays, specifically, Passover (provided all the ingredients are kosher) and Hanukkah. This is a derivation on the traditional dish, but is tasty anytime.

INGREDIENTS | SERVES 4–6

1 cup flour

4 teaspoons sugar

2 teaspoons brown sugar

2 teaspoons baking powder

½ teaspoon cayenne powder

4 teaspoons curry powder

2 teaspoons ground cumin

1 teaspoon plus 1 dash salt

¼ teaspoon ground black pepper

4 eggs, beaten

½ cup milk

2 pounds sweet potatoes, peeled, trimmed, and grated

½ cup vegetable oil

1. Stir together the flour, sugars, baking powder, and spices in a large bowl. Whisk together the eggs and milk in a smaller bowl. Pour the egg mixture into the dry ingredients. Stir till it is barely combined. Add the grated sweet potatoes to the mix and stir till evenly coated.

2. Place a skillet over medium heat. Once it is heated, add ¼ cup of the oil to the skillet.

3. Once the oil has come to temperature, drop the potato mixture into the hot oil by the tablespoonful and flatten slightly. Cook for 2 minutes on each side.

4. Place latkes on a wire rack over paper towels and let them drain. Sprinkle them while they're hot with a dash of salt.

Chapter 3

Recipes for One
in a Small Skillet

Garlic Confit

The garlic should be stored separately from the oil, in the refrigerator, for no more than one week. Botulism spores, which are odorless and tasteless, can be present on the garlic and will thrive in the oil.

INGREDIENTS | **MAKES ½ CUP**

1 head of garlic
½ cup olive oil

The Many Uses of Garlic
Spread the garlic on bread, or use in any dish that you want an intense garlic flavor. Use the oil when cooking, making vinaigrette, or dipping when you want a lighter garlic flavor.

1. Preheat oven to 350°F.

2. Peel all of the garlic cloves and place them in a small skillet. Pour the olive oil on top of the garlic cloves.

3. Bake the garlic for 45 minutes to 1 hour, or until the garlic is soft and golden brown.

Chocolate Chip Skillet Cookie

If you don't have a small skillet and still want to make this recipe, bake in a 10–12" skillet for 45 minutes. Or you can wrap half of the dough tightly in plastic wrap and freeze it for up to 3 months.

INGREDIENTS | **MAKES 2 SKILLET-SIZED COOKIES**

2 cups all-purpose flour
1 teaspoon baking soda
½ teaspoon salt
¾ cup plus 1 teaspoon unsalted butter, softened
½ cup sugar
¾ cup packed brown sugar
1 egg
2 teaspoons vanilla extract
1½ cups chocolate chips

1. Preheat oven to 350°F.

2. Combine the flour, baking soda, and salt in a bowl.

3. Use the paddle attachment of a stand mixer, or a use a handheld mixer, to cream ¾ cup butter and sugars until they're light and fluffy. Add the egg and vanilla and blend on low until combined. Add the flour mixture and beat on low until it is just combined. Stir in the chocolate chips by hand.

4. Grease a 4"–6" skillet with 1 teaspoon of butter. Divide the dough in half. Transfer half of the dough to the skillet and press to flatten evenly over the bottom of the skillet. Bake for 30 minutes, or until the edges are brown and the top is golden. Repeat with the other half of the dough.

5. Leave in the pan and rest on a wire rack for 10 minutes to cool. Cut and serve.

Lemon Garlic Shrimp for Pasta

If you're using a newer skillet you can still make this dish, just squeeze the lemon juice over the cooked pasta, shrimp, and sauce.

INGREDIENTS | SERVES 1

½ teaspoon olive oil
¼ small yellow onion, halved and thinly sliced
½ teaspoon garlic powder
Juice from ½ lemon
¼ cup chicken broth
6 medium shrimp, peeled and deveined
1 serving angel hair pasta, cooked
Pinch salt
Fresh cracked pepper to taste

1. Place a small skillet over medium heat and when heated, add the olive oil and onion. Stir frequently and cook for 4–5 minutes. The onion should be translucent and just starting to turn golden brown.

2. Add the garlic powder, lemon juice, and chicken broth to the pan and stir to scrape up the fond. Add the shrimp to the skillet and cook for several minutes until they turn pink.

3. Place pasta on a plate and pour the contents of the skillet over it. Sprinkle with salt and freshly cracked pepper before serving.

Enchilada Casserole

"Enchilada" translates from Spanish to mean "in chili." But it is possible to regulate the heat to get a flavorful sauce that isn't too spicy.

INGREDIENTS | SERVES 1

½ teaspoon corn or vegetable oil
2 corn tortillas
1 cup enchilada sauce
¼ cup shredded Cheddar cheese
2 tablespoons minced onion
2 tablespoons sliced black olives

1. Preheat the oven to 350°F. Add the oil to a small skillet.

2. Cut the corn tortillas into 8 wedges and soak them in the enchilada sauce for 15 minutes.

3. Place half of the tortilla wedges in the bottom of the skillet. Sprinkle half of the cheese on top. Add the remaining tortillas, the rest of the cheese, and sprinkle the onion and olives on top. Pour the sauce over the wedges. Place the skillet in the middle of the oven and bake for 15 minutes. Cool for a few minutes before serving.

Perfect Sunny-Fried Egg

Eggs come in different sizes. Nutrition information and most baking recipes call for large eggs, but any size will work here.

INGREDIENTS | **SERVES 1**

2 eggs
2 tablespoons olive oil
Pinch salt
Pinch pepper
2 tablespoons shredded Parmesan cheese (optional)
Pinch red pepper flakes (optional)

1. Place a small skillet over low heat. Let it warm up for 5 minutes. Crack the eggs into a small bowl.

2. Add the oil to the skillet, swirl the skillet to coat the bottom and the sides. Wait 1 minute and then slowly pour the eggs into the skillet. Sprinkle salt, pepper, and cheese or red pepper flakes over the egg.

3. Cover the skillet and cook for 2–3 minutes to get a set white and a runny yolk, 3–4 minutes for a set white and a partially set-yolk, 4–5 minutes for a set white and yolk.

4. Run a butter knife or spatula along the edges of the skillet and then slide the egg onto a plate.

Bird in a Nest

To make this a one-pot breakfast, you can fry a slice of bacon in the skillet and then cook the nest in the drippings. And to make it fancier you can garnish it with pesto, a sun-dried tomato, some chopped olives, or a roasted red pepper strip.

INGREDIENTS | **SERVES 1**

1 tablespoon butter or vegetable oil
1 small garlic clove, peeled and smashed
1 piece thick-cut crusty bread
1 large egg
Pinch salt
Pinch pepper
1 tablespoon shredded cheese

1. Place a small skillet over medium-low heat. Add the butter and let it melt. Once the butter has melted add the garlic to the skillet. Fry for 1 minute on each side and then remove from the skillet.

2. Use a biscuit cutter or small glass to cut a hole in the center of the bread. Place the slice of bread in the skillet and press slightly. Crack the egg and drop it in the hole. Season with a pinch of salt and pepper.

3. Cook for 3 minutes. Once the egg has started to firm up, flip the nest over. Sprinkle the cheese on top of the nest. Cook for 2 minutes, turn off the heat and let the nest sit in the skillet until ready to serve.

Sautéed Shrimp and Mushrooms

*This is great served over rice with a side of Stewed Black Beans (page 248)
or served over boiled fettuccine.*

INGREDIENTS | SERVES 1

1 tablespoon butter
1 tablespoon olive oil
¼ cup sliced mushrooms
1 green onion, thinly sliced
Dash salt
1 small tomato, cored and diced
1 garlic clove, minced
Juice from 1 lemon
2 tablespoons dry white wine or vermouth
¼ pound medium shrimp, shelled and deveined
¼ teaspoon Old Bay seasoning

1. Place a small skillet over medium heat. Once it is heated, add the butter and olive oil. Add the mushrooms, green onion, and a dash of salt. Cook for 4–5 minutes.

2. Stir in the tomato and garlic and cook for 3–4 minutes, or until the garlic smells fragrant and the tomato is starting to break down. Stir in the lemon juice. Cook for 1 minute.

3. Stir in the wine, the shrimp, and the Old Bay. Cook for 3–5 minutes, or until the shrimp turns pink. Serve while warm.

Lean Dijon Steak Strips

The Cattlemen's Beef Board rates 29 cuts of beef as lean or extra-lean and any of them would work in this dish. Keep in mind that a serving of beef is only 4 ounces, so read package size information.

INGREDIENTS | SERVES 1

1 teaspoon olive oil
¼ small yellow onion, finely chopped
¼ pound eye round steak, fat trimmed
¼ cup beef broth
1 tablespoon fat-free sour cream
½ teaspoon Dijon mustard
½ teaspoon soy sauce
½ teaspoon garlic powder

1. Place a skillet over medium-high heat and add oil. When it is heated add the onion. Stir frequently and cook for 2–3 minutes or until the onion is translucent. Add the steak to the pan and cook for 1 minute on each side.

2. In a small bowl combine the beef broth, sour cream, mustard, soy sauce, and garlic powder. Pour over the beef. Cover the pan, reduce heat to low and cook for 3–4 minutes for a medium-done steak.

3. Remove the lid, increase the heat to medium-high and boil for 1–2 minutes until the sauce has reduced. Slice steak into thin strips. Serve immediately.

Asparagus and Leek Frittata

A 4" or 5" skillet works perfectly for this dish. Smaller skillets may be harder to find,
but they're great for single servings and for when you just need to make a small amount of food.

INGREDIENTS | SERVES 1

1 stalk of cooked asparagus, chopped

1 teaspoon unsalted butter

¼ cup chopped leeks

2 large eggs

2 tablespoons Parmesan cheese, shredded

2 tablespoons Gruyère, shredded

1 teaspoon chives, minced

Pinch salt

Pinch pepper

Frittatas, the Lazy Man's Omelet

Frittatas are the perfect way to use up small amounts of leftovers. A handful of leftover chicken, or any leftover vegetable can be substituted in this recipe. Just make sure the filling is warm when the eggs are added. It's traditional in Naples for leftover pasta to be added to a frittata. Frittatas are almost always served well done, or firm.

1. Steam the piece of asparagus if it isn't already cooked. Place a skillet over medium heat. Once it is warm add the butter and the leeks. Cook the leeks slowly and stir frequently for 8–10 minutes. Add the asparagus to the skillet.

2. Turn on the broiler. In a separate bowl, whisk together the eggs, cheese, chives, salt, and pepper. Once the leeks are soft and the asparagus is warmed, pour the egg mixture into the skillet. Let the eggs cook for 5–6 minutes without stirring.

3. Once the bottom and sides of the eggs are firm, place the skillet under the broiler about 4 inches from the heat. Let the frittata cook until the top of the eggs are lightly browned, about 4–5 minutes.

4. Remove the pan from the oven and while it is still hot, run a thin knife along the edges of the skillet to loosen the frittata. Slide the frittata onto a plate and serve immediately.

Migas

If you don't have corn tortillas, you can use flour tortillas, although the texture won't be quite the same. For this dish, canned green chilies are perfect.

INGREDIENTS | SERVES 1

2 large eggs

1 teaspoon water

1 tablespoon chunky salsa

1 tablespoon butter

1 tablespoon olive oil

4 6" corn tortillas

¼ small onion, finely chopped

2 tablespoons chopped green chilies

½ small tomato, chopped

½ avocado, sliced

1 teaspoon fresh cilantro

3 tablespoons grated Monterey jack cheese

Dollop sour cream

Eat Every Crumb

Migas is a Tex-Mex dish in America, but it started and remains popular in Spain. "Migas" means "crumbs" and refers to the use of scraps of tortillas or bread. In Spain, you're likely to have spinach, chorizo, or grapes mixed in your migas. The recipes vary from one area of Texas to the next, but this version is popular in Austin.

1. Place skillet over medium heat.

2. Crack the eggs into a small bowl and mix in the salsa and water. Set aside.

3. Once the skillet is heated, add the butter and olive oil. Once the foaming stops, tear up 2 corn tortillas and sauté them until they're soft. Add the onion to the skillet. Cook and stir for 5 minutes, or until the onion is translucent and soft. Stir in the green chilies.

4. Pour the egg mixture in the skillet and slowly fold until the eggs are cooked through. Sprinkle the tomato over the top of the eggs.

5. Remove the skillet from the heat and stir in the avocado, cilantro, and cheese. Turn out onto a plate and serve with sour cream and warmed corn tortillas.

Leek, Mushroom, and Goat Cheese Quesadilla

The 6" skillets fit a small corn tortilla perfectly.
This one-pot dinner is a great quick meal for one and easily adaptable.

INGREDIENTS | SERVES 1

1 tablespoon olive oil
¼ cup leek, chopped
¼ cup mushrooms, chopped
½ teaspoon garlic powder
Salt to taste
Pepper to taste
2 corn tortillas
¼ cup goat cheese, crumbled
½ cup salsa and sour cream, optional

1. Place a small skillet over medium heat. Once heated add the olive oil and leek. Cook for 3–4 minutes or until the leek is just starting to soften. Add the mushrooms, garlic powder, salt and pepper to taste and stir frequently for 4–5 minutes. The mushrooms should reduce and the leeks should start to turn golden.

2. Remove the contents of the skillet to a small bowl. Wipe out the skillet and add a teaspoon of olive oil. Place one corn tortilla in the skillet and add the leek and mushroom mixture on top of it. Add the cheese on top, being careful to keep it from touching the sides of the skillet. Place another tortilla on top and press down.

3. Cook for 3–4 minutes, or until the bottom tortilla is crispy. Carefully remove the quesadilla from the skillet and flip over. Cook the second side for 2–3 minutes or until crispy.

4. Remove from skillet and let it rest for 3 minutes before slicing in half and serving with or without salsa and sour cream.

Salmon with Pineapple Salsa and Polenta

*It's difficult to scale recipes back for one person, but when cooking fish,
it's often easy to make a single serving. And with a skillet that can go from the stove
to the broiler, it makes it even easier to create a full meal in one pan.*

INGREDIENTS | SERVES 1

1 6-ounce fillet of salmon

Pinch salt

1 teaspoon olive oil

3 tablespoons pineapple salsa
(see below)

1 refrigerated tube of pre-made polenta

2 tablespoons olive oil

1 lime wedge for garnish

Pineapple Salsa

To make your own, finely chop 5 pineapple rings and place in a small skillet with 2 tablespoons of minced red onion, 2 teaspoons of minced red pepper, juice from one lime, and 2 teaspoons of chopped cilantro. Place over medium heat, salt lightly, and stir frequently for 15 minutes. The juices should evaporate and the onion and pepper should soften.

1. Preheat broiler to high. Sprinkle the salmon lightly on each side with salt. Place a small skillet over medium-high heat. Once hot add the oil and place the fillet in the middle of the pan. Cook for 3 minutes on the first side and 2 minutes on the second side. Brush 1 tablespoon of the salsa on top. Place it in the oven about 4" from the flame for 30 seconds, just enough to caramelize the salsa. Place the fish on a plate and let it rest.

2. Place the skillet over medium-high heat. Slice 2½" thick slices from the tube of polenta. Once the skillet is hot, add the oil and slide the 2 patties into the skillet. Don't touch them for 4 minutes. There should be enough crust on the bottom of the polenta to keep it together. Use a spatula to flip the polenta and cook for 5 minutes on the second side.

3. Once the polenta is cooked, drain off excess oil. Place the salmon on top of the polenta, pour the remaining salsa on top of the salmon, and place the skillet back in the oven for 1 minute to warm the fish through. Serve it immediately with the lime wedge.

Chicken Breast Rotolo with Currant Stuffing

"Rotolo" translates from Italian as "coil." It's a common cooking technique used with larger sheets of pasta, or pieces of meat that are pounded flat. This dish works great with chicken breast, but would also work with a tender cut of pork.

INGREDIENTS | SERVES 1

1 chicken breast half
Pinch salt
Pinch pepper
2 tablespoons pine nuts or other nut
2 tablespoons olive oil
½ celery stalk, minced
¼ small yellow onion, minced
1 small garlic clove, minced
¼ cup fresh currants
1 tablespoon fresh thyme or basil, chopped
2 tablespoons fresh parsley, chopped

Currants are Historically Current

Currants are a tiny, tart fruit that grows on a small bush and are very high in vitamin C. During World War II, fruit that was high in vitamin C was incredibly hard to import into Britain so the British government encouraged its citizens to grow currants that were then turned into a syrup and given to children.

1. Use the flat end of a meat tenderizer or a rolling pin to pound the chicken breast until it's ⅜" thick. Sprinkle each side with salt and pepper.

2. Place a small skillet over medium heat. Place pine nuts in the skillet and shake every 30 seconds to 1 minute and turn off the heat as soon as you smell them toasting. Transfer nuts to a separate container.

3. Place the small skillet back over medium heat and once it is warm add 1 tablespoon olive oil, vegetables, and garlic. Stir the vegetables frequently for 5–7 minutes. Add the currants and cook for 1 minute until warm. Use the back of a spoon to crush them. Cook for 3–4 minutes. Once most of the juices have evaporated, stir in herbs and nuts.

4. Spoon the mixture onto the widest end of the chicken breast, and roll toward the narrow end. Use kitchen twine or toothpicks to hold it together. Wipe out the skillet.

5. Place the skillet over medium heat and once heated add 1 tablespoon olive oil. Place the chicken in the skillet and cook for 2–3 minutes, make a quarter turn and cook for another 2–3 minutes. Continue cooking and turning for 8–12 minutes. Remove twine or toothpicks and slice the chicken into ¾" rounds. Serve immediately.

Chicken Breast Stuffed with Rapini and Black Olives

Rapini is also called Broccoli Rabe. Even though it gets little broccoli-like buds that grow on stems, it is more similar to turnip greens. If you can't find rapini, or don't like its nutty, bitter taste, you can substitute chard or spinach.

INGREDIENTS | SERVES 1

1 chicken breast
Pinch salt
Pinch black pepper
1 tablespoon plus 1 teaspoon olive oil
2 ounces rapini, chopped
¼ small onion, chopped
1 garlic clove, minced
2 ounces pitted black olives, minced
1 tablespoon shredded Parmesan cheese

1. Preheat oven to 350°F. Place the chicken breast on a sturdy surface. Use the flat side of a meat tenderizer to pound the breast until it is about ⅜" thick. Sprinkle both sides with salt and pepper.

2. Place a skillet over medium-high heat. Once heated, add 1 tablespoon olive oil, the rapini, and the onion. Cook for several minutes until the leaves are wilted and the stems are softened.

3. In a bowl, combine the rapini, the garlic, the olives, and the Parmesan cheese. Place the mixture near the widest end of the chicken breast and roll toward the other end. Use cooking twine or toothpicks to keep in place.

4. Place the small skillet back over medium-high heat. Once warmed, add 1 teaspoon oil to the pan and add chicken. Brown for 1 minute on each side. Transfer the skillet to the middle of the oven and cook for 35–40 minutes.

5. Remove the twine or toothpicks and cut the roll in slices. Serve immediately.

Quinoa and Beef-Stuffed Acorn Squash

Make the Quinoa Pilaf (page 78) before making this dish. If you don't have leftovers, you can use any leftover flavored rice or grain dish in its place.

INGREDIENTS | SERVES 2

1 acorn squash
Pinch salt
Pinch pepper
2 ounces ground beef
1 serving Quinoa Pilaf
¼ cup vegetable broth
2 teaspoons Parmesan cheese

Make Your Own Frozen Dinners

If you're trying to eliminate some of the sodium and preservatives in your diet, but like the convenience of frozen dinners, many of the recipes in this chapter can be doubled and the second portion can be stored in a sealable container for later. In most cases, you'll save money, eat healthier, and still have quick meals.

1. Preheat oven to 350°F. Remove the stem and cut the squash in half lengthwise. Use a spoon to remove the seeds and strings to create a hollow in each half. Sprinkle each half lightly with salt and pepper.

2. Place a small skillet over medium heat. Once it is warm add the ground beef and stir continually with a fork, breaking the beef into small pieces. When cooked, drain off any excess grease and add the beef to a bowl with the pilaf. Stir to combine and place half of the mixture in each hollow of squash.

3. Pour half the vegetable broth and sprinkle half the cheese on each squash half. Place the squash in a small skillet in the middle of the oven for 40–50 minutes. It is ready when you can pierce the flesh with a fork through to the skin easily. Let each half cool for 5 minutes before serving.

Tofu Steak with Mushrooms

Tofu generally comes in 1 pound blocks. To prepare it for steaks, place it in the microwave for 1 minute. Drain off the water and cut the block into 4 even slices.

INGREDIENTS | SERVES 1

2 tablespoons soy sauce

1 teaspoon toasted sesame oil

1 tablespoon rice wine vinegar

Several dashes hot sauce

¼ pound firm tofu steak, pressed

2 tablespoons peanut or olive oil

¼ cup mushrooms, sliced

¼ teaspoon salt

1 green scallion, thinly sliced

Tofu Requires Extreme Flavor

Tofu is very low in fat, very high in protein, but very bland by itself. Marinating firm tofu in a very flavorful sauce and then pan-frying is the fastest cooking technique. When trying to flavor tofu, use a more strongly flavored sauce than you would if using chicken. Many Asian bottled sauces are great as a tofu marinade.

1. Combine the soy sauce, sesame oil, rice wine vinegar, and hot sauce in a small bowl. Place the drained tofu steak in the sauce and let it rest in the refrigerator for 1–24 hours.

2. Place a small skillet over medium heat. Once it is heated, add 1 tablespoon of the oil and the mushrooms. Sprinkle the salt over the mushrooms and toss to combine. Cook for 4 minutes.

3. Remove the mushrooms from the skillet and add the remaining oil. Remove the tofu from the marinade and place it in the skillet. Cook on each side for 2 minutes.

4. Return the mushrooms to the skillet. Pour the marinade over the steak and cook until the mushrooms have warmed and the sauce has reduced. Sprinkle with chopped scallion and serve while warm.

Chapter 4

Sauces

Cajun Roux

This recipe makes enough roux to thicken a large pot of gumbo.
Leftovers can be refrigerated for a week, or frozen for three months.

INGREDIENTS | MAKES 3 CUPS

1 cup vegetable oil or peanut oil

1¼ cups all-purpose flour

1 onion, chopped

1 bell pepper, chopped

3 celery stalks, chopped

2 carrots, chopped

History of Roux

Roux comes in three colors: white, blonde, or brown. It thickens sauces and adds flavor. The longer a roux is cooked, the darker, more flavorful, and less thickening it becomes. Most French roux is light-colored, but in Cajun cuisine a darker roux is used. Creole food is more likely to use a white or blonde roux to make a sauce.

1. Place a skillet over medium heat. Once it is heated add the oil. Stir the oil with a whisk in one hand while you slowly add the flour with the other. Once all of the flour is added, stir continuously for up to 25 minutes. Use the whisk to scrape the edges of the skillet to prevent the roux from browning.

2. Once the roux looks just darker than peanut butter, turn off the heat and add the vegetables. The sugars in the vegetables, and the residual heat from the hot skillet, will permit the roux to get darker and finish cooking.

Beurre Blanc

Beurre blanc (white butter) is great when served over fish fillets that are lightly seasoned.
Because lemon juice is used in this recipe, it should only be made in a well-seasoned or an enameled pan.

INGREDIENTS | MAKES 4 TABLESPOONS

1 shallot, minced

2 tablespoons white wine

4 tablespoons butter, cut into 1 tablespoon sections

Juice from 1 lemon

Salt to taste

Pepper to taste

1. Place a skillet over medium heat. Once it is heated, add the shallot and wine. Stir continually until the liquid has reduced by half and is starting to get a syrup-like consistency.

2. Reduce the heat to low and add 1 tablespoon of butter. Whisk the sauce continually until the butter is almost melted. Add the next pat while there are bits of butter in the skillet. Repeat until all of the butter is melted and the sauce can easily coat the back of a spoon.

3. Whisk in the lemon juice and taste before seasoning with salt and pepper. Serve immediately.

Chipotle Orange Sauce

Chipotle in adobo sauce can often be found in small cans.
If you can't find canned chipotle peppers, you can substitute with jalapeño peppers.

INGREDIENTS | MAKES 1 CUP

1 teaspoon vegetable oil

½ small onion, finely chopped

1 7-ounce can chipotle in adobo sauce

1 cup orange juice

Juice from 1 lime

1 teaspoon ground cumin

2 garlic cloves, minced

2 tablespoons brown sugar

Salt to taste

1. Place a skillet over medium-high heat. Once it is heated, add the oil and the onion. Cook for 5–7 minutes or until the onion has softened and has started to turn brown.

2. Stir in the remaining ingredients and simmer for 10 minutes, or until it has reduced and thickened. Taste and season with salt as necessary. Use as a condiment or with Pan-Seared Skirt Steak (page 152).

Toasted Peanut Sauce

This Thai condiment is often served as a sauce for satay, spring rolls, potstickers,
or brushed on vegetables. For a quick meal or snack, pour on cooked pasta
and sprinkle sesame seeds or chopped scallion on top.

INGREDIENTS | MAKES 3 CUPS

1 13-ounce can coconut milk

2 ounces red curry paste (or use Green Curry Paste, page 54)

¾ cup unsweetened peanut butter

½ tablespoon salt

½ cup sugar

2 tablespoons apple cider vinegar

½ cup water

¼ teaspoon spicy red pepper flakes

1 teaspoon toasted sesame oil

1. Place an enameled pot over medium heat. Add all ingredients and bring to a boil, whisking continually.

2. Reduce the heat to low and simmer for 4 minutes, stirring occasionally.

3. Remove from the heat and serve immediately or place in an airtight container in the refrigerator for up to 1 month. (Refrigerated sauce will be thick, but will thin when heated.)

Vietnamese Chili Garlic Sauce

This Vietnamese condiment is great stirred into noodle soups, served on meats, used as a dipping sauce for egg rolls, or stirred into any sauce that you would like to be spicier. It will keep in an airtight jar in the refrigerator for at least 1 month.

INGREDIENTS | **MAKES 1 CUP**

6 ounces Thai, serrano, cayenne, or red jalapeño peppers

4 garlic cloves, chopped

1 teaspoon salt

2 teaspoons honey

2 tablespoons apple cider vinegar or rice wine vinegar

1–2 tablespoons water (optional)

1. Place all of the ingredients in a blender or food processor. Pulse until the mixture is smooth. Add 1–2 tablespoons of water if necessary.

2. Place a skillet over medium heat. Once it is heated, pour the mixture into the skillet and bring to a simmer.

3. Reduce the heat to low and simmer uncovered for 10 minutes. It should lose its raw smell and develop a richer smell. Transfer to an airtight jar.

Applesauce

If you have a food mill or tomato press, you can bake the apples with the skins on and extract them using the mill. Tart apples are better for this recipe.

INGREDIENTS | **SERVES 4**

6 large apples

Water, as needed

¼ cup sugar

¼ teaspoon salt

1 teaspoon cinnamon

¼ teaspoon nutmeg

2 whole cloves

2 tablespoons butter

1. Core and peel the apples. Place them in a small saucepan with 1" water. Bring to a boil over medium heat and cook for 15 minutes.

2. Remove the apples from the water and either run them through a food mill or through a blender (using some of the water to help create a purée).

3. Place the apple mash, sugar, salt, and spices in a skillet over low heat. Simmer for 30 minutes, stirring occasionally.

4. Stir in the butter and taste. Add more sugar or spices as necessary. Serve warm or cold.

American Piccalilli

There is a dish by this name in Britain that is more mustardy and less sweet. Use the American version on cold meats, sausages, roasts, or even mixed into riceor vegetable dishes.

INGREDIENTS | MAKES 1 PINT

2 green tomatoes

½ green bell pepper

½ red bell pepper

1 small onion, peeled

1 cup chopped cabbage

¼ cup salt

½ cup brown sugar

¼ teaspoon celery seed or celery salt

¼ teaspoon mustard seed

2 whole cloves

½ teaspoon ground cinnamon

½ teaspoon ground allspice

⅓ cup apple cider vinegar

1. Chop all vegetables. Sprinkle them with salt and place in a covered bowl overnight.

2. The next day, lightly rinse the vegetables with cold water to remove the salt.

3. Combine the vegetables with the remaining ingredients and place in a skillet. Bring to a boil and reduce the heat to low.

4. Simmer for 15 minutes. If desired, purée with a stick blender or run through a stand blender after it has cooled. Store in an airtight jar for up to 1 month.

Caramelized Onion and Fennel

Raw fennel has a fairly strong anise flavor. But when it cooks, that flavor almost disappears.

INGREDIENTS | CREATES 1 QUART

2 heads fennel

2 tablespoons olive oil

2 large sweet onions, peeled and thinly sliced

2 small tomatoes, cored and sliced

1 teaspoon salt

Caramelized Fennel and Onion Tart

To make a quick appetizer, mix 2 cups of this mixture with 1/4 cup of grated Parmesan cheese. Spread it on a pre-made pie shell. Place it in a 350°F oven for 20–30 minutes or until the crust and top have browned.

1. Cut off the green part of the fennel and the base. Discard. Separate the pieces and rinse well to remove any dirt. Slice thinly.

2. Place a Dutch oven over medium heat. Once it is warmed, add the olive oil and the vegetables. Sprinkle the salt across the top and stir to combine. Cover the pan with a lid and reduce the heat to low. Stir the vegetables every 3 minutes, three times.

3. Add a little more oil if the pan seems dry and let it cook for about an hour, stirring every 15 minutes. The mixture should be very juicy. Turn the heat to high and stir frequently for 5 minutes, or until the liquid evaporates.

Pasta Puttanesca

This it is a quick dish to make and the ingredients are very affordable.

INGREDIENTS | SERVES 4

1 pound dry spaghetti
3 tablespoons olive oil
1 garlic clove, minced
2 anchovies, finely sliced
¼ cup olives, pitted and sliced
2 tablespoons capers
¼ cup fresh parsley, chopped
1 pinch dried chili pepper flakes
1 28-ounce can whole, peeled tomatoes
Salt to taste

1. Cook 1 pound of spaghetti according to package directions. Place a skillet over low heat. Once it is warm, add the oil and the garlic. Cook garlic for 1 minute before adding the anchovies. Cook for 3 minutes, stirring continually. The anchovies should begin to dissolve. Add the olives, capers, parsley, and pepper flakes and toss to combine.

2. Pour in tomatoes and gently chop apart while stirring constantly. Let the mixture come to a boil and reduce heat to medium-low. Cook uncovered for about 15 minutes. Stir frequently to prevent sticking. Taste before seasoning with salt, and pour over the pasta.

Green Curry Paste

This is a fairly mild curry paste. If you prefer a hot paste, use serrano chilies instead of jalapeños. This is used in the Vegetable Green Curry (page 71).

INGREDIENTS | MAKES ½ CUP OF CURRY PASTE

2 stalks lemongrass
2" piece ginger, peeled and sliced
½ bunch cilantro
4 jalapeños, seeded
1 small yellow onion, peeled and quartered
3 garlic cloves, peeled
Zest from 1 lime
1 teaspoon ground coriander
1 tablespoon ground cumin
1 teaspoon honey
1 tablespoon soy sauce
3 tablespoons peanut oil

1. Remove the bottom 3" from the lemongrass and the dried fibrous tops. Cut into 1" pieces. Add to a food processor with the ginger, cilantro, peppers, onion, garlic, and lime zest. Pulse for several minutes until it is a smooth paste.

2. Add the coriander, cumin, honey, soy sauce, and oil and pulse until it is combined.

3. Place a skillet over medium heat. Add the curry paste, spreading it out evenly. Cook for 7–10 minutes, stirring frequently, until the pepper smell is overpowering. If the mixture sticks, add a tablespoon of oil.

4. Once the paste is ready, remove from the skillet. Store refrigerated for 2 weeks or frozen for up to 6 months.

Chicken Gravy

Gravy requires practice and repetition to make it perfectly.
If you use a whisk, keep a spoon nearby so you can test for your preferred thickness and flavor.

INGREDIENTS | SERVES 6

2 tablespoons chicken drippings,
or other oil

1 cup chicken broth (or juice, or beer,
or wine)

1–2 tablespoons flour

Salt and pepper as needed

Reheating Leftover Gravy

You can refrigerate leftover gravy in
a sealed container for 2–3 days. It will
become solid when cold. Reheat it in a
pan over medium heat or in the microwave
for 2–3 minutes. Whisk in a tablespoon or
two of chicken broth or other liquid to get
the desired consistency.

1. Place a skillet over medium-high heat and add the drippings. Pour in half the broth. In a separate container, stir 1 tablespoon of flour into the remaining half-cup of liquid and whisk until it is lump-free.

2. Once the liquid in the skillet starts to boil, slowly pour the flour and liquid mixture into the skillet, whisking continually. Once it returns to a boil it will start to thicken. Reduce the heat to medium and keep stirring.

3. After 3–4 minutes, if it isn't thick enough sprinkle 1 teaspoon of flour across the top of the gravy, stirring continually to prevent lumps. Cook for another 2 minutes before adding more flour.

4. If the gravy gets too thick, add a few tablespoons of liquid to thin it, and boil again before removing. If you keep the gravy in the pan, it will continue to cook even if the burner is turned off, so stir frequently. Add salt and pepper to taste.

Bolognese Sauce

This dish comes from Bologna, Italy, and is most often served on a wide noodle called tagliatelle.
It is wider than fettuccine and is easier to find fresh than dried.
The width makes sauce stick more easily.

INGREDIENTS | **SERVES 6–8**

3 tablespoons butter

3 tablespoons olive oil

½ small yellow onion, chopped

½ carrot, chopped

½ celery stalk, chopped

¾ pound lean ground beef

1 cup dry white wine

½ cup whole milk

⅛ teaspoon ground nutmeg

1 28-ounce can of chopped Italian tomatoes

1 teaspoon of salt (as desired)

1. Place a Dutch oven over medium heat and add the butter and oil. Once the butter has melted, add the onion, stirring continually for 1 minute until slightly translucent. Stir in the celery and carrot and cook for 2 minutes.

2. Add the ground beef and stir continually, breaking the meat into small pieces while it cooks. Once the meat is slightly more brown than red, turn the heat up to medium-high and add the wine. Leave uncovered and simmering vigorously. Stir occasionally for 10 minutes to prevent it from sticking while the wine evaporates.

3. Add the milk and the nutmeg and lower the heat to medium. Stir continually until it stops boiling vigorously. Continue to stir it frequently for about 6–8 minutes until the milk evaporates. Add the tomatoes and reduce the heat to low. You want it to bubble occasionally, but barely simmer.

4. Cooking time will vary between 3½ and 5 hours. Once all of the liquid has evaporated you'll be left with a meaty, gravy-like sauce. Taste and add salt if necessary.

Kansas City-Style Barbecue Sauce

Because this recipe uses a lot of acidic tomato sauce,
use a well-seasoned or enameled Dutch oven.

INGREDIENTS | **MAKES 3–4 PINTS OF SAUCE**

1 large yellow onion, chopped
4 garlic cloves, minced
1 teaspoon salt
2 tablespoons vegetable oil
1 26-ounce can tomato sauce
1 6-ounce can tomato paste
¼ cup dark molasses
1 cup mango juice
3 tablespoons cocoa powder
1 can dark beer
1 can cola (or other soda with caramel coloring)
2 tablespoons Worcestershire sauce
1 pinch cayenne powder
¼ cup cider vinegar
1 tablespoon cumin
1 tablespoon paprika
1 tablespoon coriander
1 tablespoon dried oregano
1 tablespoon dried mustard powder
1 teaspoon ground black pepper
1 teaspoon ground cinnamon

1. Place a Dutch oven over medium-high heat and when it is heated, add the onion, garlic, salt, and oil. Stir frequently and cook for 5 minutes until the onions are translucent. Turn the heat to low and cook for 15 minutes. Stir occasionally. When the onions start to caramelize and turn a light brown, add the remaining ingredients, stirring after every few items are added. Once everything is incorporated, cover with a lid and cook for 30 minutes. Stir occasionally to prevent from burning.

2. Remove the lid and simmer for 1½ hours. Some of the liquid will evaporate to create a thicker sauce. Taste and add extra salt, spice, vinegar, or sugar if desired.

Spaghetti Carbonara

This dish has to be made fresh in small batches in order to have its full flavor potential.
It is a rich dish, so try it as a side instead of a main dish.

INGREDIENTS | SERVES 2

4 ounces dried spaghetti

3 tablespoons prosciutto, pancetta, or bacon

2 eggs

¼ cup Parmesan cheese, grated

¼ teaspoon ground black pepper

Pinch nutmeg

1 cup white wine or vermouth

2 tablespoons butter

1. Place a pot of water over high heat, cover it and let it come to a boil. Cook the pasta according to package directions.

2. Place a skillet over medium-low heat. Chop the meat into matchstick-sized pieces and add to the skillet when it is warm. Cook until crispy. Drain off all but 1 tablespoon of the drippings.

3. In a small bowl, whisk the eggs, cheese, pepper, and nutmeg. Increase the heat on the skillet to medium and add the wine. Stir occasionally and let the wine reduce until it is a light syrup. Add the butter and stir it until it melts. Reduce heat to low and let the skillet sit until the pasta is cooked.

4. Drain the spaghetti and pour it into the skillet. Toss to coat the spaghetti evenly with the sauce. Pour the egg mixture over the pasta and stir vigorously until the noodles are coated and the egg has set. Serve immediately.

Roasted Tomatillo and Green Chili Sauce

You can either purée this sauce until smooth and use in a dish like the Enchilada Casserole (page 37) or you can keep it chunky and use it like salsa with chips.

INGREDIENTS | MAKES 1 PINT

10 tomatillos
1 tablespoon olive oil
1 small onion, quartered
2 cloves garlic, peeled
2 Anaheim chilies, seeded
Juice from 2 limes
Salt to taste

Tomatillos, the Distant Tomato Cousin

Tomatillos look like green tomatoes wrapped in a green, papery husk. The Aztecs in Mexico domesticated the tomatillo around 800 B.C. They're generally smaller than apricots. They have a tart, slightly bitter taste when raw, but roasting them brings out the sugars and the tartness mellows to a refreshing flavor.

1. Preheat oven to 350°F. Remove the papery husks from the tomatillos and wash them. Remove the core and cut into quarters.

2. Place a large skillet over medium heat and once it is heated, add the olive oil, vegetables, garlic, and chilies. Shake the pan frequently to keep ingredients from sticking. Cook for about 10 minutes. Place the skillet in the middle of the oven.

3. Roast for 30 minutes. Remove the pan from the oven and cool.

4. Place the vegetables in a blender or food processor. Add the lime juice. Pulse several times to get the desired texture. Taste and add salt as needed. Place in a tightly sealed container and refrigerate for up to one week.

Ethiopian Berberé Red Pepper Paste

Berberé is the official language of Ethiopia, where this intensely spicy sauce is used as a condiment. To reduce the heat, use less or omit the cayenne pepper. You can also use this paste as a rub on meat before grilling.

INGREDIENTS | **MAKES 1½ CUPS OF PASTE**

1 teaspoon ground ginger

1 teaspoon ground cardamom

1 teaspoon ground coriander

¼ teaspoon ground nutmeg

⅛ teaspoon ground cloves

⅛ teaspoon ground allspice

½ teaspoon ground cinnamon

2 tablespoons onion, minced

2 garlic cloves, minced

2 tablespoons salt

1½ cups water

1 cup sweet paprika

½ cup smoky paprika

2 teaspoons ground cayenne pepper

½ teaspoon black pepper

1. Place a dry cast-iron skillet over medium heat. Once it is hot, add the ginger, cardamom, coriander, nutmeg, cloves, allspice, and cinnamon and cook for 1 minute. They should start to smell nutty.

2. Pour the spices into a blender and add the onion, garlic, salt, and ¼ cup of water. Blend into a paste.

3. Reduce the heat on the skillet to low. Add the paprika, cayenne pepper, and black pepper in the skillet. Toast for 1–2 minutes. Stir in the rest of the water, ¼ cup at a time. Once the water is combined stir in the blended mixture.

4. Stir continuously for 10–15 minutes. Transfer the paste to a jar and cool to room temperature. Store in the refrigerator for several weeks, as long as there is a film of oil on top of the paste.

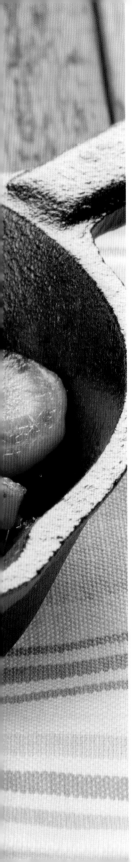

Chapter 5

Vegetables in a Skillet

Sour Creamed Greens

Most people make creamed greens dishes with a lot of heavy cream.
But you can substitute sour cream (even the fat-free variety) to get a similar and healthier dish.

INGREDIENTS | SERVES 4

1½ pounds fresh mustard greens, spinach, or chard

½ cup chicken broth

1 tablespoon butter

1 tablespoon olive oil

1 medium onion, chopped

2 cloves garlic, minced

Salt to taste

Pepper to taste

½ cup sour cream

1. Rinse the greens well and cut out tough stems if necessary. Tear the leaves into smaller pieces. Place a skillet over medium heat. Add the greens and the chicken broth. Boil for about 10 minutes. They should be bright green. Place the greens in a bowl temporarily.

2. Add the butter and oil to the skillet. Once the butter is melted, add the onion and garlic. Cook for about 5–7 minutes or until the onions are soft and starting to brown. Add the greens back into the skillet and season with salt and pepper.

3. Cook for 1–2 minutes until warmed through. Slowly stir in the sour cream. Cook for 1 minute. Serve hot.

Sautéed Okra and Tomatoes

Okra cooked with tomatoes is a classic Southern dish, and by pan-frying the okra
first before mixing in the tomatoes, you prevent them from becoming sticky.

INGREDIENTS | SERVES 6–8

1 pound okra pods, stemmed and sliced into rings

3 tablespoons vegetable oil

1 small yellow onion, chopped

3 large fresh tomatoes, seeded and chopped

2 garlic cloves, minced

1 tablespoon apple cider vinegar

Salt to taste

Pepper to taste

1. Wash the okra pods, cut off the stem ends, and slice the pods into ¼" slices. Pat them dry to prevent oil splatters. Place a skillet over medium-high heat. Once it is heated, add the oil, onion, and okra. Cook them for several minutes on each side. The onion should be golden brown about the same time that the okra is crispy on the cut sides.

2. Add the tomatoes and garlic, stirring continually for 2–3 minutes, or just until the tomatoes are cooked through. Pour into a bowl and sprinkle with the apple cider vinegar. Stir to combine and taste before adding salt and pepper.

Sautéed Radishes with Scallions

Radishes are members of the mustard and horseradish family.
Their pungent flavor turns off many people, but when cooked their flavor becomes very mild.

INGREDIENTS | SERVES 4

1 tablespoon butter

2 bunches red radishes, cleaned, stemmed, quartered

1 scallion, chopped into rings

½ cup chicken stock

Salt to taste

1. Place a skillet over medium heat. When it is heated, add the butter. Once the butter has melted, add the radishes and stir frequently for 2–3 minutes, or until the radishes have started to soften.

2. Sprinkle the scallion over the radishes and pour the chicken broth into the skillet. Cover the skillet and let the radishes cook for about 4 minutes.

3. Once the radishes are tender, uncover and increase the heat. Boil rapidly until the liquid has evaporated. Stir frequently to keep them from sticking. Sprinkle lightly with salt and serve immediately.

Caramelized Carrots

Parsnips can be substituted in this dish. If using parsnips,
cut them into long, skinny strips instead of rings so they cook evenly.

INGREDIENTS | SERVES 6–8

1 pound carrots, peeled and cut into ¼" thick slices

½ cup apple juice

Water, as needed

1 lemon

2 tablespoons butter

2 tablespoons olive oil

¼ cup brown sugar

¼ cup slivered or sliced almonds

1. Place a skillet over medium heat. Add the carrots and apple juice. Add enough water to just cover the carrots. Simmer for about 5–7 minutes, or until the thickest pieces can be pierced with a fork. Drain off the water.

2. Use a Microplane or zester to remove about 1 tablespoon of peel from the lemon. Squeeze the lemon to get 2 tablespoons of juice. Place the skillet back over medium heat and add the lemon zest, lemon juice, butter, oil, and brown sugar. Stir to combine. Once it starts to bubble, reduce the heat slightly and stir frequently to keep the carrots from sticking. Cook for about 5 minutes. They should be soft and glazed. Serve while hot and garnish with the almonds.

Roasted Broccoli with Parmesan

This is a great recipe for using up a head of broccoli that may be slightly past its prime.

INGREDIENTS | **SERVES 6**

3 pounds broccoli

6 tablespoons olive oil

¾ teaspoon red pepper flakes

Pinch salt

Pinch pepper

¾ cup grated Parmesan cheese

⅓ cup white wine vinegar

1. Preheat oven to 450°F. Place a skillet in the middle of the oven. Trim the bottoms off the broccoli stems. Peel the stems and cut them into skinny florets. Place in a bowl and toss with the oil, pepper flakes, salt, and pepper. Spread the broccoli throughout the skillet. Sprinkle the cheese over the broccoli.

2. Place the pan in the middle of the oven and cook for 20–25 minutes, or until the stems have softened.

3. Place the broccoli on a serving platter. Pour the vinegar into the skillet and stir, scraping the caramelized bits off the bottom. Pour the pan juices over the broccoli and serve.

Cauliflower with Chickpeas and Mustard Seeds

This dish makes a lot of food but the leftovers can easily be substituted in Shepherd's Pie (page 174).

INGREDIENTS | **SERVES 6–8**

1 medium white onion, chopped

1 tablespoon olive oil

5 tablespoons of yellow or black mustard seeds

1 head cauliflower, divided into florets

Pinch salt

1 can chickpeas, drained and rinsed

¼ cup white wine

1. Place a skillet over medium heat. Once the skillet is heated add the onion, olive oil, and mustard seeds. Stir frequently and let the onion cook until it starts to turn brown.

2. Add the cauliflower florets to the skillet with a sprinkle of salt.

3. Stir to combine and cook for 4 minutes. Add the chickpeas to the skillet with the white wine. Stir to combine.

4. Cover the skillet and cook for 3–4 minutes. Remove the lid and let the liquid evaporate. Serve when the cauliflower is fork tender.

Asian Potatoes with Chili and Shallots

Serve these potatoes with the Coconut Milk Fried Chicken (page 236).

INGREDIENTS | SERVES 4

3 shallots, or 1 small yellow onion

2 serrano chilies

½ teaspoon plus 1 pinch salt

1½ pounds Yukon Gold potatoes, cut into 6 wedges

¼ cup peanut oil

1 teaspoon apple cider vinegar

1. Mince the shallots and chilies finely. Place in a bowl, sprinkle ½ teaspoon salt, and toss to combine. Let sit for 10 minutes. Smash the vegetables into a slight paste.

2. Place a skillet over medium-high heat. Add the oil, then add the potatoes when the oil is warmed. Nudge them for 3 minutes to keep from sticking. Turn them over and cook for 3–5 minutes. Once the outsides are crispy, place on paper towels to drain.

3. Drain off most of the oil. Place over medium heat and add the paste. Stir continually for 4–5 minutes. Once it smells toasty, add the potatoes and toss until they're well-coated and warmed. Sprinkle vinegar and pinch of salt over the potatoes and serve immediately.

Icelandic Sugar-Glazed Potatoes

This dish is fantastic only on the day it's made. Leftovers can be chopped up and served in another dish, but are disappointing if you try to reheat them. Serve this dish with Icelandic Sweet and Tangy Pork (page 129).

INGREDIENTS | SERVES 8–10

Water as needed

2 pounds waxy potatoes

4 tablespoons sugar

3 tablespoons butter

¼ cup very hot water

1. Place a large pan of water over high heat. Boil the potatoes whole for 20 minutes. When you can insert a knife to the middle of the potato, it is ready. Remove them to cool. Peel skins and cut into thick slices.

2. Place a skillet over medium heat. Add the sugar and butter. If the sugar starts to smoke, lower the temperature. Whisk them together. Add 1–3 tablespoons of water that the potatoes were boiled in.

3. Place the potatoes in the skillet one at a time and stir to coat. If the mixture won't coat, increase the temperature slightly and add 1–2 tablespoons of water. When all of the potatoes are coated in sugar and warm, serve.

Pommes Fondantes

It's best to use potatoes that are no larger than 2" across for this dish.

INGREDIENTS | SERVES 4–6

2 pounds baby red potatoes

2 cups chicken or vegetable broth

2 tablespoons olive oil

1 tablespoon butter

1 tablespoon chopped sorrel or thyme

½ teaspoon salt

What Happens When You "Melt" Potatoes

"Pommes Fondantes" translates from French as "melted potatoes." Slow cooking these potatoes makes the inside creamy and then frying them in butter makes the outside crispy. These are likely to stick so use a well-seasoned skillet for this dish.

1. Wash the potatoes and remove the eyes. Arrange as many as possible in a 10"- or 12" skillet. Add all of the remaining ingredients. Bring the pan to a boil, reduce the heat to medium, then cover with a lid that is slightly ajar. Cook the potatoes for 15–20 minutes or until a fork can be inserted easily.

2. Make sure the liquid covers half of the potatoes and add more broth if necessary. Use the bottom of a sturdy drinking glass to lightly smash the potatoes so the skins barely crack. Place the pan over medium-high heat and cook until all of the liquid has evaporated and the potatoes are brown on one side, about 10–12 minutes.

3. Use a pair of tongs to gently turn the potatoes. Cook for 5–7 minutes until brown on the other side. If necessary, add another tablespoon of olive oil.

4. Remove the pan from the heat and let the potatoes rest for about 5 minutes before sprinkling with a little extra salt to serve.

Potatoes Au Gratin

Cooking this dish in a cast-iron skillet should give you crunchier edges and crust. Use a very well-seasoned skillet when making this dish to prevent sticking.

INGREDIENTS | SERVES 6

2 tablespoons olive oil

1 tablespoon butter

1 small onion, finely chopped

1 large clove garlic, minced

1 tablespoon flour

1¼ cups milk

1½ cups heavy cream

1 cup Gruyère cheese, shredded

¼ cup Parmesan cheese, shredded

2½ pounds potatoes sliced ⅛" thick

Salt to taste

Pepper to taste

Melty Cheese Substitutes

Gruyère and Emmenthaler are great cheeses to use in dishes like this when you want a subtly complex flavor and smooth melting. But if you can't find Gruyère cheese, or are looking for a more economical substitute, you can substitute Monterey Jack for a milder flavor or a mixture of Provolone and Cheddar cheese for a stronger flavor.

1. Preheat oven to 350°F and place a rack in the center of the oven.

2. Place a skillet over medium heat. Once it is heated add the olive oil, butter, and onion. Cook for 3–5 minutes until translucent but not brown. Add the garlic and cook for 1 minute.

3. Add the flour to the skillet and stir for 1 minute. Slowly add the milk, stirring continually to prevent lumps. Slowly add the cream, stirring continually, until it just comes to a simmer. Reduce the heat to low and simmer until slightly thickened.

4. Add the Gruyère cheese and stir until it melts. Turn off the heat. Sprinkle the salt and pepper on the potatoes. Slowly add them to the pan, a few at a time. Use the spoon to push the potatoes to the bottom of the skillet and make even layers.

4. Once all of the potatoes are in the skillet, sprinkle the Parmesan cheese on top and bake for 45 minutes. Let it rest for 10 minutes before serving.

Tortilla Española

This is great for breakfast. To spice it up, mix in some chopped peppers,
serve it with salsa, or sprinkle some shredded cheese on top.

INGREDIENTS | SERVES 4

½ cup olive oil

1 pound russet potatoes, peeled, quartered, and sliced

1 medium onion, halved and thinly sliced

5 eggs

Pinch salt

Pinch pepper

Secrets to Tortilla Success

This dish is more about technique than ingredients. To get a perfect dish, make sure the potatoes are evenly sliced, and make sure to use a very well-seasoned skillet. The skillet must be very hot when you put the egg-coated potatoes back into it. The hot skillet will cook the eggs quickly and help prevent them from sticking.

1. Place a skillet over medium-high heat. Once it is warm add the oil. Add the potatoes and onion. Cook for 20 minutes, folding the mixture every other minute. The potatoes should be soft, but not brown.

2. Place a colander in a bowl to catch the oil. Pour the potatoes into the colander and let them drain for a few minutes.

3. Crack the eggs into a large bowl. Whisk in some salt and pepper. Stir the drained potato mixture into the eggs.

4. Place 1 tablespoon of the oil into the skillet over medium heat. Once the skillet and oil are hot add the egg and potato mixture. Reduce the heat to medium-low. Shake the pan frequently to keep the mixture from sticking. Cook for 8–10 minutes or until the edges are cooked but the center isn't cooked through.

5. Place a large plate on top of the skillet and invert the pan to remove the potato mixture. Place a tablespoon of oil into the pan and slide the potato mixture into the skillet with the cooked side up. Cook for 3 minutes. Slide the tortilla onto a cutting board and cool for 10 minutes. Cut into wedges and serve with more salt and pepper.

Vegetable Green Curry

Use Green Curry Paste (page 54) for this dish.

INGREDIENTS | SERVES 4

¼ cup Green Curry Paste

2 cups vegetable broth

1 large sweet potato, peeled and cut into ½" cubes

¼ pound green beans, stems removed

8 ounces sliced button mushrooms

8 ounces fresh spinach leaves

Juice from 1 lime

1 can of coconut milk

Thai Curry Dishes versus Indian Curry Dishes

Even though both cuisines call their dishes curry, they're fairly different. Thai dishes use a paste made mostly from fresh ingredients and vegetables and usually involve coconut milk. Indian dishes are usually flavored with a dried spice mixture. Indian curries can either be dry or cooked with tomato sauce or broth and clarified butter.

1. Place a skillet over medium heat. Once it is heated, add the curry paste and the vegetable broth and stir to combine.

2. Stir in the sweet potato cubes, cover, and cook for 15–20 minutes or until you can pierce them with a fork. Stir the contents occasionally to keep them from sticking.

3. Turn up the heat to medium-high and remove the lid. Add the remaining vegetables and cook for 5–7 minutes, stirring frequently.

4. Once the liquid has reduced, lower the heat to medium-low and add the lime juice and coconut milk. Keep the coconut milk from boiling and cook for 2–3 minutes. Serve in bowls with cooked white rice.

Kale with Bacon and Tomatoes

If you can't find kale, substitute spinach or Swiss chard and reduce the cooking time from 15 minutes to 5. You can also keep more of the bacon fat and omit the olive oil to get a truly flavorful dish. Be sure to taste the dish before adding more salt.

INGREDIENTS | SERVES 6–8

2 pounds kale

4 slices bacon

1 tablespoon olive oil

1 small onion, chopped

2 garlic cloves, minced

Salt to taste

Pepper to taste

2 Roma tomatoes, seeded and chopped

2 tablespoons balsamic vinegar

All Hail Kale

Kale has been cooked in so many parts of the world, and for so long, that food historians don't know where it originated. Because it grows easily in all climates, it has migrated with travelers throughout most of the world. It's incredibly high in vitamins and minerals and has helped sustain people during rough times.

1. Strip all the stems from the leaves and discard. Wash the leaves thoroughly and shake or drain until fairly dry. Chop or tear the leaves into large pieces and set aside.

2. Place a large skillet over medium-high heat and when heated, add the strips of bacon. Cook till crisp, remove from the pan, and let cool. Pour off all but 1 tablespoon of the bacon fat.

3. Add the olive oil to the skillet with the bacon fat and the chopped onion. Cook for 5-7 minutes, or until the onion is soft and starting to brown. Stir in the minced garlic clove.

4. Add a large bunch of kale to the skillet and sprinkle with salt and pepper. Cover with a lid for 1 minute to wilt the kale. Use a spoon to move the wilted kale to the outsides of the skillet. Repeat until all of the kale has been added. Stir frequently and cook for 15–20 minutes till tender.

5. Crumble the cooked bacon and sprinkle on top with the tomato. Sprinkle the balsamic vinegar over the kale and toss to combine. Remove to a bowl and serve immediately.

Spicy Mustard Greens

Mustard greens are less bitter than kale or collard greens, and have a much more peppery flavor, similar to arugula. But a splash of spicy vinegar will help combat any remaining bitter flavor.

INGREDIENTS | **SERVES 6**

2 large bunches mustard greens

3 tablespoons olive oil

2 medium onions, chopped

6 garlic cloves, minced

1 teaspoon ground cumin

1 teaspoon dried crushed red pepper flakes

1 cup chicken or vegetable broth

Salt and pepper to taste

Spicy vinegar as condiment

1. Remove the veins from the leaves and rinse them thoroughly in cold water. Shake dry and tear into large pieces.

2. Place a skillet over medium-high heat and once heated, add the oil and onion. Stir frequently until they're soft and starting to turn brown, about 10 minutes.

3. Stir in the garlic, cumin, and crushed red pepper and cook for 3 minutes.

4. Add one batch of the greens and cover for 1–2 minutes until the greens wilt. Repeat with the other batches until all the greens have been added and have wilted.

5. Add the broth, cover, and reduce the heat to low. Let the greens cook for 30–45 minutes. They should be very tender. Taste before adding salt and pepper. Serve while hot with spicy vinegar for people to garnish as they wish.

Fried Tomato and Corn Salad

This dish is good served cold, which makes it great for taking to a summer barbecue.

INGREDIENTS | **SERVES 4–6**

1 pint cherry or grape tomatoes

1 poblano pepper

1 tablespoon olive oil

Kernels from 2 ears of sweet corn or 2 cups of frozen corn

1 small onion

2 teaspoons sherry or rice wine vinegar

Salt to taste

Pepper to taste

⅓ cup chopped cilantro

1. Place the tomatoes in the freezer for at least 2 hours, or overnight.

2. Use long tongs to hold the pepper over a burner set on high heat. Rotate and move the pepper until all of the skin has blackened and bubbled. Wrap it in a paper towel and roll it tightly in foil for 2 minutes. Remove the foil and use the paper towel to rub the skin off the pepper. Be careful not to burn yourself. Remove the stem and the seeds from the pepper and dice it finely.

3. Place a skillet over high heat and add the oil. Once it starts to smoke, add the tomatoes to the skillet. Wear an oven mitt around your wrist or use a splatter screen to protect yourself if the tomatoes pop. Shake the skillet back and forth frequently. Once the tomatoes start to thaw and release their juice, drain them and add the corn. Toss to combine and cook for 2–3 minutes. Drain again if necessary and add the onion and pepper and cook for an additional 2–3 minutes. The onions should be soft.

4. Stir in the vinegar and season with salt, pepper, and the fresh cilantro and serve either hot, warm, or cold.

Bulgur Salad with Roasted Chickpeas and Lemon

Bulgur is whole pieces of wheat that have been cleaned, parboiled, dried, and sorted into sizes. It's healthier than rice or pasta, and just as easy.

INGREDIENTS | **SERVES 4**

1¼ cups water
1 cup coarse bulgur
1 medium red onion, thinly sliced
2 tablespoons olive oil
Juice from 1 lemon
2 bay leaves
1 teaspoon cumin seeds
½ teaspoon ground turmeric
½ teaspoon ground paprika
1 pinch cayenne pepper
1 15-ounce can chickpeas, rinsed and drained
Salt to taste
Pepper to taste

1. Preheat the oven to 400°F.

2. Bring the water to a boil in a saucepan and add the bulgur and a pinch of salt. Let it sit for 20 minutes until all of the water has been absorbed.

3. Place a skillet over medium heat. Once it is heated, add the onion, oil, lemon juice, bay leaves, cumin, turmeric, paprika, and cayenne. Stir until the onions are coated with the spices. Cook the onions for 5–7 minutes until they're soft and the spices smell toasted. Stir the chickpeas into the onions and cook until they start to sizzle.

4. Place the skillet into the middle of the oven for 20 minutes and stir halfway through. Remove the skillet from the oven, discard the bay leaves, and season with salt and pepper as necessary. Pour over the bulgur and serve while hot.

Matar Palak: Peas and Spinach Indian Style

This dish tends to be fairly spicy. If you prefer a mild dish you can use 1 jalapeño instead of several of the green chilies.

INGREDIENTS | SERVES 4

16 ounces frozen spinach, thawed

3–4 green chilies, with or without the seeds

1 cup chicken broth

1 potato, peeled and chopped

1 tomato, seeded and chopped

1 tablespoon oil

1 medium onion, chopped

1 tablespoon ground cumin

1 garlic clove, minced

2 cups frozen peas

1 teaspoon turmeric

Salt to taste

Pepper to taste

1. Place the spinach and chilies in a food processor. Cut out the seeds to reduce the spiciness. Pulse until you get a paste, scraping the sides of the bowl when necessary.

2. Place a skillet over medium heat. Once it is heated add the chicken broth and potato. Simmer for 10 minutes, or until potatoes can be pierced with a fork but are not soft. Pour off the remaining broth and add the chopped tomato.

3. Add the oil, onion, cumin, and garlic. Stir until combined and cook for 5 minutes, or until the onion is soft and the cumin smells toasted. Stir in the spinach and chili mixture, and let it cook for 10 minutes.

4. Add the peas to the skillet and cook for 5 minutes. They should be warmed and tender. Stir in the turmeric and season with salt and pepper.

Palak Paneer: Indian Spinach with Fresh Cheese

This Indian dish may also be called saag paneer. "Palak" and "saag" are often used to mean "spinach" or similar green. Paneer is an unsalted and unaged cheese. If you can't find paneer you can substitute feta or firm tofu.

INGREDIENTS | **SERVES 4 AS A SIDE, 2 AS A MAIN COURSE**

1 tablespoon vegetable oil

1 small yellow onion, chopped

½ teaspoon ground turmeric

1 teaspoon ground cumin

1 teaspoon garam masala powder

1 pound frozen spinach, thawed, squeezed, and chopped

1 green jalapeño (optional), seeded and chopped

1 garlic clove, minced

1 small tomato, chopped

¼ cup chopped cilantro

1 teaspoon salt

12 ounces chicken broth

1 cup plain Greek yogurt

8 ounces paneer

1. Place a skillet over medium heat. Once it is warm, add the oil and the onion. Stir the onion frequently for 4–5 minutes, or until translucent.

2. Add the dried spices and stir continually for 2 minutes. The spices should be very fragrant.

3. Add the spinach to the skillet and stir, scraping any bits of spice off the bottom if necessary. Add the jalapeño, garlic, tomato, and cilantro. Cook for 10 minutes.

4. Add the salt and broth to the skillet and stir to combine. Let the liquid evaporate before stirring in the yogurt and cheese. Stir for 1–2 minutes until the cheese and yogurt are warmed. Serve immediately over cooked basmati rice.

Quinoa Pilaf

If you can't find quinoa at your local grocery store, you can substitute couscous.
Quinoa is a grain, but couscous, like pasta, is made from semolina flour.
Follow the cooking times on the package when following this recipe.

INGREDIENTS | SERVES 2

1 tablespoon olive oil

½ small onion, chopped

¼ teaspoon ground cinnamon

½ teaspoon ground coriander

½ teaspoon ground turmeric

Pinch red chili flakes

1 cup vegetable broth

1 small garlic clove, minced

½ cup quinoa

½ can red kidney beans, rinsed and drained

1 roma tomato, chopped

6 olives, chopped

2 tablespoons dried currants or cranberries

Salt

Pepper

1. Place a skillet over medium heat and when warm add the olive oil and onion. Cook for 5–7 minutes, stirring occasionally. The onion should be soft and just starting to turn golden. Add the cinnamon, coriander, turmeric, and chili flakes. Stir continually for one minute and then add the vegetable broth.

2. Use your spatula to loosen any spices or onion that may have stuck to the skillet. Add the garlic, quinoa, and beans. Reduce the heat to low, cover the skillet and simmer for 15 minutes. The water should be mostly absorbed.

3. Add the tomato, olives, and dried fruit. Stir and cook for 5 more minutes, or until the water is evaporated. Fluff with a fork and serve immediately.

Quinoa: Superfood

Quinoa is a grain-like crop from the Andes mountains in South America. Cultivated by the Incas, it was called the "mother of all grains," and is very high in protein and fiber. Quinoa grows with an outer coating but most quinoa sold in America has this coating removed and is ready to use.

Romanesco with Mushroom and Wine Sauce

If you can't find romanesco you can substitute cauliflower or broccoli.
If you substitute broccoli, skip the steps related to boiling the vegetable.
This dish is great served over rice or egg noodles.

INGREDIENTS | **SERVES 4–6**

1 head romanesco

1 teaspoon salt

Water, as needed

1 pound button mushrooms, sliced

3 shallots or 1 small yellow or red onion, sliced

3 tablespoons butter or olive oil

½ cup port, or other heavy red wine

½ teaspoon Dijon mustard

Romanesco, a Cousin of Cabbage

The Italians call it broccolo romanesco and the French call it chou romanesco. Like broccoli and cauliflower, it is a cousin of cabbage. Pick heads that are very firm with densely packed curds. Avoid any that are more yellow than green, or that have mold on them. The stalks are inedible, but the curds can be eaten raw.

1. Rinse the romanesco and break the clusters, or curds, off the stalks. Add salt to a pot of water with a steamer basket and bring to a boil over high heat. Once the water comes to a boil, add the romanesco and cover. Cook for 5 minutes. Remove from the water and drain well.

2. Place a skillet over medium heat and add the mushrooms, shallots and butter. Cook for 10–12 minutes, stirring every few minutes, until the shallots and mushrooms have softened and browned. Add the wine and mustard and reduce the heat to low.

3. After the romanesco has drained, add it to the skillet. Cook uncovered for an additional 5–10 minutes until the romanesco has reached the desired tenderness and the wine sauce has reduced.

Basic Sautéed Swiss Chard

Swiss chard is a hardy green with large leaves and a thick stem.
It has a much milder and less-bitter taste than mustard or collard greens.
Avoid leaves that are wilted, yellow, or that have holes in the spines.

INGREDIENTS | SERVES 2–3

1 pound Swiss chard

1 tablespoon olive oil

½ small onion, chopped

1 garlic clove, minced

Pinch crushed red pepper flakes

1 tablespoon cider or balsamic vinegar

Pinch nutmeg

½ cup chicken stock

Salt to taste

Pepper to taste

1. Run the chard under cold water to remove any leftover dirt. Cut the thick part of the stem out of the leaves and set aside. Tear the leaves into several pieces and place on a towel. Chop the stems into ½" pieces.

2. Place a skillet over medium heat. Once it is hot, add the oil, the stem pieces, and the onion. Cook for 5–7 minutes, or until the onion is translucent and just starting to brown.

3. Add the garlic, pepper flakes, vinegar, nutmeg, and stock. Stir to combine and bring to a boil.

4. Add the leaves and stir, cooking for 2–3 minutes before covering. They should be starting to wilt. Cook for 4-5 minutes, or until the leaves are cooked through and limp.

5. Remove the lid and stir frequently as the liquid evaporates. Taste and add more vinegar, salt, or pepper as needed. Serve immediately.

Chapter 6

Chicken and Poultry in a Skillet

Turkey Fillets with Anchovies, Capers, and Dill

Turkey breast is often cheapest after Thanksgiving. If wrapped tightly in plastic this dish can be frozen for 3 months. To make your own fillets, slice the breast into ⅜" slices.

INGREDIENTS | SERVES 4

2 tablespoons olive oil

6 anchovy fillets, or 1 tablespoon anchovy paste

4 turkey fillets, 4–6 ounces each, pounded thin

¼ cup chicken broth

1 tablespoon capers, chopped

2 tablespoons dill, chopped

1. Place a skillet over medium heat. Once the skillet is heated, add the oil and the anchovies. Cook for 5 minutes, stirring continually, or until they fall apart.

2. Place as many turkey fillets in the skillet as possible without overlapping. Cook on each side for 3 minutes, or until they're nicely browned. Repeat as necessary and remove the cooked fillets to a plate and keep warm.

3. Add the chicken broth to the pan and use a spoon to scrape up any bits from the bottom of the pan. Stir in the capers. Cook for 1 minute until the sauce reduces.

4. Pour the sauce over the turkey fillets and sprinkle them with chopped dill. Serve while warm.

Ginger Chicken

This dish freezes fairly well in case you'd like to make a larger batch for leftovers.

INGREDIENTS | SERVES 4

4 boneless, skinless chicken breasts

1 cup flour

2 teaspoons ground ginger

1 teaspoon salt

½ teaspoon ground black pepper

3 tablespoons vegetable oil

¼ cup soy sauce

¾ cup brown sugar

1 20-ounce can crushed pineapple, drained

½ cup water

1. Rinse the chicken breasts and pat dry. Mix the flour with the ground ginger, salt, and pepper. Dredge the chicken in the flour and shake to remove excess flour.

2. Place a skillet over medium heat. Once it is warmed add the oil and the chicken breasts. Cook on each side for 2–3 minutes. Remove from the pan and set aside.

3. Stir the remaining ingredients in a bowl and pour into the hot skillet. Once the mixture starts to boil, lower the heat to medium-low and return the chicken to the pan. Cook on each side for 12 minutes.

4. Once the center of the chicken is no longer pink, remove it from the skillet and serve over rice.

Traditional Sunday Roast Chicken

This is a perfect introductory recipe for either a new cook or a new skillet.
Serve with Chicken Gravy (page 55).

INGREDIENTS | SERVES 4–6

1 whole roaster chicken (5–7 pounds)

2 garlic cloves, sliced

3 tablespoons chopped fresh herbs, or 1 tablespoon dried oregano, basil, or thyme

1 teaspoon salt

¼ teaspoon pepper

3 tablespoons butter

1 tangerine or small orange

2 baking potatoes

1. Preheat oven to 425°F. Remove any giblets or other loose bits from the cavity of the chicken and rinse it inside and out with cold water. Pat dry. Mix the garlic slices, herbs, spices, and 2 tablespoons of butter together.

2. Starting at the breast near the neck, slide your fingers between the skin and the meat. Spread half the butter mixture between the skin and the breast meat. Spread the remainder of the butter and herb mixture between the skin and meat on the thighs and legs. Sprinkle with salt and pepper.

3. Roll the orange across a counter, and poke several holes in it. Place inside the cavity of the chicken.

4. Place a 10" or 12" skillet over medium heat. Spread the remaining tablespoon of butter over the bird. Place breast side up in the skillet and turn off the heat. Place the skillet into the center of the oven. Cook for 10 minutes. Wash the potatoes and cut into long strips no more than ¾" thick. Sprinkle with salt and pepper. Set aside.

5. Turn the oven down to 375°F and remove the pan. Turn the bird on its side. Pile the potatoes around the chicken to keep it from falling over. Return the pan to the oven for 15 minutes. Turn the bird to its other side, and cook for 15 more minutes.

6. Carefully turn the chicken on its back and cook for 30 minutes. Use a thermometer to make sure that the meat of the thickest part of the thigh is at least 165°F. Remove from the pan and place on a cutting board or platter. Cover loosely with foil to keep warm and let rest for 15 minutes before cutting and serving.

Pressed and Roasted Cornish Game Hens

The pressing technique used in this recipe permits the chicken to cook quickly since it is pressed thin. And use the other hot, empty skillet in the oven to make Oven-Fried Potatoes (page 14).

INGREDIENTS | SERVES 4

2 Rock Cornish hens

Salt and pepper to taste

Small handful of fresh oregano, tarragon, or thyme leaves, minced

3 tablespoons softened butter

1 shallot, minced

¼ cup vegetable or chicken stock

1. Preheat oven to 400°F. Place two cast-iron skillets in the middle rack of the oven. One skillet must be able to fit inside the other and the skillet that will be on top must be large enough to cover both hens.

2. Rinse the hens. Cut the spines off the bird to they can be flattened out. If necessary, snip the breast bone to permit the bird to flatten. Pat the birds dry and sprinkle both sides lightly with salt and pepper.

3. Mix the minced herbs into the softened butter. Slide your fingers between the skin and the meat of the chicken. Rub the butter under the skin and on top of each bird evenly.

4. Remove the bottom skillet from the oven, place the birds skin side down, and cook over medium-high heat for 3–4 minutes. Flip them, and place in the middle of the oven with the other skillet on top. Cook for 25 minutes, or until the internal temperature of the breast is 160°F. Place the birds on a plate, cover loosely with foil and set aside to rest.

5. Place the skillet that held the chicken over medium-high heat. Let most of the liquid boil off, but stir to remove any bits stuck to the pan. Once the liquid in the skillet turns light brown, add the shallot and cook for 2–3 minutes. Add the stock to the skillet and stir vigorously. Once the liquid has evaporated, turn off the heat.

6. Cut each chicken in half. Place each half on a plate and spoon out some of the shallot and pan sauce over the chicken. Serve immediately.

Chicken Thighs Stuffed with Apricots and Cheese

If you don't have dried apricots, you can use any dried fruit.
Dates would work great as would cranberries or cherries.

INGREDIENTS | **SERVES 4**

2 tablespoons olive oil

1 large onion, thinly sliced

1 carrot, thinly sliced

1 stalk celery, thinly sliced

4 boneless, skinless chicken thighs

½ cup dried apricots, chopped

½ cup provolone cheese, cubed

¾ cup panko or unseasoned bread crumbs

1 tablespoon chopped fresh thyme

Pinch salt

Pinch pepper

Chicken Thighs— the New Chicken Breasts?

Boneless skinless chicken breasts are the most common cut at grocery stores, which means other cuts are often cheaper. Chicken thighs do have about 10% more of your recommended daily allowance of fat than breast meat, but they have only about 50 more calories.

1. Place a skillet over medium-high heat. Once it is heated, add the oil and onion and cook for 10–12 minutes. Remove half of the onion mixture from the skillet and put into a bowl.

2. Add the carrot and celery to the skillet and cook for 4–5 minutes, or until the celery is just starting to soften. Turn off the heat.

3. Trim any excess fat from the thighs and lightly pound them so they're flat. Add the apricot, cheese, panko, thyme, and a sprinkle of salt and pepper to the bowl. Toss lightly and add ¼ of the mixture to each thigh.

4. Roll the thigh starting with the widest edge and rolling toward the smallest edge. Use toothpicks or kitchen twine to hold it together. Place it back in the skillet over medium-high heat. Move the vegetables to the edges of the skillet. Sear the chicken on each side for 3–4 minutes, or until it is lightly browned on all sides.

5. Reduce the heat to medium-low, cover, and cook for 20 minutes, until the center measures 150°F. Turn off the heat and let it rest for 5 minutes before serving.

Bourbon-Glazed Chicken

Cooking with liquor is a good way to infuse a lot of flavor into a dish.
As long as the liquid comes to a boil, the alcohol content is significantly reduced.

INGREDIENTS | SERVES 4

2 tablespoons vegetable oil

2 carrots, grated

1 stalk celery, thinly sliced

1 small yellow onion, diced

¼ cup chicken broth

4 boneless, skinless chicken breasts

Pinch salt

Pinch pepper

2 tablespoons bourbon

2 cups cooked white rice

¼ cup almond slivers

1. Place a skillet over medium heat. Once it is heated, add the oil, carrots, celery, and onion and cook for 5–7 minutes, stirring frequently. The vegetables should be soft and the onions should be turning brown.

2. Pour the chicken broth over the vegetables. Sprinkle the breasts with salt and pepper and place on top of the vegetables. Cover the skillet and steam for about 15 minutes.

3. Remove the lid and place the chicken on a plate and keep warm. Increase the heat and add the bourbon. Let the liquid boil for 10–15 minutes, or until it becomes very thick.

4. Return the chicken breasts to the pan with the almond slivers. Cook the chicken for 2 minutes on each side to warm and become coated in sauce.

5. Place a ½ cup of rice in the middle of a plate with a chicken breast on top. Spoon the vegetables and glaze over the chicken. Serve while hot.

Sour Cream Chili Bake

Because of the tomato sauce in this dish, this isn't a good recipe for a fairly new skillet. Tomato sauces can remove seasoning from a new skillet.

INGREDIENTS | SERVES 4–6

1 pound lean ground chicken

½ small onion, finely chopped

1 teaspoon ground cumin

1 10-ounce can enchilada sauce

1 8-ounce can tomato sauce

1 15-ounce can pinto beans

6 ounces crushed tortilla chips

2 cups shredded Cheddar cheese

Salt to taste

1 cup sour cream

6 ounces tortilla chips

Spice It Up!

This is a weeknight-easy dish that can be made to suit your family's spice level. Mild enchilada sauce will result in a tame dish. You can also use spicy enchilada sauce, or double the mild sauce and leave out the tomato sauce. You could also substitute 1 cup of salsa for the plain tomato sauce to add even more flavor and texture to the dish.

1. Preheat oven to 350°F. Place a skillet over medium heat. When the skillet has warmed, crumble the ground chicken into the skillet, breaking it into chunks. Cook for several minutes using a wooden spoon or spatula to cut and toss the meat.

2. Sprinkle in the onion and cumin. Continue stirring and chopping until the meat is more brown than pink. Drain any excess fat. Add the enchilada sauce, tomato sauce, beans, crushed chips, and 1½ cups cheese. Stir to combine so the cheese melts evenly. Taste and add salt and cumin if desired. Place the skillet in the middle of the oven and bake for 30 minutes.

3. When the edges of the casserole are crispy and the mixture is lightly bubbling, sprinkle the remaining cheese across the top and bake for 2–3 minutes or until the cheese melts.

4. Serve with chips and sour cream as a garnish.

Chicken and Broccoli Stir-Fry

Almost any vegetables can be used instead of broccoli in this dish.

INGREDIENTS | SERVES 4

3 scallions, thinly sliced

2 cloves garlic, minced

1" piece ginger, peeled and thinly sliced

1 tablespoon soy sauce

1 tablespoon honey

1 tablespoon cornstarch

1¼ teaspoons salt

1 tablespoon sherry

1 tablespoon sesame oil

1 pound boneless, skinless chicken breast, cut into cubes

1 broccoli head

3 tablespoons vegetable oil

2 tablespoons cold water

1 tablespoon hoisin sauce

1 tablespoon toasted sesame seeds, optional

1. Mix the scallion, garlic, ginger, soy sauce, honey, cornstarch, 1 teaspoon of the salt, sherry, and sesame oil in a bowl. Stir to eliminate all lumps of cornstarch. Add the chicken, toss to coat, and let the bowl sit at room temperature for 15–30 minutes.

2. Cut broccoli florets into bite-sized pieces. Slice the stalks into pieces about ¼" thick and no more than 2" long. Place a large skillet over high heat. Add 1 tablespoon of the oil along with the broccoli stems. Stir frequently for 30 seconds. Add the florets and 2 tablespoons of water. Toss and cook for 2 minutes before transferring to a bowl.

3. Add the remaining 2 tablespoons of oil. Remove the chicken from the marinade and add to the skillet. Toss continually for 3 minutes, or until the chicken starts to turn brown. Add the hoisin sauce and the broccoli and toss to combine. Add the marinade and stir continually until the sauce thickens.

4. Taste and season with salt and pepper before serving over cooked white rice. Sprinkle some toasted sesame seeds over the dish.

Chicken Étouffée

*Étoufée comes from the French étouffer, which means "to smother,"
and is basically a meat smothered in sauce and then poured over rice.*

INGREDIENTS | SERVES 6–8

1½ pounds bone-in chicken thighs

Pinch salt

Pinch pepper

½ cup all-purpose flour

½ cup vegetable oil

2 medium onions, chopped

2 medium bell peppers, chopped

2 jalapeño peppers, seeded, stemmed, and minced

15 garlic cloves, peeled and minced

2 teaspoons dried thyme

2 teaspoons dried sage

3 cups chicken broth

½ cup cooked white rice per serving

Hot sauce to taste

Substitution Options

Making this dish with 1 pound of crawfish meat is most common in Louisiana, but since they're hard to get outside of the area, you can substitute 1 pound of peeled shrimp or chicken. If using chicken, the dish will be much more flavorful if you use bone-in chicken thighs.

1. Season the chicken with salt and pepper and coat them with flour. Heat a skillet over medium-high heat. Add the oil. Once the oil is heated add the chicken and cook for 7 minutes on the first side. Flip the chicken and cook for 6–7 minutes more. Don't crowd the chicken, cook it in batches. Place the cooked chicken on a plate and keep it warm.

2. Stir the remaining flour into the pan to make a roux. (See Cajun Roux, page 50.) This roux should be light. Add the onions, peppers, and garlic.

3. Reduce the heat to low and stir in the thyme and the sage. Add the broth, slowly whisking the flour mixture to prevent lumps. Once you have a smooth sauce, return the chicken to the pot and bring to a boil.

4. Reduce the heat to low, cover, and cook for 20 minutes. The chicken should be very tender. Stir and flip occasionally.

5. Skim off any fat that may come to the top. Serve it over bowls of hot rice with hot sauce to taste.

Date and Balsamic Marinated Chicken Breast

The marinade in this dish is a great sauce, so serve the chicken over some rice or even mashed potatoes. You may also want to serve this dish over a pile of steamed cauliflower.

INGREDIENTS | SERVES 4

1 cup dried dates (about 12)
½ cup honey
½ cup balsamic vinegar
½ teaspoon salt
½ teaspoon Hungarian paprika
1 cup flour
4 boneless, skinless chicken breasts
3 tablespoons vegetable oil

1. Remove the pits from the dates and chop finely. Place them in a bowl with all of the other ingredients except the chicken and oil. Microwave in 20 second increments while stirring until the honey and vinegar can be easily combined. Pat the chicken breasts dry and place them in the marinade. Cover the bowl and let it sit on the counter for 30–60 minutes.

2. Place a skillet over medium-high heat and add 2 tablespoons of oil. Remove each breast from the marinade and let the excess marinade drip off. Once the oil is hot, add the chicken to the skillet so the pieces don't touch. (Cook in batches if necessary.) Cook the first side for about 3 minutes. Turn and cook the second side for 3 minutes.

3. Reduce the heat to medium and cook until the center is no longer pink. Remove the breasts from the pan and let them rest. Pour the remaining marinade into the skillet and bring to a boil before pouring over the breasts.

Coconut and Basil Chicken

Even if you don't like spicy food, keep the jalapeño for its flavor. To significantly reduce the heat in this dish, cut away the jalapeño's seeds and white veins, which contain most of the heat.

INGREDIENTS | **SERVES 4**

1 scallion, chopped with white and green separated

2" piece ginger, peeled and cut into matchsticks

1 cup coconut milk

1 cup Thai basil leaves

3 garlic cloves

2 teaspoons honey

1 teaspoon fish sauce

½ pound boneless, skinless chicken breast or thighs

Salt to taste

Pepper to taste

1 tablespoon vegetable oil

1 jalapeño pepper, seeded and thinly sliced

½ cup chopped cilantro, for garnish

2 tablespoons toasted coconut for garnish

2 lime slices for garnish

4 cups cooked white jasmine rice

1. Combine the scallion, ginger, coconut milk, basil, garlic, honey, and fish sauce in a blender and purée until smooth.

2. Remove any fat or skin from the chicken, cut the meat into 1" cubes and sprinkle the chicken with a little salt and pepper.

3. Place a skillet over medium-high heat and when it is warm, add the vegetable oil. Add the chicken. Cook for 3 minutes on each side, or until lightly browned. Reduce heat to medium-low.

4. Pour the coconut sauce and jalapeños over the chicken. Cover and cook for 8–10 minutes until the sauce just starts to bubble. Once the chicken is firm and no longer pink in the middle, it is ready to serve with the garnishes over cooked rice.

Garnishing Asian Dishes

People from many Asian cultures don't consider a meal complete without garnishes, which differ from cuisine to cuisine. This dish takes its influence from Thai cuisine and many Thai recipes are served with lime wedges, soy sauce, toasted coconut, chopped cilantro, or a spicy pepper sauce.

Chicken Asapao

This chicken stew is fairly typical of a classic Puerto Rican dish often served with rice.

INGREDIENTS | SERVES 4

1 pound boneless, skinless chicken breasts

3 cups chicken broth

2 medium potatoes

1 8-ounce can tomato sauce

¼ cup sofrito

1 teaspoon salt

2 bay leaves

¼ cup small green olives

Juice from 1 lime

Sofrito

Peel one large onion and cut into quarters. Put it into a food processor with 3 cubanelle peppers that have had the stems and seeds removed, 3 garlic cloves, half a bunch of cilantro, 3 tomatoes with the stems removed, and 1 green bell pepper with the stem and seeds removed. Pulse until it is well-blended. Leftovers can be frozen.

1. Place a Dutch oven over medium heat. Once it is heated add the chicken breasts and the chicken broth. Add water if necessary so the breasts are covered. Cook for 30 minutes. Remove the breasts from the pan and cut into ¼" cubes.

2. Return the chicken cubes to the pan with everything except the lime. Stir to combine. Reduce the heat to low and cover. Simmer for 45–60 minutes or until the chicken is soft.

3. Remove the bay leaves and stir the lime juice into the pan. Serve it over rice with a sprinkle of freshly chopped cilantro and hot sauce if desired.

Malaysian Turmeric and Honey Chicken Legs

Turmeric is a root commonly used in Asian and Middle Eastern cooking.
It has a mild flavor and turns dishes a pleasant golden yellow.

INGREDIENTS | SERVES 4

4 chicken breasts, boneless and skinless
1 bottle ginger ale or beer
Juice from 2 limes
3" section of ginger, peeled and grated
1 teaspoon ground turmeric
½ teaspoon salt
2 teaspoons ground cinnamon
1 teaspoon ground cardamom
2 garlic cloves, minced
3 shallots, sliced
1 serrano or finger pepper, thinly sliced
2 tablespoons peanut or vegetable oil
2 tablespoons honey

1. Rinse the chicken breasts and remove any excess fat.

2. Combine all of the remaining ingredients except for the oil and honey in a large plastic bag. Nestle the chicken into the marinade and let it rest in the refrigerator for 4–12 hours before cooking.

3. Remove the chicken and shallots from the marinade. Place a skillet over medium heat. Once it is heated add the oil to the skillet and several pieces of the chicken, being sure not to crowd. Cook for 5 minutes before rotating a quarter turn. Repeat until the chicken is cooked through. Remove to a platter and keep warm.

4. Place the shallots in the skillet and cook for 5–7 minutes. Add the marinade into the skillet, deglazing the pan. Simmer for 10 minutes or until the marinade is reduced by half. Add the honey and stir until combined. Return the chicken to the pan, tossing until it is well coated. Serve with white rice.

Mourgh: Afghan-Style Chicken

Because Afghanistan is located between a number of countries with a variety of cooking techniques and cuisines, Afghani food blends these influences. It tends to be richly flavored and not too hot.

INGREDIENTS | SERVES 4

2 cups and 2 tablespoons plain yogurt

4 cloves garlic, minced

1 teaspoon cumin

4 whole chicken legs, skinned and separated

4 cups chicken broth

1 14-ounce can garbanzo beans

1 medium onion, chopped

1 celery stalk, sliced

1 large carrot peeled and sliced

1 zucchini, halved lengthwise and sliced

1 teaspoon salt

¼ teaspoon ground pepper

¼ cup chopped fresh dill

Juice from 2 lemons

Afghanistan, Country of Hospitality

Afghanistan is usually pictured as a country of political upheaval. But the people of Afghanistan take delight in showing off their food, generosity, and hospitality to guests. A large sheet will be spread on the floor and rice, meat, vegetables, breads, sweets, and more will be served in a communal meal.

1. Place 2 cups of the yogurt, garlic, cumin, and chicken pieces in a sealable bowl or bag. Rub so the chicken is evenly coated and place it in the refrigerator to marinate overnight.

2. Place a skillet over medium-high heat. Remove the chicken from the yogurt and add it to the skillet with the broth, garbanzo beans, onion, celery, carrot, zucchini, salt, and pepper. Cover and simmer for 30 minutes. Remove the lid and cook for 15 minutes, or until the chicken is cooked through.

3. The broth should have reduced by half. Stir in the reserved 2 tablespoons of yogurt, dill, and lemon juice until thoroughly combined.

4. Serve warm over long grain white rice.

Saag Murg: Indian Chicken and Spinach with Spices

This dish is common in northwestern India where a lot of grain is grown.
Traditionally this dish would be eaten with paratha, a flat bread that is pan-fried and buttered.
But rice is an acceptable side.

INGREDIENTS | SERVES 4

1 pound boneless chicken breasts

2 tablespoons peanut oil

2 large onions, finely chopped

¼ teaspoon ground pepper

1 teaspoon salt

6 garlic cloves, minced

1" piece fresh ginger, peeled and grated

1 teaspoon ground cardamom

1 teaspoon of ground coriander

1 teaspoon ground cumin

1 teaspoon spicy paprika

1 teaspoon ground turmeric

1 teaspoon chili powder

2 tomatoes, seeded and chopped

1½ pounds fresh spinach, rinsed and chopped

½ cup water

1. Rinse the chicken breasts and pat dry. Place a skillet over medium heat. Once it is warmed, add the oil and chicken breasts. Cook for 5–7 minutes on each side, or until they're well-browned and almost cooked through. Set aside.

2. Add the onions to the skillet and cook for 5–7 minutes, or until they're softened and starting to turn golden. Add the pepper, salt, garlic, ginger, and the dried spices. Cook for 3–4 minutes, or until the spices smell toasty.

3. Add the tomatoes and spinach to the skillet, stir to combine, and cook for 4–5 minutes, or until the spinach has wilted.

4. Cube the chicken breasts, and add to the skillet with ½ cup of water. Stir frequently until the water has evaporated. Season with salt as needed and serve with basmati rice.

Picante Chicken and Black Beans with Pasta in an Ancho Chili Sauce

Dried chilies are a great way to add a lot of flavor to dishes. Ancho chilies are the most common variety and they tend to be fairly mild. If you prefer a spicier pepper, look for chipotles, which are ripened jalapeño peppers.

INGREDIENTS | SERVES 4

Water, as needed

1 pound whole wheat farfalle

2 dried ancho chilies, stemmed and seeded

1 tablespoon olive oil

½ small onion, chopped

½ yellow bell pepper, chopped

½ pound chicken breast tenderloins, cubed

2 small tomatoes, chopped

¼ teaspoon ground cumin

1 cup chicken broth

1 can black beans, drained and rinsed

Ancho Sauce

Stem and seed several dried peppers. Cover with boiling water, and soak for 30 minutes. Place the softened peppers in a blender with ¼ of 1 onion, 1 tablespoon vegetable oil, 1 tablespoon honey, 1 teaspoon oregano, and 1 teaspoon cumin. Purée until smooth. Add water as needed. Refrigerate in a sealed container for up to 1 month.

1. Place a large pot of water over high heat to boil. Once it comes to a boil, add the pasta and cook according to the package directions.

2. Cover the chilies with hot water for 30 minutes to soften. Remove them from the water and finely chop. Reserve the water.

3. Place a skillet over medium-high heat. Once it is heated, add the oil, chilies, onion, bell pepper, and chicken. Cook for 4–5 minutes. Add the tomatoes, cumin, chicken broth, and 1 cup of the water the chilies soaked in. Stir to combine.

4. Once the chicken is cooked through, add the beans and bring to a simmer. Divide the cooked pasta in equal portions into 4 bowls. Pour the chicken and sauce over the pasta and serve immediately.

Seared and Baked Duck Breasts with Fruit Compote

Duck fat is flavorful and has a high smoke point. You can keep the leftover fat in a jar in your refrigerator for a month and substitute it for oil or butter when pan-frying vegetables, potatoes, or even other meat.

INGREDIENTS | SERVES 2

1 quart warm water

¼ cup table salt

2 tablespoons sugar

2 boneless, skin-on duck breasts

Savory Fruit Compote, as desired (see below)

Savory Fruit Compote

Mince 1 shallot and place it in a hot skillet with 2 tablespoons of duck fat. Cook for 3 minutes. Stir in ½ cup fruit jam, ¼ cup sherry, crème de cassis, or a similar liqueur, and 2 tablespoons balsamic vinegar. Cook for 1 minute before spooning it out of the pan and over the sliced duck breast.

1. Place the water, salt, and sugar in a small saucepan over medium heat. Stir until the salt and sugar have dissolved. Transfer to a large sealable container. Place the duck breasts on a cutting board and drag a knife across the skin in diagonal lines that are 1" apart. Rotate the breast and cut again to create a diamond pattern. Place the duck in the brine in the refrigerator. Let it rest for at least 8 (but no more than 24) hours.

2. Preheat oven to 400°F. Heat a skillet over medium heat. Remove the duck from the brine and pat dry. Place the breasts skin side down in the skillet and cook for 1 minute. Nudge the breasts to loosen them if necessary and cook for 5 more minutes.

3. Turn off the heat and drain the fat. Flip the breasts over so they're skin side up and place skillet in the middle of the oven for 5 minutes.

4. Remove from the oven. Cover the skillet with a lid, and let sit for 4 minutes. Remove the breasts from the pan and place on a plate loosely covered with foil for 5 minutes.

5. Cut the breasts in ½" thick slices on an angle. Fan out on a plate before pouring compote over them to serve.

Spicy Cumin and Chili Rubbed Turkey Breast

Turkey breasts are easier to cook than an entire turkey and one breast can serve 6–8 people. Turkey breasts with the skin on and bone-in are often much cheaper.

INGREDIENTS | SERVES 6–8

1 4- or 5-pound turkey breast

3 tablespoons ground cumin

1 teaspoon table salt

½ teaspoon ground black pepper

½ teaspoon chili powder

1 teaspoon garlic powder

1 teaspoon onion powder

2 tablespoons olive oil

½ cup chicken or turkey stock

2 tablespoons flour

1. Rinse the turkey breast. If desired, remove the skin and bones before cooking. Pat the breast dry.

2. Combine all of the spices in a small bowl and stir to combine. Rub the spice mix over the meat. Place it in a sealable container and store in the refrigerator for 4–24 hours.

3. Preheat oven to 325°F. Place a skillet over medium-high heat. Add the oil and the turkey breast. Cook on each side for 4–5 minutes, or until it is lightly seared.

4. Place the pan in the center of the oven and cook uncovered for 1½ hours, or until a meat thermometer registers 155°F. Remove the meat from the pan, cover, and let it rest for 10 minutes.

5. Add the stock to the pan and scrape to remove any stuck on bits from the bottom of the pan. Add the flour, whisking continually for several minutes. Place the pan over medium heat and cook until thickened. Slice the turkey and serve the pan sauce over the slices while warm.

Turkey Mole

Most true mole sauces are cooked for hours and require a lot of work.
But this cheater-style mole gives a lot of the same flavor without a lot of the work.

INGREDIENTS | SERVES 6–8

1 tablespoon vegetable oil

1 turkey breast, 3–5 pounds

8 dried New Mexico chilies, stemmed and seeded

1 onion, chopped

4 garlic cloves, smashed

½ cup chopped peanuts

1 teaspoon dried oregano

2 tablespoons cumin

1 teaspoon salt

½ teaspoon pepper

¼ cup cocoa powder

Water, as needed

The Legend of Mole

No one really knows how mole came about. Some say nuns witnessed an angelic vision revealing how to stretch their meager rations into a feast for a visiting archbishop. It's also rumored that Montezuma served the dish to the conquistadors who he thought were gods.

1. Preheat oven to 275°F. Place a Dutch oven over medium heat. Once it is heated, add the oil and the turkey. Cook on each side for 3–4 minutes, or until lightly browned. Remove it from the pan.

2. Place the peppers in a layer on the bottom. Sprinkle the onion, garlic, peanuts, spices, and cocoa on top. Place the turkey breast on top of the seasonings. Add just enough water so the meat is covered.

3. Place it in the center of the oven, cover, and cook for 2½ hours. Remove the breast from the pan and cover it to keep warm. Place all of the chilies, onions, garlic, and peanuts into a blender. Add 2 cups of the cooking liquid. Purée until smooth. Discard the rest of the cooking liquid.

4. Return the puréed broth to the Dutch oven over medium-low heat. Slice the turkey breast on an angle into thin slices. Return the turkey to the pan and cook until warm. Serve the mole with rice and beans.

Alsatian Chicken

*This would be a great dish to serve with Pommes Fondantes (page 68)
and Garlic Soup (page 270).*

INGREDIENTS | SERVES 4

4 tablespoons butter
4 chicken thighs
1 medium onion, sliced
8 ounces mushrooms, sliced
2 tablespoons brandy
1 cup Riesling wine
1 tablespoon ground mustard powder
Salt to taste
Pepper to taste
¼ cup whole milk

Taste Alsace

Cast-iron cookware is common in Alsace, France, a region near Germany. This dish, like many other dishes of the region, combines elements of classic French and German cooking to create a very flavorful one-pot meal. You could also add a few chopped potatoes and carrots before step 5.

1. Preheat oven to 350°F.

2. Place a skillet over high heat. Once it is warmed, add 3 tablespoons butter. When it's melted, add the chicken thighs, skin side down. Cook for 6–7 minutes, or until the skin is golden brown. Turn the chicken over and cook for an additional 5 minutes.

3. Place the chicken on a plate and keep it warm. Reduce the heat to medium, add the sliced onion, and cook for 5 minutes. Sprinkle the mushrooms over the pan and cook for 5 minutes.

4. Add the brandy, wine, and the ground mustard to the skillet and increase the heat slightly. Stir to scrape any stuck-on bits. Once the liquid starts to simmer, turn off the burner and place the chicken back in the skillet.

5. Place the skillet in the middle of the oven and cook for 1 hour and 15 minutes. Then place the chicken onto a clean plate and keep it warm. Place the skillet over a medium-high burner and let the liquid reduce until 1 cup is left. Season with salt and pepper to taste.

6. Stir the milk and 1 tablespoon butter into the sauce. Melt the butter and quickly whisk the sauce before pouring it over the chicken to serve.

Chapter 7

Fish and Shellfish in a Skillet

Smothered Whitefish

You can use either the Onion Marmalade (page 242)
or the Caramelized Onion and Fennel (page 53) in this dish.

INGREDIENTS | SERVES 4

4 6-ounce whitefish fillets

Salt to taste

Pepper to taste

1 tablespoon olive oil

1 cup caramelized onions

1. Preheat oven to 350°F. Sprinkle the fillets with salt and pepper on each side. Place a skillet over medium heat to preheat. Once it is heated add the oil and the fillets.

2. Turn off the heat and cover each fillet with ¼ cup of the onion mixture. Place the skillet in the oven and cook for 20 minutes. The fish is cooked through when it starts to flake apart. Serve hot.

Simple Salmon Fillets

If you'd like to add a little more flavor to this dish,
you can substitute butter for vegetable oil.

INGREDIENTS | SERVES 4

4¼ pounds salmon fillets

2 tablespoons vegetable oil

1 lemon

1 teaspoon salt

Pepper to taste

1. Rinse the fillets and remove any loose scales or bones. Pat the salmon dry and rub 1 tablespoon of the oil on the fillets. Squeeze a little of the lemon on the flesh side of the fillets. Sprinkle them with salt and pepper.

2. Place a skillet over medium-high heat and once it is warmed add 1 tablespoon of oil. Place the fillets in the pan flesh side down.

3. Cook for 3 minutes before flipping over. Cook for 2 minutes. Remove pan from the heat and let rest for 1 minute. When it is cool enough to touch, you should be able to grab a corner of the skin and peel it off. Serve immediately

Curried Crabmeat

This dish is often called Crabmeat Indienne.
"Indienne" is the name given to many curried dishes in France.

INGREDIENTS | SERVES 4

2 tablespoons butter
¼ small onion, chopped
3 tablespoons flour
2 teaspoons curry powder
2 cups chicken broth
1½ cups crabmeat

1. Place a skillet over medium heat. Once it is heated, add the butter. Once the butter stops foaming, add the onion, stirring frequently for 3 minutes, or until the onion is softened.

2. Stir the flour into the skillet with the curry powder to create a paste. Stir the paste continually for 2 minutes.

3. Slowly pour in the chicken broth, whisking continually to prevent lumps. Bring to a simmer and cook for 3 minutes.

4. Stir in the crabmeat and cook until heated. Remove from the heat and serve over rice.

Halibut Creole

If the fillet comes with the skin on it, don't try to remove it while the fish is raw.
After it cooks, you should be able to carefully grab the skin and pull it off.
The skin is edible, but many people find the texture and taste off-putting.

INGREDIENTS | SERVES 4

4 tablespoons butter
Juice from 2 lemons
Several dashes Tabasco sauce
4 8-ounce halibut steaks
Pinch salt
Pinch pepper
1 small onion, chopped
½ red bell pepper, chopped
3 large tomatoes, peeled, seeded, and chopped

1. Preheat oven to 400°F. Place a large skillet over medium heat. Add the butter, lemon juice, and Tabasco sauce. Stir until the butter has melted. Turn off the heat.

2. Season the fish on each side with salt and pepper. Sprinkle the onion and bell pepper over the bottom of the skillet. Add the fish to the skillet and pour the tomatoes over the fish.

3. Bake for 20–25 minutes, or until the thickest part of the fish is opaque. Spoon the pan juices over the fish every 10 minutes. Remove it from the pan and spoon the sauce over the fish to serve.

Tamarind Tuna

Since the price of tuna has gone up significantly in the last few years,
you can substitute salmon fillets in this dish, which may be cheaper.

INGREDIENTS | SERVES 4

½ cup tamarind pulp

1 cup water

1 pound tuna fillet

½ teaspoon salt

¼ cup peanut oil

Popularity Isn't Always a Good Thing

Tuna used to be a very cheap fish, but in the last 10 years, several types of tuna have been depleted and are close to being endangered. To make sure you're eating responsibly, avoid Bluefin or Bigeye tuna and ask for Yellowtail instead.

1. Place the tamarind pulp in a glass bowl. Heat the water and pour it over the paste. Use a spoon to combine the pulp with the water.

2. Sprinkle the tuna lightly with the salt. Cut it into 1½" strips. Add the tuna to the marinade and toss to coat. Let it sit for 30 minutes at room temperature.

3. Place a skillet over medium-high heat and when it is warmed add the oil. Pat the tuna dry and add to the oil when it's hot. Cook for 2 minutes on each side. The tuna will be dark on each side but still pink in the center. Serve over white rice.

Truly Blackened Catfish

This works best with small catfish fillets instead of large ones.
Ideally each fillet should be around 4 ounces.

INGREDIENTS | SERVES 4–6

2 sticks unsalted butter

1 teaspoon pepper

½ teaspoon thyme

1 tablespoon spicy paprika

1 teaspoon garlic powder

1 teaspoon onion powder

½ teaspoon oregano

2½ teaspoons salt

1 teaspoon chili powder

¼ teaspoon cayenne pepper

1½ pounds catfish fillets

1. Melt the butter in a shallow bowl. Combine the spices and place on a plate. Dip the fish in the butter and then sprinkle or roll the fish in the spices.

2. Heat up a charcoal or gas grill till hot. Place a cast-iron skillet over direct heat for 10 minutes. Let it sit until white ash forms in the bottom of the skillet.

3. Place the fillets in the skillet. Pour 1 tablespoon of melted butter over each fillet. Be careful of flaming butter. Cook for 2 minutes before turning over fillets and cooking for another 2 minutes. Serve with lemon wedges.

Yasa Tibs (Ethiopian Sautéed Fish)

"Yasa" means fish and "Tibs" means that the meat is served in large pieces which is reserved for guests and special occasions. Use the Ethiopian Berberé Red Pepper Paste (page 61) for this recipe.

INGREDIENTS | SERVES 4

Juice from 4 limes
1½ teaspoons Berberé Red Pepper Paste
1 pound cod fillets, cut into chunks
2 tablespoons olive oil
1 teaspoon spicy paprika
3 garlic cloves, minced
1" piece ginger, peeled and grated
¼ cup plain tomato sauce
¼ cup fish stock
¼ cup chopped cilantro

1. Mix the lime juice and berberé paste in a glass container. Marinate the fish for 1 hour.

2. Place a skillet over medium heat. Add the oil and paprika and cook for 1 minute. Add the garlic and ginger and cook for 1–2 minutes.

3. Add the fish with the marinade liquid, the tomato sauce, and the fish stock. Cook on the first side for 2–3 minutes. Turn it over to cook on the other side for 2–3 minutes. It is done when the fish is flaky. Pour the contents into a bowl and sprinkle cilantro over top. Serve with rice or flat bread.

Cajun Shrimp

You can replace the beer with soda in this recipe.

INGREDIENTS | SERVES 4

1 pound shrimp, peeled and deveined
¼ teaspoon cayenne pepper
1 teaspoon black pepper
1 teaspoon salt
1 teaspoon red chili flakes
1 teaspoon thyme
1 teaspoon oregano
1 teaspoon ground marjoram
4 tablespoons unsalted butter
3 cloves garlic, minced
2 teaspoons Worcestershire sauce
1 cup beer, room temperature

1. Rinse the shrimp and shake them dry. Combine all of the dried seasonings in a bowl.

2. Place a skillet over medium-high heat. When it is hot, add the butter and garlic and cook for 1 minute. Add the seasoning mix, Worcestershire sauce, and beer.

3. Once the sauce bubbles, add the shrimp. Cook for 4–6 minutes, stirring so they cook evenly.

4. Once the shrimp is cooked, remove from the pan and place in a serving bowl. Let the liquid simmer for 10 minutes until it is a reduced sauce. Adjust the seasonings and serve with white rice.

Grilled Barbecue Salmon

Since salmon is a high-fat fish, it holds up incredibly well when grilling. The Kansas City-Style Barbecue Sauce (page 57) is great in this dish, or you can use a bottled sauce.

INGREDIENTS | **SERVES 4**

1 tablespoon vegetable oil
Pinch salt
Pinch pepper
4 6–8-ounce salmon steaks
¼ cup barbecue sauce

1. Brush a grill pan lightly with vegetable oil and place over medium-high heat.

2. Sprinkle salt and pepper over the salmon. Brush one side of the salmon lightly with barbecue sauce. Place that side down on the warmed pan. Brush the other side with barbecue sauce.

3. Cook for 3 minutes on each side, or until it is opaque about half-way up the side of the fillet. Once the salmon is cooked through, brush it again with a light coating of barbecue sauce and serve while warm.

Fish Tacos

You need a firm fish since you'll be pan-frying these. Look for perch, grouper, catfish, or ask your fishmonger for suggestions based on availability. It is fine if the fish has the skin on.

INGREDIENTS | **SERVES 2**

½ pound firm white fish fillets
2 tablespoons peanut or corn oil
Salt to taste
1 lime
4 corn tortillas and desired toppings

White Sauce and Toppings

Fish tacos are served in warmed corn tortillas with shredded cabbage, diced tomato, and a white sauce. To make the sauce, you'll need to peel, seed, and mince a serrano pepper. Mix with ¼ cup yogurt, ¼ cup mayonnaise, and 1 teaspoon garlic salt. Refrigerate for 3 hours.

1. Rinse fish and pat dry with paper towels. Place a skillet over medium-high heat. Once it is heated, add the oil and swirl to coat. Add the fillets, skin side up. Shake the skillet to prevent sticking. Cook for 3 minutes.

2. Flip the fish over and cook for another 3 minutes. You should see the side of the fish change from translucent to opaque. Remove the fish from the pan and place it skin side up on a plate. Carefully peel off the skin.

3. Chop the fish into 1" strips and place in a bowl. Sprinkle salt and squeeze the lime over the top of the fish. Toss to coat. Serve in tortillas with toppings.

Fish Drowned in Lemon Basil

There are many types of basil. Lemon basil has a delicate lemony flavor and can be hard to find. But any type of basil, other than Thai basil, can be substituted in this recipe.

INGREDIENTS | SERVES 4

4 6-ounce fillets tilapia or a similar white fish

Salt to taste

Pepper to taste

2 tablespoons olive oil

2 small zucchini or yellow squash, sliced

1 cup lemon basil leaves

Zest from 1 lemon

Juice from 1 lemon

Which Fish Is Best?

For people who rarely eat fish at home, shopping for fish can be overwhelming. But it shouldn't be. Fish is often served as either a steak (a cross-section of the gutted fish) or a fillet (meat from one half of a fish). White fish tends to have a less fishy taste on its own and picks up flavors from sauces very well.

1. Rinse the fish fillets and pat dry with paper towels. Squeeze gently to find any remaining bones and remove. Sprinkle lightly with salt and pepper. Set aside.

2. Place a skillet over medium heat and add the oil. Slide two fillets into the skillet and cook on each side for 4–5 minutes, or until the center is almost opaque and the fish begins to flake on the tips. Place on a clean plate to keep warm. Cook the remaining fish and add to the plate.

3. If all of the oil is gone from the skillet, add another tablespoon of olive oil to the pan before adding the zucchini rounds.

4. Sprinkle the basil, lemon zest, and a pinch of salt and pepper over the zucchini. Cover the pan and steam for 1 minute before tossing. Place the fish on top of the zucchini and sprinkle with lemon juice. Cover the skillet for 2–3 minutes to warm the fish and finish cooking the zucchini. Serve immediately.

Seafood Paella

There are special pans available for paella, but a large skillet or Dutch oven will also work.

INGREDIENTS | **SERVES 4–6**

2 quarts plus 1 cup water

¼ cup salt plus 2 pinches

¼ cup sugar

Ice cubes, as needed

1 pound of large shrimp, peeled and deveined

4 tablespoons olive oil

6 garlic cloves, minced

Pinch pepper

1 red bell pepper, seeded and sliced

1 medium white onion, finely chopped

1 15-ounce can diced tomatoes

1 15-ounce can chicken broth

2 cups white rice

½ cup dry white wine

3 bay leaves

1 large pinch saffron threads

12 mussels, cleaned and debearded

1 cup cleaned squid, sliced in rings

2 cups crabmeat

1 cup frozen peas, thawed

¼ cup chopped parsley

1 lemon, cut in wedges

1. Bring 2 quarts of water to a boil. Stir in ¼ cup salt and sugar until dissolved. Add several cups of ice cubes till chilled. Add the shrimp to the brine, cover, and refrigerate overnight. Remove from the brine and pat dry. Sprinkle with 1 tablespoon of oil, 2 garlic cloves, 1 pinch salt, and pepper. Let it sit at room temperature for 30 minutes.

2. Preheat oven to 350°F with a rack just below the middle position.

3. Place a very large skillet or a Dutch oven over medium heat. Add 1 tablespoon of oil and the bell pepper. Cook for 5–7 minutes. Spoon the pepper out and set aside, but leave as much of the oil in the pan as possible.

4. Add 2 tablespoons of oil to the pan with the onion and cook for 5–7 minutes. Add the remaining garlic, stirring continually for 1 minute. Stir in 1 cup of water, the tomatoes, chicken broth, rice, wine, bay leaves, saffron, and 1 pinch salt. Increase the heat to medium-high and bring to a boil.

5. When the contents boil, cover and cook in the middle of the oven for 15–20 minutes. Gently stir the seafood into the rice. Lay the pepper strips in a pinwheel on top and sprinkle the peas across the top. Cook in the oven for 8–12 minutes.

6. Rest for 5 minutes before serving. Discard any unopened mussels and the bay leaves. Serve with parsley and lemon wedges.

Seared Tuna Steak with Tangy Cilantro Sauce

Tuna is a low-fat fish and can become dry and bland when cooked through.
By cooking it till rare, you get a pleasant combination of cooked and rare textures.

INGREDIENTS | **SERVES 2**

1 bunch cilantro, rinsed and picked over

¼ cup water

2 teaspoons plus 1 pinch salt

¼ cup rice wine vinegar

½ cup safflower or canola oil

1 12–16-ounce tuna steak

Pinch pepper

Pinch salt

2 garlic cloves, peeled and smashed

1 tablespoon olive oil

Use the Rest of the Sauce

This recipe makes a cup of sauce and you'll likely use ¼ cup or less, but don't discard the remainder. You can use it as a salad dressing, drizzle it over sliced fresh tomatoes, or mix it into potatoes or rice as a side. You can store it in a tightly sealed container for a few weeks in your refrigerator.

1. Roughly chop the cilantro. Place in a blender with the water, 2 teaspoons salt, and vinegar. Pulse on liquefy for several minutes until the contents are smooth. Pour the safflower oil in slowly while the blender runs. Taste and season with salt as needed.

2. Rinse the tuna under cold water and pat dry. Sprinkle with salt and pepper. Place a skillet over medium-high heat. Once it is heated through, add the garlic cloves and olive oil. Toss to coat and move the cloves to the edges of the pan.

3. Place the tuna in the middle of the skillet and cook for 2 minutes on the first side. Flip it to the second side and cook for 1 minute. This will make it rare.

4. If you prefer a medium-done tuna, cook for 4 minutes on the first side and 3 minutes on the second with the skillet over medium heat.

5. Slice the steak against the grain and drizzle the cilantro sauce over the fish. Serve while warm.

Tuna Almandine with Sugar Snap Peas

With sugar snap peas you eat the pod and the pea. They're younger than the peas that are shelled and served without the pod. You may want to remove the membranous string on one side of the pod of older peas.

INGREDIENTS | SERVES 2

2 tablespoons butter

½ large sweet onion, thinly sliced

½ pound sugar snap peapods

Salt to taste

Pepper to taste

1 tablespoon olive oil

2 6-ounce tuna steaks

½ cup sliced almonds

Almondine versus Almandine

Both of these words refer to the same thing. Almandine comes from the French word for almond. It's common in French cooking for green beans and fish to have a garnish of sliced or slivered almonds on top. But in American versions of these recipes the word almandine was converted to almondine. Most English dictionaries will direct you from almondine to almandine.

1. Place a large skillet over medium-high heat. Add the butter and sliced onions. Stir frequently for 8–10 minutes or until they're tender and translucent.

2. Add the peas to the skillet and season with salt and pepper. Toss them a few times and cook for 2–3 minutes. Move the vegetables to the sides of the skillet. If the butter in the skillet has evaporated, add some olive oil.

3. Place the tuna steaks in the middle of the skillet and cook on each side for 2–3 minutes. You'll want the center to be pink, so cooking to medium rare is recommended. Divide the tuna and peas between two plates and sprinkle the almonds on top.

Shrimp and Avocado Pasta with a Tequila Tomato Sauce

The avocado purée in the sauce and the addition of butter at the end help to create a richly flavored sauce that has very little fat per serving. The cilantro and avocado garnish also make this a great summertime option. This sauce is very good served on fettuccine.

INGREDIENTS | SERVES 8

1 avocado, peeled and chopped

1 28-ounce can chopped tomatoes

1 teaspoon salt

¼ teaspoon freshly ground black pepper

1 teaspoon crushed red pepper flakes

3 tablespoons cold unsalted butter

1½ pounds medium shrimp

½ cup tequila

1 pound fettuccine

¼ cup fresh cilantro, chopped

1. Put half the avocado, tomatoes, salt, pepper, and red pepper flakes in a blender and pulse several times. You don't want a thin purée but do want to chop up the tomatoes and avocado and mix with the spices.

2. Place a skillet over medium-heat and add half of the butter. Cut the other half into cubes and set aside. Once the butter has melted, add the shrimp and tequila to the skillet. Stir quickly to combine and stir every 2 minutes until the shrimp are slightly pink and the tequila has mostly evaporated. Reduce the heat to low.

3. Cook fettuccine according to package directions. Add the contents of the blender and the remaining butter to the skillet. Stir to combine. Add the remaining avocado and cilantro as garnish on the final dish. Once the pasta is cooked through, drain and divide into bowls. Pour the sauce and shrimp over each dish and garnish with avocado and cilantro.

Shrimp in Fra Diavolo Sauce

Fra is Italian for "brother" and diavolo means "devil" and is often used to name recipes that are spicy. This name seems to be an Italian-American name and is not commonly seen in Italy.

INGREDIENTS | SERVES 4–6

1 pound linguini

3 tablespoons olive oil

1 pound of deveined and shelled shrimp (31–40 count)

1 teaspoon red pepper flakes

1 teaspoon salt

¼ cup sweet white wine

4 cloves garlic, thinly sliced

1 15-ounce can chopped tomatoes

1 cup dry white wine

¼ cup parsley, chopped

Cooking with Wine When You Don't Drink It

Common advice on choosing cooking wine is "if you wouldn't drink it, then don't cook with it." But what do you do if you don't drink wine? Avoid cooking wine because it is full of preservatives and salt that will clash with many dishes. Look for dry or sweet on the label and match it to the recipe.

1. Cook the linguini according to the package directions. Place a skillet over medium heat. Once it is heated add 1 tablespoon of olive oil, shrimp, red pepper flakes, and salt. Stir frequently for 2 minutes to keep everything from sticking.

2. Turn off the heat and pour in the sweet wine. Toss and let sit for 2 minutes. The residual heat should cause most of the wine to evaporate. Pour the contents into a bowl and set aside.

3. Return the skillet to the stove over low heat. Once it is heated, add 2 tablespoons of olive oil and the garlic. Cook for several minutes. Once it starts to turn golden brown, remove from the oil and set aside to drain. If the oil gets frothy, lower the heat.

4. Stir in more red pepper flakes if desired, tomatoes, and the dry wine. Increase the heat to medium and simmer for 10 minutes to reduce. Stir in parsley. Divide pasta and top with the shrimp and sauce.

White Beans with Shrimp

*If you can't find Great Northern beans you can substitute
cannellini beans, or any other small bean you can find.*

INGREDIENTS | SERVES 6

1 tablespoon olive oil

1 carrot, peeled, cut in half lengthwise
and sliced

1 small onion, peeled and chopped

2 garlic cloves, minced

1 celery stalk, sliced

2 tablespoons parsley, chopped

2 tablespoons thyme, chopped

Pinch red pepper flakes

4 tablespoons unsalted butter

1 pound large shrimp, peeled and
deveined

2 cans Great Northern beans, drained
and rinsed

Juice from 1 lemon

1. Place a large skillet over medium heat and once it
   is heated, add the oil, carrot, and onion. Cook for
   5–7 minutes or until the vegetables are softened
   but not browned. Add the garlic and celery. Stir to
   combine before adding in the herbs, red pepper
   flakes, and butter.

2. Stir continually until the butter is melted and starts to
   turn brown. Swirl the skillet occasionally.

3. Place the shrimp in the skillet and cook on each side
   for 1–2 minutes. Stir in the beans and lemon juice and
   cook until warmed through. Serve immediately.

French or Belgian Steamed Mussels

Some mussels won't open during cooking.
They should be discarded before serving.

INGREDIENTS | SERVES 2

Water, as needed

1 cup cornmeal

2 pounds fresh mussels

2 tablespoons butter

1 medium yellow onion, thinly sliced

1 large garlic clove, minced

2 cups dry white wine or ale

3 tablespoons fresh tarragon or thyme, chopped

Caring for Your Mussels

Discard any mussels with cracked shells. If you tap an open mussel, it should close; if it doesn't, discard it. Make sure they are wrapped in something damp and placed in a mesh bag since they need airflow. Keep them in the bottom of your refrigerator wrapped in wet newspaper for up to 48 hours, but they're best the same day they're purchased.

1. Fill a very large bowl half full of water that is cool to the touch. Sprinkle the cornmeal across the top of the water and let it settle. Use a plastic bristle brush to remove any dirt or other unwanted debris from the mussels. To remove the beard, place the back of a butter knife on one side of the beard and your thumb on the other side. Pinch the beard between your thumb and the knife and pull using a side-to-side motion.

2. Place mussels into the bowl. Shake the bowl every few minutes to keep the cornmeal floating. Let them sit in the water for 30 minutes. Every 10 minutes gently nudge the bowl to create waves. The mussels should expel any dirt they have stored and replace it with the cornmeal.

3. Place a Dutch oven over medium heat and add the butter. Add the onions and stir to coat in butter. Stir frequently until they are mostly translucent. Add the garlic and stir. Cook for 3–4 minutes. Add the wine and herbs. Cover and bring to a boil.

4. Remove the lid and gently add mussels to the pan, leaving the dirt in the bottom of the bowl. When all of the mussels are added, increase the heat to high and cook for 3–4 minutes.

5. Scoop the mussels into bowls and keep them warm. Let the liquid in the pan continue to boil for 5–10 minutes until reduced by half. Pour the liquid and onions over the mussels. Serve with crusty bread.

Oysters Rockefeller

This dish uses the skillet for presentation rather than its cooking abilities. Rock salt is often used during canning and is inexpensive. If you don't want to open the oysters yourself, ask your fishmonger to do it for you.

INGREDIENTS | SERVES 2

1 scallion, chopped, white and green parts separated

¼ celery stalk, finely chopped

2 tablespoons fresh parsley, chopped

¼ cup fresh spinach, chopped

2 tablespoons unseasoned bread crumbs

3 dashes Tabasco

¼ teaspoon Worcestershire sauce

2 tablespoons butter

½ teaspoon salt

12 large oysters on the half-shell

1 lemon cut into 8 wedges

Rock salt, as desired

1. Preheat oven to 450°F. Combine the white part of the scallion, celery, parsley, and spinach. Chop them together till very fine. Place into a bowl with the bread crumbs, Tabasco, and Worcestershire sauce.

2. Cream the butter and salt into the breadcrumb mixture until you get a fine paste. Pour 1" of rock salt over the bottom of the skillet. Nestle the oysters in the salt.

3. Divide the butter and breadcrumb mixture over the oysters. Bake for 10 minutes, or until the mixture has melted. Sprinkle a pinch of green scallion on top of each oyster and serve while warm with lemon slices.

Rich Rockefeller

This dish was created at Antoine's in New Orleans, the country's oldest family-run restaurant. It was created in 1899 and named after John D. Rockefeller, who was then the richest man in the country. Snails were popular at the time, but these oysters were a substitute using local ingredients. The recipe has been replicated many times, but never duplicated exactly.

Scallops Seared in Clarified Butter

Dry-packed scallops will brown and cook better. If you use wet-packed scallops, rinse them and let them drain for an additional 10 minutes.

INGREDIENTS | SERVES 4

12 whole scallops
3 tablespoons clarified butter
Pinch salt
Pinch pepper
2 tablespoons butter
2 garlic cloves
1 teaspoon dried thyme
1 cup dry white wine
1 lemon, cut into wedges

Making Clarified Butter

To make clarified butter at home, melt unsalted butter over medium-high heat until boiling. Lower heat to medium and simmer until any foam or white bits sink to the bottom. Strain melted butter through a coffee filter. Store in sealed container in refrigerator for up to 6 months.

1. Use several paper towels to pat the scallops dry. Wrap them in paper towels and let them sit at room temperature for 15 minutes. If there is a tough muscle on the side, remove it.

2. Place a skillet over medium-high heat. Once it is warmed add the clarified butter. Season the scallops with salt and pepper and place in the pan.

3. Cook for 2–3 minutes or until the bottom edges start to turn golden brown. Flip them over and cook for 2–3 minutes, or until the sides are opaque.

4. Remove the scallops from the pan. Add the butter, garlic, thyme, and wine. Scrape the bottom to remove the crust. Let the wine boil for 5 minutes. Pour it over the scallops and serve with lemon wedges.

Chapter 8

Pork in a Skillet

Kielbasa, Potatoes, and Peppers

*This dish, using Polish smoked sausage, is quick to make and comforting.
If you like mustard with your sausages, add 3 tablespoons of mustard with the chicken broth.*

INGREDIENTS | SERVES 4

3 tablespoons vegetable oil
4 medium potatoes, cut into ¼" slices
1 small onion, chopped
1 bell pepper, seeded and cubed
1 pound kielbasa, cut into 1" pieces
½ cup chicken broth
1 tablespoon Worcestershire sauce
2 teaspoons salt
¼ teaspoon ground black pepper

1. Place a skillet over medium heat. Once it is heated, add the oil and the potatoes. Cook for 3 minutes. Stir and cover with a lid. Cook for another 5 minutes, stirring occasionally.

2. Add the onions and the peppers. Cook for 3 minutes, covered. Add the kielbasa and chicken broth. Cook for 8–10 minutes, or until the kielbasa is cooked through and the potatoes are browned. Stir in the Worcestershire sauce, and season with salt and pepper to taste.

Oven-Roasted Spareribs

This very simple preparation lets the flavor of the spareribs truly shine. If the simple flavor won't make your diners happy, feel free to brush on 2 cups of barbecue sauce during the last 30 minutes of cooking time.

INGREDIENTS | SERVES 4

4 pounds spareribs
Salt to taste
Pepper to taste

1. Preheat the oven to 350°F. Season the spareribs generously with salt and pepper on all sides.

2. Place the ribs in a large skillet in the middle of the oven. Bake for 30 minutes.

3. Turn them over and bake for another 30 minutes. If the ribs aren't crispy on the outside, increase the heat to 425°F and bake for 10 minutes. Serve while warm.

Southern-Style Pork Chops

To make this soul food dish healthier, bake the pork chops in a 375°F oven for 45 minutes.

INGREDIENTS | SERVES 6

6 pork chops, cut 1" thick

2 teaspoons salt

2 teaspoons garlic powder

1½ teaspoons ground mustard

1 teaspoon smoked paprika

½ teaspoon black pepper

¼ teaspoon onion powder

½ teaspoon dried oregano

½ cup flour

½ cup vegetable oil

1. Rinse the pork chops and pat dry. Combine all of the dried spices together in a wide, shallow bowl. Place the flour in another wide, shallow bowl.

2. Rub the seasoning mix into each piece. Dredge the pork chops in the flour and shake off the excess. Place chops on a wire rack for 30 minutes before cooking.

3. Add the vegetable oil to a skillet and place over medium heat. When the oil is shimmering and hot, slide 2 pork chops into the skillet and cook on each side for 10–12 minutes. Place the cooked pork chops on paper towels and keep warm. Repeat with the other pork chops. Serve while warm.

Italian Sausage with Escarole and White Beans

If you can't find cannellini beans you can also use Great Northern beans or any other white or light-colored bean available.

INGREDIENTS | SERVES 4–6

1 bunch escarole

1½ pounds Italian sausage links, mild or hot

3 tablespoons olive oil

3 garlic cloves, minced

1 can cannellini beans

½ teaspoon red chili flakes

¼ cup Romano cheese, grated

1. Remove the thick stems and any thick veins from the escarole. Rinse the leaves in cold water to remove any dirt. Shake to dry or pat dry between a few towels.

2. Slice the sausage into ¼" slices. Place a skillet over medium-high heat and add the oil and sausage once the skillet is heated. Sprinkle garlic over the sausage. Toss to combine. Add the can of beans, including the juice, and chili flakes. Cook until the liquid has mostly evaporated.

3. Reduce the temperature to low and add the greens. Cover the pan with a lid and steam for 5–7 minutes to wilt and warm the greens. Dish onto plates and sprinkle with 1–2 teaspoons of the cheese.

Grits and Ham Bake

In America, cornmeal porridge is called "grits," but in other cultures the same dish is called polenta. It uses the same ingredients, with a similar cooking technique, but the flavorings can be different.

INGREDIENTS | SERVES 4

Butter, as needed

3 cups water

¾ cups instant grits

6 ounces evaporated milk

1½ cups Cheddar cheese

1 teaspoon garlic powder

¼ teaspoon ground black pepper

Several dashes Tabasco sauce

8 ounces ham, cubed

1 egg, beaten well

¼ cup shredded Monterey Jack cheese

1. Preheat oven to 350°F. Butter the bottom and sides of a skillet. Boil the water in a small saucepan over medium heat, add the grits, and cook according to the package directions until done.

2. Stir in the milk, cheese, spices, and ham. Stir the egg into the mixture and pour into the skillet.

3. Bake in the middle of the oven for 45 minutes. Sprinkle the Monterey Jack cheese on top and bake for 5–10 minutes.

4. Let the mixture cool in the skillet for 10 minutes before serving. Leftovers can be refrigerated for several days.

Choucroute

This dish is pronounced "shoe-croote," and is French for "sauerkraut."
As the sauerkraut cooks the taste becomes very mild. Because of the acidic
nature of sauerkraut, it's better to use an enameled skillet for this dish.

INGREDIENTS | SERVES 6–8

4 slices bacon

1 large yellow onion, chopped

3 garlic cloves, sliced

2 apples, cored and sliced

1 quart sauerkraut, fresh, jarred, or bagged

1 bottle non-bitter beer, or ½ bottle Riesling

7 juniper berries, or ½ cup gin

8 peppercorns

2 bay leaves

1 tablespoon brown sugar

¼ pound ham, cubed

1½ pounds German sausages (knackwurst, bratwurst, garlic sausage, kielbasa)

1. Place a skillet over medium heat. Once it is heated, add the bacon to the skillet and fry until is cooked through but not crispy. Add the onion and cook for 5–7 minutes or until the onion starts to brown. Add the garlic and cook for 1 minute, stirring continually.

2. Add the apples, sauerkraut, and beer. Stir to combine. Add the juniper berries, peppercorns, bay leaves, and the sugar. Reduce the heat to low, cover, and simmer for 1 hour.

3. Stir the ham into the skillet and add the sausages. Cook for 1½ hours, covered. Add water to the pan if it seems like it is getting too dry. When the sausages are cooked through, serve while warm with boiled and buttered potatoes.

City Chicken

Before the Depression, pork and beef were cheaper to serve than chicken.
Serving chicken in rural areas was more common because they were easier to raise.
But in the cities, raising chickens was harder and before refrigeration, they didn't store well.

INGREDIENTS | SERVES 4–6

1 pound pork, trimmed of excess fat and cut into 1" cubes

1 pound lean beef, trimmed of excess fat and cut into 1" cubes

1 egg, beaten

1½ cups bread crumbs

1 teaspoon salt

½ teaspoon ground black pepper

2 tablespoons butter

3 tablespoons olive oil

1 cup chicken broth

1 tablespoon cornstarch

1. Place alternating cubes of pork and beef on skewers, making sure the meat is touching. Place the egg in a shallow dish large enough to hold an entire skewer. Combine the bread crumbs with the salt and pepper and place in an equally large dish. Dip the skewers in the egg. Roll the skewers through the bread crumbs.

2. Place a large skillet over medium heat. Add the butter and oil. Once the oil is heated, add a few of the skewers and cook for 2–3 minutes on each side, or until they're browned. Repeat with the other skewers.

3. Return all of the skewers to the skillet. Add half the chicken broth. Cover the pan, reduce heat to medium-low, and simmer for 25–30 minutes. Remove the skewers from the pan and keep them warm.

4. Dissolve the cornstarch in the rest of the chicken broth and slowly whisk it into the skillet. Stir constantly until the sauce has thickened. Pour some of the sauce over each skewer and serve.

Icelandic Sweet and Tangy Pork

This dish is served in restaurants in Iceland and is very similar to a cooking technique used with puffin. Since puffin is hard to find, pork makes a nice stand-in. This dish goes great with the Icelandic Sugar-Glazed Potatoes (page 67).

INGREDIENTS | **SERVES 8–10**

3 pounds pork tenderloin

1 teaspoon paprika

½ teaspoon salt

½ teaspoon sugar

Large pinch of mustard powder

½ teaspoon of chili powder

½ teaspoon ground cumin

Large pinch black pepper

½ teaspoon garlic powder

Large pinch cayenne pepper

1 tablespoon vegetable oil

1 14-ounce can beef broth

1 pound pitted dates, chopped

1 pint heavy cream

3 tablespoons stone-ground mustard

1. Cut the pork tenderloin into 2" chunks. Mix all spices together in a bowl. Rub the spices over the pork. Let sit in the refrigerator for 2–24 hours.

2. Place a large skillet over medium-high heat. Once it is heated add the oil and the pork. Don't crowd the pan, so do this in batches if necessary. Cook for about 2 minutes on each side. When all of the pork is browned, return all the pork to the skillet, lower the heat to medium-low, and add the beef broth.

3. Add the dates to the skillet and cook for 15–20 minutes. The pork should be barely pink in the middle.

4. While the pork cooks, place a small saucepan over medium heat and add the cream. Once it's heated, stir in the mustard until dissolved. Once dissolved, pour into the skillet. Place the cover on the skillet and cook for another 10 minutes. The pork should be completely cooked through and still tender.

Chicago-Style Deep-Dish Sausage Pizza

Using a cast-iron skillet for this is perfect because it makes the dough crispy and keeps the sides from flopping over.

INGREDIENTS | MAKES 2 PIZZAS

1 package active dry yeast

1 tablespoon sugar

1 cup warm water

5 tablespoons melted butter

½ cup fine cornmeal

1 teaspoon salt

4 cups all-purpose white flour

1 teaspoon cream of tartar

8 ounces shredded mozzarella cheese

8 ounces cooked Italian sausage crumbles

1 jar prepared pizza sauce

Save Time with a Refrigerator Rise

Bread recipes tell you to let the dough rise at room temperature. To save time, you can make the dough the night before and refrigerate it in a sealed container. When you preheat your oven, remove the dough from the bowl, punch it down and let it sit for 20 minutes to warm up. The longer rise will make the dough taste yeastier, too.

1. Combine the yeast, sugar, and water in the mixing bowl of a stand mixer, or in a large mixing bowl. Let it sit for 10 minutes, or until the yeast becomes frothy. Add 3 tablespoons of the melted butter and stir to combine. Using a dough hook on a low setting, or mixing with a fork by hand, stir in the cornmeal, salt, 2½ cups flour, and the cream of tartar. Add more flour in ¼ cup intervals until the dough holds together in a ball and isn't sticky.

2. Flour a surface and knead the dough for a few minutes until it is smooth and elastic. Pour ½ tablespoon of melted butter into a clean bowl. Divide dough in half and shape into balls. Roll dough in the butter to coat. Cover the bowl and let it rest in a warm and draft-free area for 2 hours, or until it has doubled in size.

3. Preheat oven to 450°F. Punch the dough and let it rest for 10 minutes. Stretch and roll 1 ball into a round that overlaps your skillet by a couple of inches on each side. Brush the inside of the skillet with the remaining butter up to the top edge. Place the disk in the skillet and pinch the dough so it climbs up over the edge of the skillet. Use a fork to pierce the bottom of the crust repeatedly.

4. Bake for 10 minutes. Remove from the oven, layer half the cheese, the sausage, the remaining cheese, and cover the toppings entirely in sauce. Bake for 30 minutes or until the crust is golden brown and the cheese is bubbling up through the sauce. Serve with a fork and knife.

5. Repeat steps 3 and 4 with the other ball of dough to make a second pizza.

German Ham Hocks

In German this dish is called Schweinshaxe. *Most recipes call for the hocks to be simmered in beans or stewed to make the meat tender. But in this recipe, the skin turns into a crispy crust and the juicy meat falls off the bone.*

INGREDIENTS | SERVES 2

2 fresh ham hocks

1 teaspoon salt

½ teaspoon ground black pepper

1 teaspoon powdered sage

1 teaspoon dried rosemary, ground

1 tablespoon butter or bacon grease

1½ cups chicken broth

1 onion, peeled and quartered

1 carrot, peeled and cut into 1" pieces

3 celery stalks, cut into 1" pieces

10 peppercorns

¾ cup sour cream

2 tablespoons flour

1. Preheat oven to 350°F. Using the tip of a thin, sharp knife, loosen the meat near the bone slightly. Mix the salt, pepper, sage, and rosemary together. Rub the spice mixture over the hocks.

2. Place a skillet over medium-high heat and add the butter. Once it has melted and stopped foaming, add the hocks and sear on all sides for 3 minutes.

3. Add the chicken broth and onion, cover the pan, and bake in the oven for 2 hours. Turn the hocks every 30 minutes to keep them coated in the liquid. Add more broth if they seem to be getting dry. Add the carrots, celery, and peppercorns for the last 45 minutes of cooking time.

4. Remove the hocks and vegetables and keep warm. Place the skillet on the stove over medium heat. Scrape the bottom of the skillet to remove any stuck-on bits. Remove any fat from the surface of the liquid.

5. Stir the sour cream and flour together and slowly stir the mixture into the hot liquid, whisking continually. Once it simmers, reduce the heat to low and stir frequently while it thickens for 3–4 minutes. Taste and season if desired.

6. Remove the meat from the ham hocks and return to the skillet with the vegetables and any reserved liquid. Stir in and serve over egg noodles or boiled potatoes with sauerkraut.

Apricot-Stuffed Pork Roast

The apricots are tart and sweet and complement the pork and the sauce.
This dish is fairly easy to make but the apricot nestled in the meat looks impressive once it is sliced.

INGREDIENTS | SERVES 6

1 3-pound pork roast

2 teaspoons finely chopped fresh oregano (or 2 tablespoons dried)

3" piece fresh ginger, peeled and cut into 10 slices

5 garlic cloves, cut into halves

5 apricots, cut into halves

1 tablespoon caraway seeds

1 teaspoon salt

¼ teaspoon ground black pepper

2 tablespoons olive oil

2 cups chicken stock

2 shallots, minced

½ cup balsamic vinegar

1 tablespoon butter

1. Preheat oven to 425°F. Trim away most of the fat from the roast, but leave a thin layer on top. Cut ten evenly spaced holes that are 1½" deep. Rub a pinch of oregano into each hole. Add a piece of ginger, a piece of garlic, and a piece of apricot into each hole. Combine the rest of the oregano with the caraway seeds, the salt, and the pepper. Rub the roast with 1 tablespoon of oil, and rub the herb and spice mixture over the roast.

2. Place a skillet over medium-high heat. Once the skillet is heated, add the roast, fat-side down, and cook on each side for 5 minutes.

3. Once all of the sides are browned, remove the skillet from the heat and place it in the middle of the oven. Roast for 40–60 minutes or until the center of the roast registers 150°F. Remove the roast from the pan, cover with foil, and let it rest for 10 minutes while you make the sauce.

4. Place the chicken stock, 1 tablespoon of oil, shallots, and the balsamic vinegar in the skillet and place over medium heat. Use a spoon to scrape up any stuck-on bits. Cook for 8 minutes, or until slightly reduced. Whisk in the butter and season to taste with salt and pepper. Remove from the heat and serve in a bowl to pour over the roast.

Jamaican Pork and Mango Stir Fry

Jamaican cuisine often combines spicy food with fruit to cut the heat.
It's also common to find ginger, nutmeg, and vanilla added to savory and sweet dishes.

INGREDIENTS | SERVES 4

1 pound pork tenderloin

1 teaspoon Jamaican Spice Mix (see below)

2 teaspoons olive oil

1" cube fresh ginger, freshly ground

1 mango, peeled and cubed

1 red bell pepper

⅔ cup orange or apple juice

1 teaspoon cornstarch

1 Scotch bonnet pepper, minced

¼ cup sliced green onion

Jamaican Spice Mix

Combine 2 tablespoons brown sugar with 1 tablespoon kosher salt, coriander, ginger, garlic powder, and ½ tablespoon of ground black pepper, cayenne pepper, ground nutmeg, and ground cinnamon. Store the mixture in an air-tight container. The flavors will start to diminish after 3 months but should be usable for up to a year.

1. Trim any excess fat from the meat and slice into 1" rounds. Cut slices into ¼" strips. Sprinkle the spice mix over the pork and let it rest in the refrigerator for 4–8 hours, or on the counter for 30 minutes.

2. Place a skillet over medium heat. Once it is heated add the oil and pork. Toss continually for 2 minutes. Add the ginger, mango, and bell pepper and cook for another 2–4 minutes, or until the pork is no longer pink.

3. Whisk the orange juice, cornstarch, and the Scotch bonnet pepper in a small bowl. Pour into the skillet, stirring continually. Cook for 2–3 minutes till the sauce has thickened.

4. Sprinkle the green onion over the dish and serve it over rice while warm.

Lumpia Filled with Ground Pork, Mushrooms, and Carrots

Lumpia is a Filipino dish similar to Chinese egg rolls or Thai spring rolls.
A prepared mixture is placed into a wrapper and either fried or served fresh.
This variety is easy to make at home since you wrap the mixture in leaf lettuce before eating.

INGREDIENTS | SERVES 4

1 tablespoon peanut or vegetable oil

2 carrots, finely chopped

1 small yellow onion, finely chopped

1 pound ground pork

12 ounces button mushrooms, thinly sliced

1" chunk ginger, peeled and finely diced

3 tablespoons soy sauce

¼ cup rice wine vinegar

1 tablespoon honey

2 tablespoons sesame oil

¼ teaspoon Chinese five spice

Pinch chili powder or cayenne powder

1 head green leaf lettuce or iceberg

The Wonder and History of Chinese Five Spice

The Chinese strive to balance all flavors in a dish. They believe there are five flavors—sour, bitter, sweet, pungent, and salty—and this mix combines them all. Make your own by combining ¼ teaspoon each of freshly ground black pepper, ground cloves, ground anise, ground cinnamon, and ground fennel seeds.

1. Place a skillet over medium-low heat. Add the oil once it is warm, then add the carrots. Cook for 2–3 minutes before adding the onion. Crumble the ground pork across the skillet surface and use a wooden spoon to cut it into small pieces. If the ground meat starts to stick, add a little more oil. Once the meat is mostly cooked, add the mushrooms and stir until they start to soften. Remove the skillet from the heat and drain any excess oil.

2. Mix the ginger, soy sauce, vinegar, honey, sesame oil, and spices. Place the skillet over medium-low heat and pour the sauce over the meat. Stir to combine and cook until the liquid has evaporated and the sauce has permeated the meat. Remove it from the pan and place into a serving bowl.

3. Rinse the lettuce leaves under cold water and shake, spin, or pat dry. Cut off any thick stems. Place on a plate for serving.

4. To assemble the lumpia, place a leaf in one palm. Place a heaping tablespoon of the meat mixture on the lettuce leaf. Roll it into a tube and hold the base pinched closed while you eat to keep the filling from falling out of the bottom.

Mexican-Inspired Pork Tenderloin

*Sherry tends to be sweet and is usually served at the end of a meal or with dessert.
A dry sherry is the least sweet but is still very flavorful. If you can't find sherry,
use a medium-dry white wine in this dish. Do not use cooking sherry.*

INGREDIENTS | SERVES 4

4 ¾"-thick pork tenderloin slices
2 garlic cloves, minced
1 teaspoon ground cumin
2 teaspoons dried oregano
1 teaspoon salt
½ teaspoon ground black pepper
½ cup dry sherry
Juice from 2 limes
2 tablespoons olive oil

1. Rinse the pork slices and pat dry with a paper towel. Add all of the remaining ingredients except for the oil in a sealable container. Stir well to combine and add the pork slices to the marinade. Refrigerate overnight. Shake the dish a few times.

2. Place a skillet over medium-high heat and add the oil when heated. Shake off the excess marinade from the pork and place in the skillet so they don't touch. Cover the skillet with a splatter screen. Cook for 2 minutes on each side.

3. The meat should register at least 150°F. Place the slices on a plate, cover, and let them rest for 5 minutes before serving.

4. While they rest, pour the marinade into the still-hot skillet and use a spatula to scrape up any stuck-on bits. Stir continuously and let the sauce reduce by half. Pour the reduction over the meat before serving.

Pork Chop Cacciatore with Potatoes and Peppers

If you can't find juniper berries you can use two bay leaves as a substitute.
If you have gin, you can also add 3 tablespoons of gin to this dish.

INGREDIENTS | SERVES 4

½ cup olive oil

6 garlic cloves, minced

1 tablespoon dried rosemary, crushed

6 juniper berries, crushed

4 bone-in pork chops, ½" to ¾" thick

Salt to taste

Pepper to taste

2 large baking potatoes, halved and cut into thick slices

2 bell peppers, seeded and cut into large pieces

Cacciatore

"Cacciatore" means "hunter" in Italian. This style of cooking refers to meat cooked with easy-to-find vegetables like peppers, onions, mushrooms, and tomatoes. Wine is often included, but not necessary. This dish uses juniper berries and rosemary, which can be gathered from a forest.

1. Preheat oven to 450°F. Combine the olive oil, garlic, rosemary, and juniper in a bowl. Rub half the mixture on the pork chops and sprinkle with salt and pepper. Toss the potatoes and peppers in the bowl to coat with oil and spices. Sprinkle with salt and pepper.

2. Place a large skillet over medium-high heat. Once it is heated through, add the pork chops and cook on each side for 2–3 minutes. Remove from the heat.

3. Add the potatoes and peppers to the skillet, placing the chops on top of the vegetables. Bake for 15–20 minutes, or until the chops are just cooked through.

4. If the chops cook before the vegetables are done, remove the meat from the pan and set aside to keep warm. Change the oven to broil and cook for a few minutes while stirring frequently to prevent it from burning.

Pork Chops with Capers and Mustard Sauce

If you can't find capers, substitute finely chopped green olives in this dish.

INGREDIENTS | SERVES 4

4 9-ounce pork chops (1¼" thick)

Salt to taste

Pepper to taste

1 tablespoon olive oil

1 cup low-sodium chicken or vegetable broth

⅓ cup capers

2 tablespoons Dijon mustard

2 tablespoons sweet cream butter

Capers

Capers are immature flower buds that have been pickled in vinegar, most commonly used in Mediterranean cuisines. Most capers are about the size of a corn kernel. Once the fruit flowers it becomes a berry (called a "caperberry"), which can also be pickled and served. Because of its volcanic soil, the Greek island of Santorini is known for having the most flavorful capers.

1. Trim off any excess fat from the pork chops. Rinse and pat dry. Sprinkle each side lightly with salt and pepper.

2. Place a large skillet over medium-high heat. Once it is heated, add the oil and pork chops. Cook on each side for 5 minutes until evenly browned. Place them on a plate and cover with foil.

3. Pour the broth into the pan and use a spoon to remove any stuck-on bits. Boil. Whisk in the capers, mustard, and butter. Once the butter has melted, return the chops to the skillet and continue cooking for 3–5 minutes until no pink juices run from a small cut in the center. Place them on a plate and cover with the foil again.

4. Turn the heat up to high and reduce the liquid in the pan by half before pouring over the chops and serving.

Pork-Stuffed Chili Relleno

This flavored meat is tasty and can be mixed into scrambled eggs or served in tacos, on tostada shells, or even on a bun. Save the leftover broth to add to bean soups.

INGREDIENTS | **SERVES 6**

2 pounds pork, cut into 1" cubes

1 white onion, chopped

7 garlic cloves

1 teaspoon salt

Water, as needed

3 tablespoons vegetable oil

½ teaspoon ground black pepper

1 teaspoon ground cinnamon

1 teaspoon ground cumin

1 15-ounce can tomato purée

6 poblano chilies

1. Preheat oven to 375°F. Place a skillet over medium heat. Once it has heated, add the pork. Cook for 2 minutes on each side until browned. Cook in batches if necessary. Once the pork is seared, add half the onion, 4 smashed garlic cloves, and 1 teaspoon salt.

2. Add water to the skillet until the meat is barely covered. Braise in the oven for 45 minutes until the meat is tender but not soft. Remove the skillet from the oven and cool at room temperature until the pork can be handled. Shred the meat and discard any large pieces of fat or cartilage. Strain the broth and set aside. Discard the garlic and onion.

3. Wipe the skillet clean and place over medium-high heat. Once it is heated, add the oil and the remaining onion. Cook for 4–5 minutes. Add 3 minced garlic cloves and cook for 1 minute, stirring continually.

4. Add the meat and sprinkle the pepper, cinnamon, and cumin on top. Stir to combine and cook for 10 minutes. Add the tomato purée and cook for 10 minutes, or until the sauce has mostly evaporated. The mixture should be moist but not juicy.

5. Preheat the broiler. Cut the top off the poblano peppers and remove the seeds. Stuff about ½ cup of pork mixture into each pepper.

6. Lay the stuffed peppers in a clean skillet and place the skillet 6" from the flame. Roast evenly on each side for 3–4 minutes, or until the skins of the peppers just start to blacken and crack. Serve.

Pork Scallopine with Red Wine and Mushrooms

"Scallopine" simply refers to a thin and tender cut of meat that is dredged in flour and cooked at a high temperature for a short time.

INGREDIENTS | SERVES 4

1½ pounds pork tenderloin cut into 4 slices

Salt to taste

Pepper to taste

½ cup all-purpose flour

4 tablespoons butter

2 large shallots, chopped

2 garlic cloves, minced

16 ounces button mushrooms, sliced

1 tablespoon dried thyme

2 cups dry red wine

Pork Trivia

Pigs were domesticated as early as 5000 B.C. in Asia. They are omnivorous, unlike other livestock. Until the 1900s pigs were often only slaughtered in the fall and were only born in the early spring. Now, due to mass production, pigs are born and slaughtered year-round.

1. Use a meat tenderizer to pound the pork till it is ¼" thick. Season with salt and pepper. Dredge the pieces in flour and shake off the excess.

2. Place a large skillet over medium-high heat. When it's heated, add 2 tablespoons butter. Once it is melted and frothy, slide the pork into the skillet and cook for 1–2 minutes on each side. Remove them from the pan and set aside to stay warm.

3. Add the rest of the butter and the shallots to the skillet. Cook for 1 minute. Add the garlic to the pan and cook for 30 seconds.

4. Sprinkle the mushrooms, thyme, and salt over the pan's surface. Cook for 5 minutes, stirring frequently until the mushrooms are tender.

5. Add the wine to the skillet and simmer for 10 minutes or until it's reduced by half. Taste and season as needed. Serve over rice or mashed potatoes.

Stuffed Pork Chops

If you don't want to make your own stuffing mix,
you can use a boxed mix to save time.

INGREDIENTS | **SERVES 4**

4 thick-cut boneless pork chops
2 tablespoons olive oil
1 small yellow onion, chopped
4 ounces button mushrooms, chopped
1 garlic clove, minced
5 slices stale bread, air dried and crumbed
1 tablespoon parsley flakes
1 teaspoon sugar
1 teaspoon dried oregano
2 tablespoons Parmesan cheese
1 teaspoon salt, plus more to taste
¼ teaspoon pepper, plus more to taste

Boneless Pork Chop Substitute

If you can't find boneless pork chops, you can cut a pork tenderloin into 1½" to 2" thick rounds. They'll be smaller than boneless pork chops, but they'll cook just as quickly and be just as juicy.

1. Rinse the pork chops. Pat dry. Preheat oven to 400°F.

2. Place a skillet over medium heat. Once it's heated add 1 tablespoon of the oil and the onion. Cook for 5–7 minutes. Add the mushrooms and cook for 7–10 minutes or until they've softened and released their juices. Stir in the garlic clove and cook for 1 minute. Stir in the bread crumbs, parsley flakes, sugar, oregano, cheese, 1 teaspoon salt, and ¼ teaspoon pepper.

3. Cut a pocket in each pork chop. Season the pork chops inside and out with salt and pepper. Divide the stuffing into 4 portions and stuff 1 portion into each chop.

4. Place a skillet over medium-high heat. Once heated, add the remaining oil and as many pork chops as will fit without touching. Cook on each side for 3–4 minutes until they're golden brown.

5. Place all the chops in the skillet and cook in the oven for 10 minutes until they're cooked through. Remove and let rest for 5 minutes before serving.

Sweet and Sour Pork

This dish is a great way to use leftover pork. To determine how far your leftovers will go, each serving of pork is approximately the size of your fist.

INGREDIENTS | **SERVES 4**

¼ cup ketchup

Juice from 1 lemon

2 teaspoons soy sauce

1 15-ounce can pineapple chunks in juice

1 tablespoon cornstarch

¼ cup cold water

1 pound cooked pork, cubed

1. Place a skillet over medium heat. Combine the ketchup, lemon juice, and soy sauce. Add the sauce to the skillet.

2. Stir in the juice from the can of pineapple. Combine the cornstarch and water in a small bowl. Once the sauce is bubbling, whisk in the cornstarch mixture.

3. Let the sauce simmer for several minutes until it starts to thicken. Stir in the pork cubes and pineapple chunks. Cook until the sauce has thickened again and the pork is warmed through. Serve over white rice.

Chapter 9

Beef in a Skillet

Swiss Steak

This is a cross between pot roast and stew. It's a great way to use a tough cut of meat from the hind leg or shoulder of a cow. Those tough cuts are very flavorful and soften up nicely after cooking over low heat for a long time.

INGREDIENTS | SERVES 4

1½ pounds rump, round, or chuck roast

2 tablespoons flour

1 teaspoon salt

½ teaspoon ground black pepper

2 tablespoons vegetable oil

1 medium onion, thinly sliced

2 garlic cloves, smashed

1 15-ounce can stewed tomatoes

1 teaspoon smoked paprika

1 tablespoon Worcestershire sauce

1 cup beef broth

1. Preheat oven to 325°F. Trim any exterior fat from the steak. Mix the flour, salt, and pepper in a small bowl. Sprinkle half of the flour mixture over the roast and use the base of a sturdy glass to pound the flour into the meat. Repeat with the other side.

2. Place a skillet over medium heat. Once the skillet is heated, add the oil and the meat. Cook on each side for 5 minutes until the meat is browned.

3. Remove the meat from skillet and add the onion. Cook for 5 minutes, stir in the garlic. Chop the tomatoes and add. Stir in the paprika, Worcestershire, and broth. Cook covered in the oven for 2 hours, or until the meat is tender.

Thai Mussamun Curried Beef with Potatoes

Mussamun is a type of Thai curry paste that is popular in Southern Thailand, especially among those who are Muslim. It is an intensely flavored, but lightly spicy curry paste.

INGREDIENTS | SERVES 4

2 tablespoons peanut oil

1 large yellow onion, sliced

1 teaspoon dried chili powder

1 teaspoon ground coriander

1 teaspoon ground cumin

½ teaspoon black pepper

½ teaspoon ground nutmeg

1" piece ginger, peeled and shredded

1 serrano or Thai chili, thinly sliced

1 lemongrass stalk

1 15-ounce can coconut milk

½ pound beef sirloin, cut into cubes

1 teaspoon soy sauce

2 teaspoons sugar

1. Place a skillet over medium heat and once it's heated add the oil and onion. Stir frequently and cook for 7–9 minutes or until the onion is lightly browned. Stir in the dried spices, the ginger, and the chili and cook for 3–5 minutes, or until the spices are fragrant.

2. Remove the outer leaves from the lemongrass stalk. Cut off the base end and the top dried portion. Cut the stalk in half lengthwise and then into 1" chunks. Stir the lemongrass and the coconut milk into the skillet.

3. Add the cubed beef, soy sauce, and sugar to the skillet. Stir to combine and cook for 7–10 minutes. Serve over Jasmine rice.

Sloppy Joes

If you use lean ground beef and fat-free Cheddar cheese, this is a very low-fat dish.
To cut calories you can omit the brown sugar.

INGREDIENTS | SERVES 4–6

1½ pounds lean ground beef
1 medium onion plus ¼ onion, chopped
2 garlic cloves, smashed
1 8-ounce can tomato paste
1 12-ounce can tomato sauce
1 red bell pepper, finely chopped
2 tablespoons Worcestershire sauce
2 tablespoons brown sugar
2 tablespoons prepared mustard
1 tablespoon cider vinegar
1 teaspoon chili powder
4–6 hamburger buns
½ cup Cheddar cheese, shredded

1. Place a large skillet over medium heat. Once it's heated, add the ground beef. Chop the ground beef with a wooden spoon or a spatula into small pieces.

2. Once the beef is cooked, drain off the fat and then put the beef in a bowl. Add 1 chopped onion and the garlic to the skillet and sauté.

3. Return the meat to the skillet and combine all of the other ingredients except for the ¼ onion, hamburger buns, and cheese. Reduce the heat to low and simmer for 20 minutes. Once the liquid has evaporated and the pepper is softened, move the meat mixture to a serving bowl. Serve with chopped onion, hamburger buns, and shredded Cheddar cheese for garnish.

Carne Guisada

"Carne guisada" means "stewed beef" in Spanish. Every region of Central America and many of the Spanish-speaking islands have their own version of this dish. This one isn't spicy, but some are. It's best to serve this version with white rice in bowls.

INGREDIENTS | SERVES 6

2 tablespoons vegetable oil

1½ pounds beef stew meat, trimmed and cubed

1 large onion, cut into eighths

1 red bell pepper, seeded and sliced

4 garlic cloves

1 celery stalk, chopped

8 ounces button mushrooms, sliced

1 cup beer

1 14-ounce can stewed tomatoes

2 fresh jalapeño peppers, stemmed, seeded, and diced

1 teaspoon ground cumin

2 cups beef broth

1. Place a Dutch oven over medium-high heat. Add the oil and beef when it is heated. Cook for 5 minutes so all sides are browned. Remove the beef and set aside.

2. Add the onion and peppers and cook for 5 minutes while stirring frequently. Add the garlic, celery, and mushrooms and cook for 5 minutes. Once the celery has softened, add the beer. Stir to loosen the fond.

3. Add the tomatoes, jalapeños, cumin, and beef broth. Return the meat to the pan and stir until everything is well combined. Turn the flame to the lowest setting and cover. Cook for 3–3½ hours. The meat should fall apart when you pick it up. Serve immediately.

Restaurant-Style Ribeye

This technique works well with almost any cut of tender steak. In addition to ribeye, you can use a New York strip, T-bone, porterhouse, tenderloin, or a filet mignon.

INGREDIENTS | SERVES 2

2 1" thick choice-grade steaks
1 tablespoon vegetable oil
1 tablespoon butter
Salt to taste
Pepper to taste

Steak Temperatures

When following this recipe, begin testing the steak after cooking 3 minutes. Remove the steak when the center of the steak is done to these temperatures: rare: 120°F; medium-rare: 125°F; medium: 130°F; medium-well: 145°F; well: 155°F. The steak temperature will rise 5° while it rests.

1. Let your steaks sit at room temperature for 30 minutes before cooking. Preheat oven to 425°F. Place a skillet large enough to hold two steaks on a burner over high heat. Turn on a vent if you have one or open a window.

2. Pat the steaks dry and brush both sides of each steak with the oil. Sprinkle salt and pepper on each side of the steaks. Test the skillet temperature by placing a drop of water in the center. If it sizzles, you know it's ready. Place the steaks in the skillet so they aren't touching and let them sit without moving for 2 minutes. Carefully flip each steak over. Cook on the other side for 2 minutes.

3. Turn off the burner. Cut the butter into two pieces and put a piece on the middle of each steak. Move the skillet to the middle of your oven. The cut, thickness, and quality of the meat will determine cooking time.

4. Once the steaks are done, place them on a plate, cover with a piece of foil, and let them rest for 5 minutes.

Grilled Flank Steak with Chimichurri Sauce

If you can't find flank steak, ask for ½" cuts of a bottom round roast. If neither are available, look for a piece of beef that is no more than ¾" thick and pound it slightly before cooking.

INGREDIENTS | **SERVES 4**

1½ pounds flank steak, trimmed of excess fat

1 pinch plus 1 teaspoon salt

1 pinch plus ¼ teaspoon ground black pepper

2 teaspoons vegetable oil

2 cups packed parsley leaves

4 garlic cloves, quartered

1 scallion, roughly chopped

¼ cup apple cider vinegar

¼ cup red wine vinegar

½ teaspoon ground paprika

1 large pinch red chili flakes

¼ cup olive oil

Chimichurri: Jimmy McCurry's Sauce

Chimichurri is a popular condiment served on grilled meats in Argentina and other Latin American countries. It's believe the sauce was invented by an Irishman named Jimmy McCurry who was traveling with an army in the late 1800s during Argentina's fight for independence. But since his name was hard to pronounce, it became known as chimichurri sauce.

1. Place a grill pan over high heat. Season the steak with a pinch of salt and pepper on both sides. Brush vegetable oil across the surface of the pan once it is heated.

2. Place the steak in the pan and cook for 4 minutes. Turn it and cook for 4 minutes for medium-rare, 5 minutes for medium, and 6 minutes for medium-well. Place the steak on a cutting board, tent with foil, and let it rest for 5 minutes.

3. Place the parsley in a food processor or blender and pulse several times. Scrape down the sides and add the garlic, scallion, and vinegars. Pulse a few times. Add in 1 teaspoon salt, ¼ teaspoon pepper, and the rest of the spices and pulse until smooth. While the food processor runs, slowly add the olive oil to create an emulsion.

4. Cut the steak diagonally against the grain into ½" thick slices. Serve with the sauce.

Japanese Caramelized Ribeye Steaks

The wasabi in this dish gives the steak its punch. If you don't have wasabi you can substitute 1 teaspoon of prepared horseradish or 1 tablespoon of dried mustard powder.

INGREDIENTS | SERVES 4

Juice from 4 limes
½ cup soy sauce
3 garlic cloves, minced
1 teaspoon wasabi powder
1 cup Sweet Chili Sauce (see below)
4 6-ounce ribeye steaks
2 tablespoons olive oil

Sweet Chili Sauce

This is a great dipping sauce for egg rolls, won tons, or grilled meat. In a blender add 4 minced garlic cloves, 2 tablespoons honey, juice from 4 limes, 2 tablespoons fish sauce, and 1–2 Thai red chili peppers that have been stemmed and chopped. Purée until thin and add more lime juice if you want a thinner texture.

1. Preheat oven to 450°F and place a rack in the center of the oven.

2. Whisk together the lime juice, soy sauce, garlic, wasabi powder, and chili sauce.

3. Place a skillet over medium-high heat. Once it is heated add half of the oil and two of the steaks. Cook on each side for 2 minutes. Repeat with the other steaks.

4. Turn off the heat, place all of the steaks in the skillet, and pour the sauce on the steaks. Cook in the oven for 7–10 minutes; 7 minutes for medium-rare and 10 minutes for medium-well.

5. If the steaks don't sit flat in the skillet, flip them halfway through the cooking time. Serve with white rice.

Corned Beef Hash

If you happen to have any leftover Corned Beef Brisket (page 256), Basic Beef Roast (page 255), Oven-Braised Pork Roast (page 263), or Braised Beef Shank (page 158), you can use it to make this dish.

INGREDIENTS | SERVES 4–6

1 tablespoon butter

3 tablespoons olive oil

1 medium onion, finely chopped

1 garlic clove, minced

2–3 cups chopped, cooked beef or pork roast

2–3 cups peeled, chopped potatoes

Salt to taste

Pepper to taste

Better with an Egg on Top

You can turn this into a one-pot meal with eggs cooked on top. Once the hash is crispy all over, use a spoon to dig out four holes that are about 2" from the skillet edge and evenly spaced apart. Crack an egg into each one. Cover the skillet and cook for 3–5 minutes, depending on how well-done you like your eggs.

1. Place a skillet over medium heat. Once it is heated through add the butter and oil. Stir in the onion and cook for 4–5 minutes. Add the garlic and cook for 1 minute.

2. Add the beef and potatoes to the skillet. Spread them evenly across the surface of the pan and increase the heat to medium-high. Press down on the mixture frequently with a spatula. Do not stir.

3. Cook the first side for 6–9 minutes. Lift a section in the middle up to see if the bottom is browning. Once it is browned, flip the contents over in sections so the other side can brown. Cook the second side for 4–7 minutes.

4. Remove it from the heat, season with salt and pepper and serve with crusty bread and fried eggs for breakfast.

Pan-Seared Skirt Steak

If you can't find skirt steak, substitute flank steak or thin-cut bottom round steaks.
Serve with the Chipotle Orange Sauce (page 51) or the Chimichurri Sauce (page 149).

INGREDIENTS | SERVES 4

1½ pounds skirt steak
Pinch salt
2 tablespoons vegetable oil

Quick Savory Grits

Grits are rarely served in the North, but they're a great side dish with steak and are easy to make. They tend to be bland, but adding flavoring (particularly garlic, onion, or leeks) to the simmering milk adds zest. Follow the package directions and add 2 chopped scallions, 1 chopped leek, or 2 minced garlic cloves to the milk while cooking.

1. Trim as much of the silver skin and fat from the steak as possible. Cut each steak with the grain into 2 even pieces that are between 4"–5" long.

2. Sprinkle the meat with salt. If desired, toss the steak in a sauce or a marinade.

3. Place a skillet over high heat. Once the skillet is hot but not smoking, add 1 tablespoon of oil to the pan. Slide half of the meat into the skillet. Cook for 3–4 minutes, or until browned. Shake the skillet frequently to keep the meat from sticking.

4. Use tongs to flip the steak to the other side and cook for 3–4 minutes. The meat should be medium to medium-rare. Cooking past medium will make the steak very tough. Remove the meat from the skillet and tent with foil to keep warm. Repeat with remaining meat.

5. Let the second batch of meat rest for 5 minutes. Slice thin against the grain and serve with a sauce of your choice while warm.

Beef Stroganoff

*This dish comes from Russia and was made popular in the 1950s
by servicemen returning from Europe after WWII.*

INGREDIENTS | SERVES 4

1 pound beef stew meat

1 tablespoon vegetable oil

¼ pound mushrooms, sliced

½ small onion, chopped

2 garlic cloves, minced

½ teaspoon dried oregano

¼ teaspoon salt

¼ teaspoon pepper

¼ teaspoon dried thyme

1 bay leaf

1½ cups beef broth

¼ cup sherry

½ cup sour cream

¼ cup all-purpose flour

2 tablespoons water

½–¾ cup cooked noodles per person

1. Preheat oven to 325°F. Trim any excess fat from the beef and cut the meat into 1" cubes. Place a skillet over medium-high heat. Once it is warmed, add the oil and the meat. Let the beef cook until each side is browned. Drain the fat.

2. Add the mushrooms, onion, and garlic. Cook for 5–7 minutes. Add the oregano, salt, pepper, thyme, bay leaf, broth, and sherry, stirring to combine. Cook in the middle of the oven for 1½ hours. Discard the bay leaf. Remove the beef from the pan and cover to keep warm.

3. Place the skillet over a low flame on the stovetop. In a small bowl, combine the sour cream, flour, and water. Slowly pour 1 cup of hot liquid from the pan into the sour cream mixture. Once everything is combined, stir the dairy mixture into the skillet and whisk to combine. Stir in the reserved meat and simmer for an additional 3 minutes.

4. Pour the stroganoff mixture over the noodles and serve immediately.

Swedish Meatballs

This recipe is part of traditional smorgasbords and served with lingonberry preserves. If you can't find this, you can substitute with cranberry sauce.

INGREDIENTS | SERVES 4–6

1 teaspoon plus 1 pinch salt

1 small onion, minced

2 slices white sandwich bread, crust removed

1 large egg, beaten lightly

3 tablespoons milk

8 ounces lean ground beef

8 ounces ground pork

Large pinch nutmeg

Large pinch allspice

Large pinch pepper

1–2 cups vegetable oil

1 tablespoon butter

1 tablespoon all-purpose flour

2 cups chicken broth

2 teaspoons honey

2 bay leaves

½ cup milk

Juice from 1 lemon

1. Sprinkle 1 teaspoon salt over the onion and set aside. Cut the bread into cubes and place in a large bowl. Add the egg and milk and mash into a paste. Add the beef, pork, the onion, nutmeg, allspice, and pepper. Mix together with your hands. Use a tablespoon to create evenly sized meatballs.

2. Place skillet over medium-high heat and add enough oil so it is ½" deep. Once the oil is heated, add a single layer of meatballs so they don't touch. Roll them frequently so they brown evenly for 8–10 minutes. Reduce the heat if the oil starts to smoke. Place the meatballs on paper towels to drain and keep warm.

3. Drain the oil from the pan, but leave the brown bits. Add the butter; when it has melted and is just starting to turn brown, sprinkle the flour over the surface and whisk for about 1 minute.

4. Stir in the broth, honey, and bay leaves, whisking and scraping the bottom of the skillet. Bring the mixture to a simmer and cook for 5 minutes.

5. Once the sauce has thickened, stir in the milk. Return the meatballs to the skillet and simmer for about 5 minutes so they're heated through. Discard the bay leaves, stir in the lemon juice, and taste before adding salt and pepper. Serve with boiled egg noodles.

Large Meatballs with Peppers and Potatoes

These large meatballs are great as a meal on their own or can be served over boiled pasta for a more traditional Italian-style dinner.

INGREDIENTS | SERVES 4

1½ pounds lean ground beef

¼ cup plain bread crumbs

½ cup grated Parmesan cheese

2 eggs, beaten

1 teaspoon salt

½ teaspoon pepper

1 large baking potato, peeled and shredded

4 cups bottled pasta sauce

8 jarred or fresh cherry peppers, quartered

¼ cup chopped fresh basil

Some Cherries Are Spicy and Sweet

Cherry peppers are small, sweet, and mildly spicy and are called cherry because they resemble the fruit. They're bright red and 1" to 2" in diameter. They may be called Hungarian peppers. They're frequently pickled or brined but are great fresh as well. As with all peppers, you can remove the seeds to reduce the heat.

1. Preheat oven to 375°F. Use your hands to combine the ground beef, bread crumbs, Parmesan cheese, eggs, salt, and pepper in a large bowl. Divide it into eight evenly sized balls.

2. Place the shredded potato on sturdy paper towels and squeeze to remove as much of the water as possible.

3. Place a skillet over medium heat. Once it is heated, add the pasta sauce. Stir in the cherry peppers and potatoes. Cook 3–4 minutes until it simmers.

4. Nestle the meatballs into the skillet. Season if desired. Cover and cook in the middle of the oven for 25–30 minutes. Serve with chopped basil on top.

Beef Teriyaki

This dish is similar to Teriyaki Pork (page 220) but the fruit juice and vinegar additions match well with the more flavorful beef.

INGREDIENTS | SERVES 4

1 garlic clove, minced

1 teaspoon ginger juice

3 tablespoons soy sauce

3 tablespoons rice wine vinegar

1 teaspoon toasted sesame oil

3 tablespoons pineapple juice or pomegranate juice

1½ pounds sirloin, cut into ¼" strips

2 tablespoons peanut oil

3 cups frozen broccoli

Juicy Root

Ginger root actually has a very high water content even though it is a fibrous plant. The juice is where all the flavor is. Slice a root and purée it in a food processor. Place a couple layers of cheesecloth together over a bowl. Pour the ground ginger into the cheesecloth and squeeze to remove all the juice. The leftover fiber can be discarded.

1. Whisk together the garlic, ginger juice, soy sauce, vinegar, sesame oil, and fruit juice. Place it in a sealable glass bowl. Add the beef strips to the marinade and let it rest in the refrigerator for 4–24 hours. Stir once or twice.

2. Place a large skillet over medium-high heat. Add the peanut oil once the pan is heated. Add half of the beef strips, stirring frequently. Cook for 4–5 minutes, or until browned. Remove the beef from the skillet and repeat with the rest of the beef. Return the first batch of the beef to the skillet and cook until most of the liquid has evaporated.

3. Add the frozen broccoli to the skillet and toss to combine. Pour the marinade over the skillet contents and toss to combine for about 3 minutes or until the broccoli is cooked through. Serve over rice.

Bi Bim Bap

*Bi Bim Bap translates as "mixed rice" and is a comfort food eaten for any meal.
It can also be made with pork, chicken, seafood, or tofu and often comes with hot sauce on the side.
If you can find spicy kimchi, serve it on top.*

INGREDIENTS | SERVES 4–6

2 cups bean sprouts

1 medium carrot, peeled and grated

1 medium cucumber, peeled, halved, and sliced in half rounds

1 cup rice vinegar

8 ounces sirloin cut into ¼" thick slices

2 tablespoons soy sauce

¼ cup vegetable oil

12 ounces shiitake mushrooms, minced

4 garlic cloves, minced

1 pound spinach, cleaned, stemmed, and chopped

Pinch salt

Pinch pepper

6 cups cooked rice, warm

4–6 large eggs

1 tablespoon sesame oil

1. Place the bean sprouts, carrots, cucumber, and vinegar in a small glass bowl. Toss to combine, press the vegetables so they are submerged, and let sit in the refrigerator for 4–24 hours. Drain the vegetables before serving.

2. Toss the beef and soy sauce together in a bowl. Cover and let sit for 30 minutes at room temperature. Preheat oven to 200°F and insert 4–6 oven-safe bowls.

3. Place a skillet over medium-high heat. Once it is warmed add 1 tablespoon of oil, the beef, and the mushrooms. Cook for 2 minutes. Add 1 tablespoon of the oil and the garlic. Cook for 30 seconds. Add the spinach, sprinkle with salt and pepper, and toss until the spinach is wilted. Place a serving of rice into each bowl. Divide the beef and vegetables over the rice and place the bowls back in the oven.

4. Wipe the skillet clean and add 2 tablespoons of oil to the skillet. Place it over medium-high heat. Crack 2 eggs into 2 coffee mugs. Once the skillet is heated, pour the eggs into the skillet at the same time. Do not to break the yolks. Sprinkle salt and pepper on top, cover the skillet with a lid and cook for 2–3 minutes. The whites should be set, but the yolks should be runny. Repeat with remaining eggs.

5. Remove the bowls and slide 1 egg onto each bowl. Drizzle the sesame oil over the eggs, and add a portion of the pickled vegetables to the bowl. Serve while hot.

Braised Beef Shank with Potatoes, Carrots, and Cauliflower

Beef shanks are horizontal cuts from the front leg of the cow. They have a lot of connective tissue, which dissolves into a gelatinous broth. This cut of beef is often inexpensive and very flavorful.

INGREDIENTS | **SERVES 3–4**

2 pieces beef shank, 2" thick

2 tablespoons butter

4 tablespoons vegetable oil

1 tablespoon dry peppercorns

1 large onion, chopped

1 5-ounce can tomato paste

2 quarts water

1 cup balsamic vinegar

2 tablespoons fresh thyme

2 bay leaves

4 garlic cloves, minced

4 carrots, peeled and cut into chunks

3 medium potatoes, peeled and chunked

½ head cauliflower, cut into chunks

Salt to taste

Pepper to taste

Cauliflower, the Cabbage Flower

Cauliflower is actually a member of the cabbage family and is also related to mustard. It is most commonly found as a white vegetable but can also be purple or orange. To choose the best head of cauliflower, look for produce that doesn't have brown markings or curds that seem loose. A tightly packed head is freshest.

1. Bring the meat to room temperature. Place a large skillet over medium-high heat. Add the butter and oil. Once it is heated, sear the meat on each side for 4 minutes. Add the peppercorns to the skillet and cook for 2 minutes. Add the onion to the pan and place the meat on top of the onion.

2. Stir the tomato paste into the water. Add it to the skillet with the balsamic vinegar. Bring the broth to a boil and then reduce the heat to low. Once it reduces to a simmer, skim off the foam and discard. Add the thyme and bay leaves. Cover the pan and cook for 3½–4 hours. Remove the meat and keep warm.

3. Strain the stock and return it to the pan. Add the garlic, carrots, potatoes, and cauliflower to the pan. Place it over medium heat and cook for 30 minutes, uncovered. Continue to skim off any foam as it cooks. Add salt and pepper to taste.

4. Separate the beef into pieces and pour the sauce over the meat. Serve with vegetables on the side.

Pan-Seared Sweetbreads

Sweetbreads are glands that come from the throat or near the heart of a calf or lamb. The glands near the heart tend to be more tender. Don't skip the parboiling step, this preserves the color and firms the texture of the meat.

INGREDIENTS | SERVES 4

4 veal sweetbread lobes, 6 ounces each

2 quarts water

1½ teaspoons salt

Juice from 1 lemon

¼ cup vinegar

¼ teaspoon white pepper

4 slices bacon

1 tablespoon butter

3 teaspoons honey

4 tablespoons balsamic vinegar

2 tablespoons chopped parsley

Cooking Offal

Until the last few years, it has been rare to see sweetbreads, liver, heart, or tongue on restaurant menus that didn't cater to a specific ethnic cuisine. But the recent popularity of these forgotten parts brings them to fine-dining menus again. These often-unwanted parts are usually inexpensive, especially when compared to prices at a four-star restaurant.

1. If the sweetbreads are frozen, let them thaw slowly in the refrigerator or under a running stream of cool water. Do not thaw in a microwave. Place them in a bowl of ice-water to cover for 20 minutes.

2. Place water in a stockpot with 1 teaspoon of salt, lemon juice, and vinegar over medium heat. Bring to a gentle boil, reduce the heat to low, and add the sweetbreads. Simmer for 10 minutes. Remove them from the water and plunge into a bowl of ice water. Let them rest for 10 minutes and remove any fat, outer membranes or remnants of tubes. Pat dry.

3. Slice the sweetbreads so they are ¼" thick. Place on a tray between two layers of parchment paper. Rest a heavy plate on top and refrigerate for 2 hours.

4. Sprinkle salt and pepper on each side of the sweetbreads. Place a skillet over medium heat. Add the bacon slices and cook until crispy. Remove the bacon from the pan to cool. Add the butter and slide in one layer of the sweetbreads. Cook for 4–5 minutes on each side. Cook in batches if necessary.

5. Add the honey and balsamic vinegar to the skillet and bring to a simmer before returning the sweetbreads to the skillet and tossing them to coat evenly. Sprinkle with chopped parsley and serve immediately.

Pepper Steak

If you can't find poblano or Anaheim chilies, you can use bell peppers.
Red or yellow peppers have more flavor than green peppers.

INGREDIENTS | SERVES 4

12 poblano or Anaheim chilies

2 tablespoons vegetable or olive oil

Pinch salt

Pinch pepper

1¼ pounds tenderloin

1 large sweet onion, thinly sliced

5 garlic cloves, minced

3 tablespoons red wine or rice wine vinegar

1 tablespoon soy sauce

1½ cups chicken broth

3 tablespoons cornstarch

½ cup tomato sauce

1 teaspoon dried basil

Pinch cayenne powder

3 cups cooked rice

1. Place peppers over direct flame, or in a grill pan over medium-high heat, and cook for 12–15 minutes turning frequently, until the skins are charred. Place the peppers in a tightly sealed bag and let them steam and cool for 2–3 minutes.

2. Trim the bottoms and tops off the peppers. Cut them open down one side and remove the seeds and ribs. Scrape off the charred skin and rinse clean. Slice the peppers into ½" wide strips.

3. Place a large skillet over medium-high heat. Add 1 tablespoon of oil. Sprinkle salt and pepper on the meat and add to the skillet. Cook for 3–4 minutes on each side. Once cooked, remove it from the pan and cover.

4. Add the remaining oil to the skillet with the onions. Cook for 5–7 minutes. Add the garlic and cook for 1 minute. Add the vinegar and soy sauce and stir to scrape up any stuck-on bits. Add 1 cup of chicken broth.

5. Stir the cornstarch into the remaining chicken broth until there are no lumps. Stir the broth briskly into the pan to prevent lumping. Stir in the tomato sauce and basil. Bring the contents to a simmer.

6. Add the pepper strips and cayenne powder. Taste the broth and season if needed. Simmer for 3 minutes. Return the beef and warm for 2 minutes. Serve over rice.

Ropa Vieja

Serve this dish with cooked white or yellow rice, black beans, and tortillas.

INGREDIENTS | SERVES 4

1 teaspoon cumin

1 teaspoon paprika

1 teaspoon mild chili powder

1 teaspoon ground coriander

1 teaspoon dried oregano

1 pound flank steak

2 teaspoons olive oil

1 carrot, sliced

1 onion, sliced

1 celery stalk, sliced

1 poblano pepper, sliced

1 red bell pepper, sliced

2 garlic cloves, minced

2 tablespoons tomato paste

4 large tomatoes, roughly chopped

¼ cup sherry vinegar

2 cups beef broth

Salt to taste

Pepper to taste

1. Combine the five spices in a bowl. Trim the excess fat, and press spices into the meat. Cut the meat into pieces small enough to fit in the skillet.

2. Place a Dutch oven over high heat and add the oil. Sear meat for 2 minutes on each side. Reduce the heat to medium, place the meat in a bowl, and cover.

3. Sprinkle the carrot, onion, celery, peppers, and garlic into the pan, stirring continuously for 7–10 minutes. Add the tomato paste, tomatoes, and vinegar, and stir. Place the meat in the pan and add enough beef broth so half of the pan is full, but don't cover the meat.

4. Turn the heat to high and as soon as the liquid starts to simmer, turn the heat to medium-low, cover with a lid, and cook on a low simmer for 1½–2 hours. Take the meat out of the pan and rest in a bowl.

5. Turn off the heat and let the pan sit for 10 minutes. Use a large spoon to skim the fat off the surface. Turn the heat up to high and boil until it is reduced to a third of its original volume. Shred the meat, then add it back to the pan. Cook for 3–5 minutes. Taste and season with salt and pepper.

Stuffed Cabbage Rolls

This dish is common in Russia and other eastern European countries.
To make it more Russian, leave out the paprika and add ¼ teaspoon ground clove.

INGREDIENTS | SERVES 6

1 head cabbage, core removed

1 teaspoon salt

½ cup cooked rice

1 small yellow onion, shredded

¾ pound lean ground beef

¾ pound ground pork

⅓ cup milk

2 teaspoons paprika

½ teaspoon pepper

1 teaspoon dried oregano

1 28-ounce can tomato purée

2 tablespoons tomato paste

2 tablespoons cider vinegar

2 tablespoons honey

1 cup water

Dealing with Leftovers

If you have leftover rice and ground meat you can substitute those in this recipe for equal portions of the raw items. And if you have leftover rolls, you can wrap them tightly and freeze for 3 months. To reheat, thaw the tightly wrapped leaves, place them in a skillet, and bake at 400°F for 25–30 minutes, or until they're warmed through.

1. Place a large pot of water over high heat. Add the head of cabbage and salt once the water has come to a boil. Cook for 5 minutes, rotating the head every minute. Remove the outer layers and let cool. If the leaves are hard to remove, cook for few minutes more. Save twenty leaves and cut out the thick part of the ribs. Shred or chop the remaining cabbage. Combine the rice, onion, meat, milk, paprika, pepper, and oregano in a bowl.

2. Add half of the chopped cabbage to a large skillet. Place 2 tablespoons of the meat mixture in the center of each leaf. Fold in the sides, then the base, and tightly roll the top of the leaf and set them seam-side down in the skillet. Sprinkle the rest of the shredded cabbage on top.

3. In a small bowl, combine the tomato purée, tomato paste, vinegar, honey, and water. Taste and season if necessary. Pour the mixture over the cabbage rolls and place on a low burner. Cook for 45 minutes until the cabbage is tender. Ladle the sauce over the cabbage rolls and serve warm.

Salisbury Steak

Salisbury steak was created by and named after Dr. J. H. Salisbury in 1897.
He believed that vegetables and starches were responsible for most health ailments,
and recommended that his followers make meat two-thirds of their daily diet.

INGREDIENTS | SERVES 4

1 can condensed cream of mushroom soup

1 tablespoon yellow mustard

2 teaspoons Worcestershire sauce

1 teaspoon prepared horseradish

1 large egg, slightly beaten

¼ cup cracker crumbs

1 small onion, chopped

½ teaspoon salt

¼ teaspoon pepper

3 tablespoons minced, canned mushrooms

1 pound ground beef

½ pound ground pork

2 tablespoons vegetable oil

½ cup chicken broth

From Health Food to USDA Regulated TV Dinner

Salisbury steak became very popular during the 1950s, and the TV dinner version was common. Because there were so many variations, the USDA stepped in to regulate how much of each patty had to be meat (65%) and how much could be starchy filler (12%). The balance is made up of vegetables and gravy.

1. Blend the soup, mustard, Worcestershire sauce, and horseradish in a small bowl. In a separate bowl, mix well the beaten egg, cracker crumbs, onion, salt, pepper, and 3–4 tablespoons of the soup mixture. Add the mushrooms, beef, and pork. Use your hands to incorporate everything into the beef.

2. Divide the beef into 8 evenly sized patties that are oval shaped and no more than ¾" thick. Place a skillet over medium-high heat. Once it is heated add the oil and several of the patties. Cook on each side for 4 minutes. Set aside and repeat.

3. Drain any fat and return the patties to the skillet. Add the chicken broth to the soup mix and pour it over the patties. Cover and cook over low heat for 12–15 minutes, or until the patties are cooked through in the middle. Serve the patties with mashed potatoes or boiled egg noodles.

Chapter 10

Lamb and Game in a Skillet

Lamb Burgers

*Lamb is more common than beef in many Mediterranean countries.
The rich flavor holds up well to strong spices. Contrast the rich flavor with
the Chimichurri Sauce (page 149) and crispy cucumber slices.*

INGREDIENTS | SERVES 4

1 pound lean ground lamb
1 cup fresh bread crumbs
1 teaspoon salt
¼ teaspoon ground black pepper
1 celery stalk, chopped
2 teaspoons Worcestershire sauce
½ teaspoon dried rosemary, crumbled
2 tomatoes, seeded and finely chopped
1 egg, beaten
2 tablespoons olive oil

1. Combine all of the ingredients but the olive oil in a large bowl. Mix together and shape into 6 patties.

2. Place a skillet over medium heat. Once it's heated add the oil and three of the patties. Cook on each side for 5 minutes, or until cooked through the middle. Serve on trimmed pita bread with fresh cucumber slices.

Seared Venison Steaks with Gin Sauce

*If you don't have gin, you can use vermouth or a dry white wine.
If you prefer a non-alcoholic substitution, use 1 cup of any tart fruit juice.*

INGREDIENTS | SERVES 4

4 venison steaks, 4–6 ounces each
¼ cup gin
1 teaspoon peppercorns
2 tablespoons olive oil
2 teaspoons Worcestershire sauce
1 onion, chopped

1. Place the venison steaks in a sealable plastic bag with the gin and the peppercorns. Let them sit at room temperature for at least 30 minutes or in the refrigerator for 2–24 hours.

2. Place a skillet over medium-high heat. Once it's heated, add the oil. Lay the steaks in the pan and cook for 2–4 minutes on each side.

3. Once the meat is cooked, remove it from the pan and keep warm. Add the gin and peppercorn sauce to the skillet with the Worcestershire and onion. Cook for 4–6 minutes. Pour the sauce over the steaks and serve while hot.

Azerbaijani Stewed Lamb

*This dish is traditionally called Bosartma, which translates as stewed lamb.
It is traditionally served with cherry plums that are commonly found in central
and eastern Europe. A darker-skinned plum is better than a lighter-skinned plum.*

INGREDIENTS | SERVES 4

3 tablespoons butter

2 pounds lamb, cut into 1" cubes

1 large onion, chopped

4 Roma tomatoes, cubed

3 tablespoons tomato paste

2 plums, pitted and chopped

3 cups chicken broth

1 tablespoon chopped dill

1 tablespoon chopped cilantro

1 tablespoon chopped mint

Juice from 1 lemon

Salt to taste

Pepper to taste

1. Place a skillet over medium-high heat. Once it's heated, add the butter. When the butter has melted, add the lamb and cook for 10 minutes, turning the meat every 1–2 minutes until it's browned on all sides.

2. Remove the meat from the skillet and add the onion. Cook for 8–10 minutes. Add the tomatoes, tomato paste, and plums. Stir until everything is well coated. Stir in the chicken broth and the herbs. Cover the skillet, reduce the heat to low, and simmer for 1 hour, or until the lamb is cooked through and soft. Stir in the lemon juice and then season to taste with salt and pepper.

Greek Lemon and Oregano Lamb

You can easily double this recipe and use an entire leg of lamb.
Ask the butcher to trim off the last several inches so it will fit in a large skillet.
The trimmed section can be used to make Lamb Shank with Chard (page 172).

INGREDIENTS | SERVES 4

2 pounds lamb leg roast, bone in

3 garlic cloves, sliced

Juice and zest from 1 lemon

1 teaspoon salt

½ teaspoon ground black pepper

2 tablespoons dried oregano

2 tablespoons butter

1 cup hot water

1½ pound potatoes, scrubbed and quartered

2 tablespoons olive oil

Salt to taste

Pepper to taste

1. Preheat oven to 350°F. Rinse and dry the lamb. Trim off any large pieces of fat or silver skin. Cut small slits into the meat and insert slivers of garlic. Mix the lemon juice, salt, pepper, and oregano in a small bowl. Rub the mixture over the lamb.

2. Place a skillet over medium-high heat. Once it's heated, add the lamb and sear it on each side for 4 minutes. Once it is browned, bake in the center of the oven for 1 hour.

3. Remove the pan from the oven and drain the fat. Rub the butter over the meat and return it to the skillet. Pour the water into the skillet and cook for 45 minutes. Toss the potatoes in the lemon zest and olive oil. Sprinkle liberally with salt and pepper and place around the lamb. Bake for 45–60 minutes, or until the potatoes and lamb are tender. Tent the skillet with foil and let it rest for 15 minutes before carving and serving.

Herb-Roasted Rack of Lamb

When you purchase the racks of lamb, ask for them to be frenched.
The top of the bone has the flesh removed to create an impressive display when cooked,
and to prevent burning. This dish isn't cheap, but it is easy to make and impressive to serve.

INGREDIENTS | SERVES 4–6

2 14–16-ounce racks of lamb

2 sprigs rosemary, leaves stripped and chopped

2 tablespoons chopped fresh thyme

2 garlic cloves, minced

¼ cup olive oil

Salt to taste

Pepper to taste

1. Trim all but a thin layer of fat from the lamb. Score the fat layer in a cross-hatch pattern, being careful to not cut through to the meat. Combine the herbs and garlic in enough oil to coat the lamb. Sprinkle salt and pepper all over the meat, and rub with the olive oil and herbs. Place in a container and seal tightly. Refrigerate for 8–24 hours.

2. Preheat oven to 425°F. Let the meat come to room temperature while the oven preheats.

3. Place a skillet over medium heat. Once it's heated add 2 tablespoons of oil. Place the lamb, fat-side down, in the skillet and cook for 6 minutes, or until well-browned. Repeat with the other rack. Remove the skillet from the heat.

4. Stand the racks in the skillet and lean them against each other with the fat side facing to the outside of the skillet.

5. Cook in the middle of the oven for 15 minutes. Reduce the heat to 325°F and roast for 5–15 minutes. Use a meat thermometer to test the meat's doneness: 130°F for medium rare, 140°F for medium, and 150°F for well done. Let it rest for 10 minutes before cutting the rack between the bones in sections of two and serve.

Indian-Style Lamb Curry

It is rare to see dishes in India called curries. The British settlers in India adopted the Tamil word "kari," which means "sauce for rice" to refer to any dish with a sauce that was served over rice.

INGREDIENTS | SERVES 4–6

1 small yellow onion, peeled and halved

1 small garlic clove

½ cup Greek-style yogurt

2 teaspoons lemon juice

1 teaspoon ground coriander

½ teaspoon salt

½ teaspoon cumin

½ teaspoon ground cloves

½ teaspoon ground cardamom

½ teaspoon black pepper

¼ teaspoon ground ginger

¼ teaspoon ground cinnamon

½ teaspoon olive oil

1½ teaspoons cornstarch

1 pound boneless lamb, cut into 1" cubes

1 tablespoon butter

1 tablespoon vegetable oil

1 cayenne pepper

1. Purée half the onion, the garlic, yogurt, and lemon juice in a blender.

2. Place a dry skillet over medium heat. Once it's heated, add the dry spices to the skillet and shake every few seconds. Cook for 2 minutes. Pour the spices into the blender with the olive oil and cornstarch and blend.

3. Pour the yogurt mixture over the lamb cubes in a sealable container. Toss so the meat is coated. Leave the meat at room temperature for 2 hours, or marinate overnight in the refrigerator.

4. Place a skillet over medium heat and once it's heated, add the butter and vegetable oil. Mince the other half of the onion. Once the butter stops foaming, add the onion to the skillet. Cook for several minutes while stirring. Add the meat and the marinade and bring to a simmer. Add the whole cayenne pepper.

5. Reduce the heat to low, and cover and simmer for 2 hours. Stir occasionally to keep the sauce from sticking. After 1 hour, taste the sauce. As soon as it seems hot enough, remove the pepper. Taste and season if needed.

Lamb and Spring Vegetable Stew

Ask for meat from the leg, the shoulder, or top round. These cuts can handle the long stewing period and they tend to be some of the cheaper cuts available.

INGREDIENTS | SERVES 4

2 tablespoons olive oil

1 large onion, chopped

1 garlic clove, minced

1 pound lean, boneless lamb, cut into cubes

Pinch salt

Pinch pepper

¼ cup dry white wine

4 cups chicken stock

1 bay leaf

1 sprig fresh thyme

2 pounds small red potatoes, scrubbed

8 ounces baby carrots

8 ounces button mushrooms, halved

8 ounces radishes, stems and roots trimmed

8 ounces frozen peas

1. Preheat oven to 350°F. Place a skillet over medium heat and add the oil and the onion. Cook for 8–10 minutes. Add the garlic and stir continually for 1 minute.

2. Season the lamb lightly with salt and pepper. Add the lamb cubes and cook for 2 minutes on each side, turning as needed, until all of the meat is browned.

3. Add the wine to the pan and scrape the bottom. Add the chicken stock, bay leaf, thyme, potatoes, carrots, and mushrooms. Bring the contents to a boil and then cover the pan. Bake in the middle of the oven for 1 hour. Add the radishes to the pan, replace the lid, and bake for 30 minutes. Add the peas, replace the lid, and bake for 10 minutes. Remove the bay leaf and thyme sprig.

4. Season the broth with salt and pepper as needed and serve while warm with crusty bread.

Lamb Shank with Chard

Part of what makes the flavor and texture of this sauce so rich is the bone marrow from the shank. You can scrape out the marrow and stir it into the final sauce to increase the texture.

INGREDIENTS | SERVES 4

4 lamb shanks, 1" of the lower bone exposed

2 teaspoons salt

1 teaspoon ground pepper

2 tablespoons vegetable oil

1 medium onion, thinly sliced

2 celery stalks, thinly sliced

2 carrots, thinly sliced

2 cups red wine

2 sprigs rosemary

2 bay leaves

1–2 cups chicken stock

1 pound Swiss chard

1. Preheat oven to 300°F. Place a skillet over medium-high heat. Sprinkle the shanks with salt and pepper. Once the skillet is heated, add the oil and two shanks. Cook for 3–4 minutes on each side or until browned. Repeat with the remaining shanks.

2. Set aside the shanks. Add the onion, celery, and carrots to the pan and cook for 12–14 minutes. Pour the wine into the pan and scrape the bottom. Remove it from the heat and add the rosemary, bay leaves, and the lamb shanks. Fill the pan with chicken stock as necessary to cover all of the meat. Cook in the middle of the oven for 3 hours. Turn the shanks every 30 minutes.

3. Once the shanks are cooked, remove them from the pan and keep warm. Skim off some of the fat before placing the pan over a burner set to high heat. Boil until the sauce is reduced and thickened. Reduce the heat to low.

4. Wash the chard, cut out the stalk, and tear the leaves into large pieces. Add the chard to the sauce, place a cover on the pan, and cook for 2–3 minutes. Pour the sauce and chard over the meat and serve while warm.

Lamb Chops with Rosemary and Wine Sauce

Lamb chops tend to be an expensive cut of meat, but are fairly lean and cook quickly.
Look for chops that are pink to light red with a fat layer that is thin and white or pink instead of yellow.

INGREDIENTS | SERVES 4

8 lamb chops
Pinch salt
Pinch pepper
2 tablespoons olive oil
1 shallot, minced
1 clove garlic, minced
1 cup dry red wine
1 teaspoon fresh rosemary, minced
1 teaspoon butter
1 teaspoon flour
2 tablespoons Dijon mustard
3 tablespoons sour cream

American Lamb versus Australian Lamb

You're just as likely to find Australian or New Zealand lamb at your local grocery as you are American lamb. American lamb is fed grain as well as grass which reduces the gamey taste sometimes found in Australian lamb. The fat on American lamb is white instead of yellowish.

1. Place a skillet over medium-high heat. Season the lamb chops with salt and pepper. Once the skillet is heated, add half of the oil and four of the chops. Cook on each side for 3 minutes. Remove them from the pan and keep warm. Repeat with the other four chops.

2. Pour off all but 1 tablespoon of the oil. Add the shallot to the pan and cook for 3–4 minutes, stirring frequently. Add the garlic and cook for 1 minute, stirring constantly.

3. Add the wine and scrape the bottom of the pan. Stir in the rosemary and increase the heat to high. Let the sauce boil for 3 minutes or until it has thickened to a syrup-like consistency.

4. Add the butter and stir until it melts. Sprinkle the flour over the pan and whisk it until it has thickened. Stir in the mustard and the sour cream. Return the chops to the pan and cook for 1–2 minutes. Taste the sauce and season with salt and pepper as necessary. Pour the sauce over the chops and serve while warm.

Shepherd's Pie

If you can't find or don't like lamb, use 2 pounds of non-lean ground beef instead of the mix of lamb and beef.

INGREDIENTS | SERVES 4–6

2 pounds russet potatoes, peeled and cubed

Water, as needed

½ cup milk

1 large egg

¼ cup sour cream

1 pound ground lamb

Salt, to taste

Pepper, to taste

½ pound lean ground beef

1 large onion, minced

2 medium carrots, peeled and sliced

3 garlic cloves, minced

2 tablespoons all-purpose flour

2 cups chicken broth

1 tablespoon apple cider vinegar

1 tablespoon Worcestershire sauce

1 teaspoon dried thyme

2 teaspoons mustard powder

1 cup frozen peas, thawed

1 teaspoon sweet paprika

Cottage Pie versus Shepherd's Pie

The term "shepherd's pie" wasn't used until the 1870s, when people in the British Isles started eating potatoes. "Cottage pie" has been cited before 1800 and refers to a crust-covered pie filled with beef instead of lamb. On current menus, you're likely to find cottage pie referring to dishes with beef and shepherd's pie referring to dishes with lamb.

1. Boil the potatoes in salted water for 14 minutes. Drain and place in a large mixing bowl. Mash lightly and use a hand-mixer to incorporate the milk, egg, and sour cream until the potatoes are smooth. Set aside.

2. Place a large skillet over medium-high heat and when heated, add the ground lamb. Sprinkle with salt and pepper and stir, crumbling the lamb. Cook for 4–6 minutes. Remove the meat, but not any fat, and place in a bowl. Add the ground beef to the skillet and cook for 3–4 minutes, stirring and breaking the meat apart. Add it to the bowl with the lamb. Drain off all but 2 tablespoons of the fat and discard.

3. Add the onion and carrot to the pan. Cook for 5–7 minutes. Stir in the garlic and cook for 1 minute. Sprinkle the flour over the vegetables and toss to coat.

4. In a small bowl combine the chicken broth, vinegar, Worcestershire sauce, thyme, and mustard powder. Stir it into the skillet. Bring to a boil and thicken slightly. Stir in the meat and the peas. Remove from the heat and smooth out the mixture.

5. Preheat the broiler and place a rack in the middle of the oven. Spoon the whipped potatoes over the contents in the skillet. Sprinkle paprika over the potatoes. Place in the oven and broil. Check every 30 seconds and remove when the potatoes are golden brown. Rotate the skillet so the potatoes brown evenly. Remove from the oven and let it rest for 5 minutes before serving.

Rabbit Legs in Mustard Sauce

If you can't find just rabbit legs at your butcher, purchase two rabbits and use the rest to make a batch of Rabbit and Dumplings (page 178). The back legs are meatier than the front. Serve one large back leg, or one smaller back leg and front leg per diner.

INGREDIENTS | **SERVES 4**

¼ cup Dijon mustard

1 teaspoon salt

¼ teaspoon ground black pepper

4 large rear rabbit legs (or 4 front and 4 rear from smaller rabbits)

1 tablespoon olive oil

¼ cup grainy mustard

1 garlic clove, minced

2 tablespoons chopped fresh tarragon

Zest from 1 lemon

2 tablespoons butter

½ cup dry white wine

½ cup chicken stock

½ cup sour cream

2 tablespoons fresh chives, chopped

Rabbit: Another White Meat

People are trying to eliminate high-fat, high-cholesterol food from their diets without compromising on taste. Rabbit is one of the leanest, low-calorie, and high protein commercially farmed meats in the United States, even better than the white meat of chicken. Most butcher shops will carry it in the freezer section.

1. Combine the Dijon mustard, salt, and pepper. Rub the mustard over the rabbit legs and let them rest in the refrigerator for 4–24 hours.

2. Preheat oven to 350°F. Place a skillet over medium-heat. Once it's heated add the oil. Remove most of the mustard from the rabbit legs and sear them for 2–3 minutes on each side. Remove them from the skillet.

3. Add the grainy mustard, garlic, tarragon, lemon zest, and butter to the skillet. Stir until the butter melts. Return the rabbit to the skillet and bake in the oven for 15 minutes.

4. Add the wine and chicken stock to the skillet. Return it to the oven and bake for 20 minutes.

5. Remove the skillet from the oven and stir in the sour cream and chives. Cover and let the skillet rest for 5 minutes. Serve over boiled potatoes or egg noodles.

Rabbit with Black Olives and Herbs

Using fresh rather than dried herbs can provide your cooking with a different flavor.
If you don't have fresh herbs, substitute half the quantity of dried herbs.

INGREDIENTS | SERVES 4

1 rabbit, quartered

Salt to taste

Pepper to taste

½ cup all-purpose flour

4 tablespoons olive oil

1 Spanish onion, chopped

1 carrot, peeled and chopped

1 celery stalk, chopped

6 garlic cloves, chopped

½ cup chicken broth

¾ cup black olives, pitted and chopped

2 tablespoons fresh thyme, chopped

1 tablespoon fresh oregano, chopped

1 tablespoon fresh basil, chopped

1. Preheat oven to 350°F. Rinse the rabbit pieces and pat dry. Season with salt and pepper. Dredge in flour and shake off any excess.

2. Place a skillet over medium-high heat. Once it's heated through, add 1 tablespoon of olive oil and half the rabbit pieces, meat-side down. Cook for 4–5 minutes. Remove them to a plate and repeat with the other pieces.

3. Add the remaining oil to the skillet with the onion, carrot, and celery. Cook for 8–10 minutes. Add the garlic and cook for 1 minute, stirring continually.

4. Add the chicken broth to the skillet and scrape the bottom of the pan. Stir in the olives, the herbs, and the rabbit pieces. Bake in the middle of the oven for 1 hour, or until the juices run clear when poked with a fork.

5. Remove the rabbit from the pan and keep it warm. Place the skillet over medium-high heat and boil until thickened. Pour the sauce over the rabbit and serve.

Rabbit and Dumplings

If you don't have rabbit, you can substitute 2 pounds of dark chicken meat with the bone in.

INGREDIENTS | SERVES 4

1 rabbit
3 tablespoons olive oil
1 cup chopped white onion
1 cup chopped celery
1 cup chopped carrot
1½ cups white wine
4 cups chicken stock
3 tablespoons butter
½ cup turnip, peeled and chopped
½ cup celery root, peeled and chopped
Salt to taste
1 tablespoon fresh rosemary (1 teaspoon dried)
3 tablespoons fresh thyme (1 tablespoon dried)
3 tablespoons fresh sage (1 tablespoon dried)
4 garlic cloves, minced
1½ cups all-purpose flour
Pepper to taste
1 teaspoon Worcestershire sauce
Pinch cayenne
Pinch ground nutmeg
1 tablespoon baking powder
1 tablespoon melted butter
1 egg
½ cup buttermilk

1. Place a large skillet over medium-high heat. Rinse the rabbit, pat dry, add it to the pan with 1 tablespoon of the oil. Cook on each side for 3–4 minutes. Remove it from the pan.

2. Add the rest of the olive oil and ½ cup each of the onion, celery, and carrots to the skillet. Cook for 10–12 minutes, stirring frequently. Add half of the wine to the pan and scrape the bottom. Add the chicken stock. Return the rabbit to the pan. Reduce the heat to medium low, cover, and simmer for 1 hour. Let the rabbit cool and remove the meat from the bones. Set aside with the broth and cooked vegetables.

3. Add 2 tablespoons of butter to the skillet over medium heat. Add the remaining onion, carrots, and celery with the turnip and celery root. Sprinkle with salt and sauté for 10 minutes. Add the herbs, garlic, and the rest of the wine, cooking and stirring continually until most of the wine evaporates. Preheat oven to 375°F.

4. Stir 1 tablespoon of butter into the skillet and add ¼ cup of the flour, stirring constantly. Cook for 5 minutes for a light roux or up to 15 minutes for a darker roux. Add reserved rabbit, vegetables, and broth. Whisk to prevent lumps from forming. Add salt, pepper, and Worcestershire sauce to taste. Leave on low heat.

5. Combine the remaining flour, ¼ teaspoon black pepper, ½ teaspoon salt, cayenne, nutmeg, and baking powder in a bowl. Combine melted butter, egg, and buttermilk into another bowl. Pour the dry ingredients into the wet and stir until the mixture just comes together.

6. Use a large spoon to drop dough into the bubbling mixture. Place the entire skillet in the middle of the oven and cook for 25–30 minutes. Serve warm.

Ostrich Scallopine with Peppercorn Crust

Ostrich fillets are the most tender cut of red meat available.
Ostrich is very lean, so be careful not to overcook it.

INGREDIENTS | SERVES 2

2 4-ounce ostrich steaks

Salt to taste

Pepper to taste

20 peppercorns, crushed

1 tablespoon olive oil

3 tablespoons balsamic vinegar

1 tablespoon butter

1 shallot minced

Ostrich: Flightless but Tasty and Healthy

Ostrich meat is higher in protein than chicken, leaner than beef or pork, and it has the appearance and texture of beef, even after it is cooked. Because it is lean, it cooks quickly and can be tough if overcooked. The eggs, while hard to find, are also edible. They weigh 3–4 pounds and are the equivalent of 24 eggs by volume.

1. Rinse the ostrich and pat dry. Place the steaks between two layers of plastic wrap and beat them with a rolling pin until they're no more than ½" thick. Sprinkle each side of the steaks with salt and pepper. Sprinkle a pinch of crushed pepper on each side and press into the meat.

2. Place a skillet over medium-high heat. Once it's heated through, add the oil and the steaks. Cook the steaks on each side for 1½–2 minutes. Remove them from the skillet and let rest for 10 minutes before serving.

3. Add the vinegar to the skillet and scrape the bottom. Add the butter and let it melt. Once it has melted, add the shallot, stirring continually for 2 minutes. Pour the shallot and vinegar mixture over the steaks and serve while they're hot.

Japanese Braised Boar on Soba Noodles

Szechuan pepper is also known as Sansho pepper and is usually available ground. It has a lemony taste. Ground black pepper can be substituted if Szechuan pepper is unavailable.

INGREDIENTS | **SERVES 4**

Salt to taste
Pepper to taste
1½ pound boar shoulder
1 tablespoon peanut oil
¼ cup sake
1 thumb-sized piece fresh ginger, peeled and matchsticked
3 cups vegetable stock
1 teaspoon honey
1 tablespoon soy sauce
⅛ teaspoon ground Szechuan pepper
1 pound dry soba noodles
1 scallion, thinly sliced

Soba Noodles

Soba noodles are native to Japanese cuisine. They're often made from buckwheat and are similar to a thick spaghetti noodle in size and shape. They're denser and chewier than Italian pastas since they're made from a different flour. In Japan they're often served cold during the summer and hot during the winter.

1. Preheat oven to 275°F. Sprinkle salt and pepper on the boar. Place a skillet over medium-high heat. Once it's heated, add the peanut oil. Sear the meat on each side for 3 minutes, or until it is browned. Remove the meat from the pan.

2. Add the sake to the pan and use a spoon to scrape any stuck-on bits. Stir in the ginger, stock, honey, soy sauce, and Szechuan pepper. Place the meat back in the pan and let the sauce come to a boil.

3. Cover and cook in the center of the oven for 3–4 hours, or until the meat is tender and close to falling apart. Remove it from the skillet and keep warm.

4. Place the skillet over medium heat and let the sauce boil until it reduces by half. Cook the soba noodles according to the package directions. Slice the meat thinly and serve it on the soba noodles. Pour some of the pan reduction over the noodles and sprinkle with scallion. Serve warm.

Wild Boar Ragú

Most boar meat comes from feral animals that are kept on a reserve.
They search for their own food and eat what is available where they live.
The taste of boar tends to be sweeter and stronger than pork.

INGREDIENTS | SERVES 6

2 pounds wild boar boneless shoulder, cut into 1" cubes

2 tablespoons salt

1 teaspoon ground black pepper

1 tablespoon garlic powder

2 tablespoons olive oil

1 large onion, diced

1 fennel bulb, diced

8 garlic cloves, diced

1 cup dry red wine

2 28-ounce cans whole tomatoes

2 tablespoons dried oregano

Polenta

Pour 6 cups of water into a large saucepan. Bring to a boil and whisk in 2 teaspoons of salt and 1¾ cups cornmeal. Reduce the heat to low and cook for 15–20 minutes, or until it thickens, stirring often. Remove from heat and add 2 tablespoons butter and ½ cup Parmesan cheese.

1. Use paper towels to pat dry the meat. Sprinkle with salt, pepper, and garlic powder.

2. Place a Dutch oven over medium heat. Once it's heated add the oil and one layer of meat. Cook for 3–4 minutes on each side, turning as needed. Remove from the pan once they're seared all over and repeat with the remaining meat.

3. Remove the last batch of meat from the pan, add more oil if necessary, and add the onion and fennel. Cook for 10–12 minutes. Add the garlic and stir continually for 1 minute. Stir in the red wine and scrape the bottom of the pan.

4. Crush the tomatoes and add them with the liquid. Add 1 can of water. Add the oregano and more pepper if desired. Return the meat to the pan and reduce the heat to low. Cover and cook for 1½–2 hours. Stir occasionally. Serve over pasta or polenta.

Lemon and Garlic Frog Legs

People generally say that frog legs taste like chicken, but they're more likely to have a seafood or fishy taste. The only part of the frog that is generally eaten are the hind legs.

INGREDIENTS | SERVES 4

2 tablespoons butter

2 shallots

2 garlic cloves, minced

2 tablespoons white wine vinegar

¼ cup water

1 bay leaf

½ teaspoon salt

¼ teaspoon ground black pepper

Juice from 1 lemon

1 tablespoon olive oil

8 frog legs

Frogs Aren't Just for the French

Frog legs are often seen as a very French dish, but they have a long culinary history in America. They were, and continue to be, popular in the South. Frogs are also eaten in Asia, southern Europe, and the Mediterranean.

1. Place a skillet over medium heat. Once it's heated add 1 tablespoon of the butter. When the butter has melted, add the shallots and stir frequently for 3–5 minutes. Add the garlic and stir continually for 1 minute.

2. Add the vinegar to the skillet and scrape the bottom. Add the water, bay leaf, salt, pepper, and lemon juice. Cook for 7–10 minutes, or until most of the liquid has evaporated.

3. Add the rest of the butter and olive oil. Once the butter has melted, add the legs and cook for 2–3 minutes on each side until browned. Remove the legs from the pan and keep warm. Remove the bay leaf.

4. Add 2 tablespoons of water if necessary to stir the pan drippings into a light sauce. Pour the sauce over the frog legs and serve while warm.

Osso Bucco

You may have to go to a butcher to get veal shank.
The preferred shank comes from the hind leg, weighs about 8 ounces and is 1½" thick.

INGREDIENTS | SERVES 4

4 veal shanks

Pinch salt

Pinch pepper

4 tablespoons olive oil

2 cups white wine

1 large onion, cut into large chunks

2 carrots, peeled and cut into ½" rings

1 celery stalk cut into ½" slices

5 garlic cloves, minced

2 cups beef broth

1 15-ounce can diced tomatoes, drained

1 bay leaf

Gremolata

Gremolata is an Italian condiment often served with veal, but it goes great with chicken, fish, or vegetables. To make, mince 3 garlic cloves, add a pinch of salt, and smash with a stainless-steel spoon into a paste. Stir in 2 teaspoons of minced lemon zest and ¼ cup chopped parsley. Let it set for an hour before serving. Can be cooked or served raw.

1. Preheat oven to 325°F and place a rack in the lower-middle. Rinse the shanks, pat dry, and season with salt and pepper. Place a large Dutch oven over medium-high heat. Once it's heated add 1 tablespoon of oil and place two shanks in the pan. Cook on each side for about 5 minutes, or until they're browned.

2. Place the shanks in a bowl and add ½ cup of wine to the pan. Scrape any stuck-on bits. Pour the liquid into the bowl with the shanks. Repeat with the other two.

3. Add the remaining 2 tablespoons of oil to the Dutch oven and add the onions, carrots, and celery. Cook for 10–12 minutes, or until the edges brown. Stir in the garlic and cook for 1 minute. Stir in the rest of the wine, broth, tomatoes, and bay leaf. Add the shanks and any juices to the pan.

4. Cover and cook in the oven for 2 hours or until the meat can be pierced with a fork but is not yet falling off the bone. Remove the bay leaf. Serve with gremolata.

Chapter 11

Recipes for a Grill Pan

Grilled Sweet Potato Sticks

Scotch bonnet peppers are native to Africa and are one of the spiciest peppers.
If you prefer a less spicy dish you can use a serrano or a jalapeño.

INGREDIENTS | SERVES 6–8

3 pineapple slices
1 Scotch bonnet pepper
¼ cup rum
2 tablespoons vegetable oil
½ teaspoon salt
1½ pounds fresh sweet potatoes
1–2 tablespoons peanut oil

1. Place everything except the sweet potatoes and peanut oil in a blender or food processor and pulse till well combined. Pour into a saucepan or small skillet over medium-high heat and boil for 10 minutes until it has reduced slightly.

2. Peel the sweet potatoes and cut them into 1" slices lengthwise. Cut slices in 1" strips. Dip them into the glaze and toss to combine.

3. Place a grill pan over moderate direct heat. Brush with peanut oil. Cook sweet potatoes on each side for 5–7 minutes. Baste with the glaze as you turn them. Serve while warm.

Grilled Okra

If you don't like okra, this recipe also works well with slices of eggplant or whole button mushrooms.

INGREDIENTS | SERVES 4–6

1 teaspoon kosher salt (½ teaspoon table salt)
1 teaspoon white sugar
2 teaspoons sweet paprika
1 teaspoon ground coriander
½ teaspoon ground black pepper
½ teaspoon cayenne pepper
¼ teaspoon celery seed
1 pound okra
2 tablespoons vegetable oil

1. Prepare a high-heat grill pan. Combine the salt, sugar, and spices in a small bowl.

2. Rinse the okra in cold water and trim off the stem, but don't cut into the pod. Shake dry and place into a large bowl. Drizzle the oil over the okra and toss with your hands to coat.

3. Sprinkle the spice mix over the okra, tossing so it's coated evenly. Insert skewers perpendicularly through the pods.

4. Place skewers on the grill and cook for 2–4 minutes on each side, using tongs to turn them over. Transfer to a platter and serve immediately.

Tuna "Fish Sticks" with Sesame Soy Sauce

Tuna fillet is better for this dish than steaks because the fillet can be cut into four even pieces to cook evenly. The crushed red pepper can be omitted if desired.

INGREDIENTS | SERVES 4

1 tablespoon rice wine vinegar

2 tablespoons soy sauce

2 teaspoons toasted sesame oil

1 teaspoon honey

½ teaspoon crushed red pepper

1½ pounds tuna fillet, cut into 4 "sticks"

1 tablespoon olive oil

1. Combine the vinegar, soy sauce, sesame oil, honey, and red pepper in a small bowl. Heat in the microwave until the honey has melted and the sauce can be stirred.

2. Place a grill pan over medium-high heat. Rub the oil over the fish sticks.

3. Place the fish on the grill pan at an angle. Cook on each side for 2 minutes, turning the sticks with tongs. Brush each cooked side with the soy sauce mixture.

4. Once the tuna has seared on each side, remove it from the pan and slice on an angle. Drizzle the remaining marinade over the tuna and serve warm.

Grilled Dijon Tomatoes

This is a simple and delicious side dish to serve with the Restaurant-Style Ribeye (page 148).

INGREDIENTS | SERVES 4

1 tablespoon Dijon mustard

1 teaspoon salt

Large pinch black pepper

3 tablespoons melted butter

¼ cup panko bread crumbs

¼ cup Parmesan cheese, shredded

2 medium tomatoes, cut in half lengthwise and seeded

1 teaspoon olive or vegetable oil

Paprika to taste

1. Preheat broiler on high and place grill pan in middle of oven. In a small bowl combine the mustard, salt, pepper, butter, bread crumbs, and Parmesan cheese.

2. Once the grill pan is hot, brush the cut side of each tomato lightly with the oil and place cut side down. Cook for 2–3 minutes. If the skin on the uncut side starts to blacken, remove tomatoes from the oven.

3. Carefully turn the tomato halves over. Place a quarter of the mustard mixture onto each tomato half and sprinkle lightly with paprika. Return the skillet to the oven and cook for 3–5 minutes until the mustard mixture is golden brown. Serve immediately.

Grilled Tenderloin with Chili and Cashews

*Filet mignon is the most tender cut of beef. It is the leanest cut
and is best cooked on high heat for a short period of time.*

INGREDIENTS | SERVES 4

1 pound Thai rice noodles

3 tablespoons Asian chili sauce

4 6-ounce filet mignon portions

Salt to taste

Pepper to taste

1 tablespoon toasted sesame oil

Juice from 2 limes

3 scallions, thinly sliced

5 ounces cashews, crushed

1. Cook the noodles according to package directions. Drain.

2. Rub 2 tablespoons of the chili sauce over the meat and season with salt and pepper. Place a grill pan over medium-high heat. Once it's heated, grill the steaks for 3–4 minutes on each side. Let rest for 5 minutes.

3. Combine 1 tablespoon of the chili sauce with the sesame oil, lime juice, and scallions. Toss the mixture over the noodles. Divide the noodles into 4 bowls.

4. Slice the beef thinly and place it over the noodles. Sprinkle the cashews over the beef and serve.

Grilled Turkey Cutlets and Mango Slices

*If you can't find a fresh mango, fresh or canned pineapple slices can be used instead.
If you can't find turkey cutlets, you can use thin slices of chicken breast or pork tenderloin.*

INGREDIENTS | SERVES 4

½ cup pomegranate juice

2 tablespoons honey

Several dashes Tabasco sauce

½ teaspoon salt, plus more to taste

¼ teaspoon black pepper, plus more to taste

4 thin-cut turkey cutlets (1¼ pounds)

Vegetable oil, as needed

2 large fresh mangos, peeled and sliced ½" thick

1. Place a small skillet or saucepan over medium heat. Combine the juice, honey, Tabasco, salt, and black pepper and bring to a boil. Boil for 10–15 minutes until the sauce is reduced and thickened slightly.

2. Place a grill pan over medium-high heat and lightly grease the ridges. Spoon the sauce over the cutlets and sprinkle with salt and pepper. Place the cutlets on the grill pan and cook each side for 2–3 minutes.

3. Dip the mango slices in the fruit sauce and place on the grill pan. Cook on each side until there are grill marks. Serve the turkey and fruit over rice or noodles. Pour the leftover sauce on each serving.

New York Strips with Mustard Herb Crust

Avoid yellow prepared mustard for this recipe. Grainy mustard is better for cooking and making vinaigrette.

INGREDIENTS | **SERVES 4**

4 6–8-ounce New York strip steaks
Salt to taste
Pepper to taste
1 tablespoon olive oil
3 tablespoons grainy mustard
¾ cup bread crumbs
½ cup parsley, chopped
2 garlic cloves, minced
3 tablespoons butter

1. Preheat oven to 425°F. Trim any extra fat from the steak. Sprinkle each side liberally with salt and pepper.

2. Place a skillet over medium-high heat. Once it's heated, add the oil. Cook the steaks for 1 minute on each side. Remove the skillet from the heat.

3. Cover both sides of the steaks with the mustard. Combine the bread crumbs, parsley, garlic, and butter in a bowl.

4. Place the steaks in a skillet and divide the bread crumbs mix over the 4 steaks. Place the skillet in the oven and bake for 12–15 minutes. Let the meat rest for 10 minutes before serving.

Skirt Steak with Chermoula

Chermoula is a non-spicy Moroccan salsa-like dish. It is great on beef or lamb but can also be used as a marinade for fish or chicken.

INGREDIENTS | **SERVES 4**

1½ pounds skirt steak
2 tablespoons vegetable oil
Pinch salt
Pinch pepper
1 small onion, diced
2 garlic cloves, minced
1 cup parsley, chopped
½ cup cilantro, chopped
1 teaspoon ground cumin
Juice from 3 lemons, zest from 1
¼ teaspoon cayenne
¼ teaspoon ground black pepper
½ teaspoon smoked paprika

1. Trim off any membrane or extra fat from the beef. Brush the meat with vegetable oil and sprinkle with salt and pepper. Let it sit at room temperature for 30–60 minutes.

2. To make the chermoula, combine the remaining ingredients in a small bowl.

3. Place a grill pan over medium-high heat. Once it's heated, cook the meat for 3–5 minutes on each side. Let rest for 10 minutes before serving.

4. Slice the steak in thin slices on an angle and place them over steamed white rice and top with the chermoula.

Deviled Chicken

Hungarian paprika is less common than sweet paprika. It is spicier, but is a really gentle way to add a touch of heat to a dish. If you don't like spicy foods you can substitute sweet paprika instead.

INGREDIENTS | SERVES 4

1 tablespoon olive oil

1 small onion, peeled and chopped

¼ cup mustard

1 teaspoon Hungarian paprika

½ teaspoon pepper

½ teaspoon salt

1 pound chicken thighs

1. Preheat oven to 425°F. Place a skillet over medium-high heat. When the pan is hot, add the oil and onion. Stir frequently and cook for 5–7 minutes. Combine the mustard and spices in a bowl.

2. Remove the skin from the chicken, rinse, and pat dry. Place the chicken on top of the onion and sear each side for 3–4 minutes. While flipping, stir the onions to prevent them from burning. Once the exterior is seared, brush the mustard mixture over the chicken.

3. Cook, covered, in the middle of the oven for 30–35 minutes. The chicken is done when the internal temperature of the meat is 160°F. Sprinkle lightly with paprika to garnish and serve immediately.

Shish Kebabs

If you prefer beef or lamb, cook them for 2–3 minutes on each side until done. Pork will take the same amount of time as the chicken.

INGREDIENTS | SERVES 8

½ cup olive oil

3 tablespoons chopped fresh herbs

3 garlic cloves

Juice and zest from 1 lemon

2 pounds boneless, skinless chicken thighs cut into 2" chunks

Salt to taste

Pepper to taste

3 red bell peppers, cut into 1" pieces

1 large Vidalia onion, cut into 1" pieces

1. Place the oil, herbs, and garlic in a food processor and blend into a smooth purée. Place ¼ cup in a separate bowl and add the lemon zest. Sprinkle the meat with salt and pepper. Place it into a container with the rest of the purée. Refrigerate 12 hours.

2. Use a skewer to spear a piece of meat, a pepper, and an onion, leaving a little room between each item.

3. Place a grill pan over medium-high heat. Once it's heated brush the pan with a little oil. Place the skewers on top, being careful they don't touch. Cook for 3–4 minutes on each side.

Bacon-Wrapped Cheese-Stuffed Jalapeños

If you leave in the peppers' ribs, it will make the dish spicy.
If you remove all of it, it will be fairly mild.

INGREDIENTS | **MAKES 14 PIECES**

7 jalapeños
4 ounces cream cheese
14 slices bacon (approximately 1 pound)

Alternate Recipe Option

The flavor of the bacon and the pepper are dominant. But if you'd like the cheese to be more prominent, you can mix 2 tablespoons shredded Cheddar cheese, 1 teaspoon garlic powder, and 1 teaspoon cumin in the cheese.

1. Trim the woody part of the stem from the jalapeños. Cut the peppers open lengthwise and scoop out the seeds and the white veins. Spread a teaspoon or two of cream cheese onto each jalapeño half.

2. Starting at the thick end, wrap the bacon slice around the pepper. Spear with a toothpick to hold it in place. If the slice of bacon is too long, trim off the extra instead of wrapping it further.

3. Preheat oven to 375°F. Place a grill pan in the middle of the oven. Add the peppers and cook for 12–15 minutes, or until the bottom of the bacon is crispy.

4. Turn on the broiler and cook for 4–6 minutes until the cheese is bubbling and the bacon is crispy. Remove to a plate and let them rest before serving.

Grilled Artichokes

Fresh artichokes are easiest to find from March through May.
Look for heads with tightly sealed leaves. The stem should be plump and not wrinkly.

INGREDIENTS | SERVES 2

Water, as needed
1 lemon, juiced
2 large artichokes
1 tablespoon olive oil
Salt to taste
Pepper to taste

1. Add 1" of water to a pot large enough to hold the artichokes, and place over medium heat. Add the lemon juice and lemon halves. Cover and bring to a boil.

2. Remove the outer ring of lower leaves. Cut off the tips of each artichoke leaf to remove the barb. Cut off the top inch of the artichoke and the last inch of the stem.

3. Place the artichokes in the water with the stem up. Reduce the heat to low, cover, and steam for 15 minutes. Remove them from the pan. Discard the water and lemon. Place the chokes on a cutting board, top down. Slice the artichoke in half. Use a melon baller or spoon to remove the fuzzy choke.

4. Place a grill pan over medium-high heat. Once it's heated, brush the olive oil on the cut side of the artichokes and sprinkle lightly with salt and pepper. Place the chokes cut side down on the grill pan and cook for 10 minutes. Turn them a quarter turn after cooking for 5 minutes. Serve with a garlic mayonnaise.

Tamarind Shrimp Kebabs

If you can't find tamarind, substitute equal parts lime juice and brown sugar.

INGREDIENTS | SERVES 4

2 tablespoons tamarind paste

½ cup chicken or vegetable broth

2 tablespoons rice wine or dry sherry

1½ tablespoons brown sugar

½ teaspoon salt

4 garlic cloves, minced

1 small yellow onion, minced

1 jalapeño, minced

1 pound of shell-on shrimp (31–40 count), deveined

1 teaspoon peanut oil

2 scallions, chopped

¼ cup cilantro, chopped

Tamarind

Tamarind is a fruit that grows in a pod and is common in Southeast Asia, parts of Africa, and Mexico. Its distinct flavor is usually found in paste form. A tablespoon or two can be added to almost any sauce or marinade to add a lot of flavor. It tends to be a bit on the salty side, so taste your dishes before salting them.

1. Combine the tamarind paste and broth in a bowl. Let it sit for several minutes and then mash the paste until it has dissolved. Add the wine, sugar, and salt, stirring to combine.

2. Trim wooden skewers to fit your pan. Combine the garlic, onion, and jalapeño, and rub on the cut side of the shrimp. Thread the shrimp onto skewers so they're barely touching. Place the skewers in a large dish and lay flat. Pour the marinade over the shrimp, cover, and place in the refrigerator for 30–60 minutes.

3. Place the grill pan over medium-high heat and brush the ridges with the peanut oil. Remove the skewers from the marinade and place one layer on the pan. Cook for 3–4 minutes on each side. Once they're pink on both sides, place on a serving platter.

4. Sprinkle the scallion and cilantro over the platter for serving. If you want to serve the leftover marinade as a dipping sauce, pour the liquid into a small skillet and bring to a boil and cook for 2–3 minutes. Serve alongside the shrimp.

Beef and Chicken Fajitas

Even though you're using the same marinade for the chicken and the beef, you can't marinate them together. Chicken has to cook at a higher temperature than beef to kill any potential salmonella.

INGREDIENTS | SERVES 6–8

12 ounces beer

½ cup vegetable oil, plus more as needed

Juice from 2 limes

5 garlic cloves, smashed

2 tablespoons Worcestershire sauce

1 tablespoon chili powder

1 teaspoon ground black pepper

1 teaspoon ground cumin

1 pound skirt or flank steak

1 pound boneless, skinless chicken breasts

Salt to taste

2 small onions, quartered

1 green pepper, cut into ½" strips

1 red or yellow pepper, cut into ½" strips

Corn or flour tortillas for 6–8 people

Chopped fresh cilantro

Lime wedges

Bottled hot sauce or salsa to taste

1. Combine the beer, ½ cup vegetable oil, lime juice, garlic, Worcestershire sauce, chili powder, pepper, and cumin and divide into 2 large sealable bowls.

2. Trim any excess fat off the steak and chicken. Use a meat tenderizer to pound the chicken to ⅜" thick. Sprinkle the meat lightly with salt and place the beef in one container and the chicken in the other. Refrigerate for 3–8 hours.

3. Place a grill pan over medium-high heat and brush the ridges with oil. Place the onions on the pan and cook until translucent. Move to a bowl and keep warm. Scatter the peppers across the grill pan and cook until soft. Place them in the bowl with the onions.

4. Apply another coating of oil on the grill pan ridges. Cook the flank steak for 4–5 minutes on each side. Let it rest on a plate. Slice the steak into strips.

5. Apply another coating of oil on the grill pan ridges. Cook the chicken breasts for 6–7 minutes on each side. Let them rest on a plate. Slice the chicken into strips. Serve meat and vegetables with warm tortillas, chopped cilantro, lime wedges, and hot sauce or salsa.

Grilled and Butter-Basted Lobster Tails

Lobster is expensive, and buying the tails alone is more expensive than buying the whole lobster. But this dish is great for a celebratory meal!

INGREDIENTS | **SERVES 2**

2½ pounds lobster tails

2 tablespoons chives, minced

2 tablespoons olive oil

2 tablespoons butter

2 garlic cloves, minced

¼ cup water

2 tablespoons chopped parsley

1. Place the lobster tail on the cutting board with the shell-side down. Cut through the belly shell from the top, through the meat, and through the back shell. Don't cut through the fin portion of the tail. Gently pull the sections of meat away from the shell. Rinse the tails in cold water.

2. Combine the chives and 1 tablespoon of olive oil in a small bowl. Rub the mixture over the meat and shell.

3. Place a grill pan over high heat. Once it's heated through, brush the surface of the pan with the remaining olive oil. Place the lobster shell-side down on the grill. Cover and cook for 1 minute. Turn the lobster and cook on the other side for 1 minute, covered. The lobster should still be pink in the middle. Remove it from the pan.

4. Lower the heat to medium and add the butter. Once the butter has melted, add the garlic and water and rotate back and forth to combine. Bring to a simmer.

5. Hold the skillet at an angle so the sauce pools to one side. Place the lobster back in the pan on the side farthest away from the flame. Use a long-handled spoon to scoop butter and pour it over the lobster. Baste with the pan at an angle for 5 minutes or until the lobster is cooked through. Sprinkle with parsley, pour the remaining sauce over the lobster, and serve.

Miso-Glazed Salmon

The ingredients for the sauce should be found in the Asian section of your grocery store, or at an Asian specialty shop. If you can't find mirin, you can substitute ¼ cup of white wine and a tablespoon of honey.

INGREDIENTS | SERVES 4

¼ cup rice wine vinegar

¼ cup mirin

¼ cup red miso

4 6-ounce salmon fillets

2 tablespoons vegetable oil

Miso Hungry

Miso is common in Japan and is made by fermenting rice, barley, and/or soybeans with salt and a special fermenting agent. The thick paste is used in soups, sauces, and for pickling meats and vegetables. It is high in vitamins, minerals, and protein and was necessary during times of drought since it could be preserved and kept for a long time.

1. Combine the vinegar and mirin in a sauce pan until it is very warm but not boiling. Stir in the miso paste and dissolve. Cool to room temperature.

2. Rinse off the salmon fillets, remove any bones, and pat dry. Place them inside a sealable plastic bag. Pour the cooled mixture over the fillets and coat. Place in the refrigerator and let it sit for at least 8 hours, but no more than 3 days.

3. Place your grill pan over medium-high heat. Brush the ridges with vegetable oil. Once the pan is heated, place the salmon skin side up. Cook for 3 minutes. Turn the fish to cook for 3 minutes on the other side. At this point the fish should be medium-rare. But if you prefer the fish cooked more thoroughly, turn the fish flesh side down and place the fish at a different angle. Cook for 2 minutes on each side.

4. Place the leftover marinade in a saucepan over medium-high heat and bring to a boil. Boil for several minutes so it reduces to a syrup and brush or pour over the fish.

Malay-Inspired Satay

This dish is commonly found in street vendor stalls in Malaysia, but it's easy enough to make at home. You can substitute flank steak for chicken if you wish.

INGREDIENTS | SERVES 6–8

1 teaspoon ground coriander

1 teaspoon ground fennel

2 stalks lemongrass cut into 1" sections

5 shallots

3 garlic cloves

2" piece ginger, peeled and thinly sliced

1 teaspoon ground turmeric

4 tablespoons brown sugar

2 tablespoons peanut oil

¾ teaspoon salt

3 pounds chicken thighs, deboned

4 tablespoons peanut oil for frying

Green Basting Brush

You need a basting brush for this recipe, but if you hate cleaning a bristle brush, this tip will make you happy. Lemongrass, especially the root end, is a very woody and fibrous plant. If you trim the root end slightly and then pound it until it frays, you have a basting brush. Not only will this brush add a little extra flavor to your dish, you won't have to clean it, and you won't regret throwing it away.

1. Place the coriander, fennel, lemongrass, shallots, garlic, ginger, turmeric, and sugar into a food processor and pulse several times until the mixture resembles creamy mashed potatoes. Scrape down the sides of the bowl and add 1–2 tablespoons of water if necessary. With the food processor running, add 2 tablespoons of oil until it is fully incorporated.

2. Cut the chicken thighs into pieces roughly 1" by 3" by ¼". Place the meat in a glass bowl, cover with the marinade, and toss to coat.

3. Put chicken pieces onto skewers 1" apart.

4. Place a grill pan over medium-high heat. Once it's heated, place a few skewers on the pan, making sure they don't touch. Baste the meat with the marinade and cook for 3–4 minutes, or until lightly browned. Turn the meat over, baste and cook for 3 minutes. Serve immediately with the Sweet and Spicy Dipping Sauce (page 236) or the Vietnamese Chili Garlic Sauce (page 52).

Pork Tenderloin Medallions Marinated in Currants

If you can't find fresh currants, use ¼ cup currant jelly or jam.
If you can't find currant jelly, you can substitute cherry or cranberry preserves.

INGREDIENTS | SERVES 4

1 2-pound pork tenderloin
Pinch salt
Pinch pepper
3 tablespoons balsamic vinegar
1 garlic clove, minced
½ cup fresh red currants
½ teaspoon hot sauce
1 tablespoon olive oil
¼ cup fresh cilantro or parsley, chopped

1. Remove any external fat and silver skin from the tenderloin. Cut into eight even slices. Sprinkle with salt and pepper on both sides.

2. Combine the vinegar, garlic, currants, and hot sauce in a sealable bag. Remove the air from the bag and use a rolling pin to break up the fruit. Add the pork to the bag and marinate from 30 minutes to 24 hours.

3. Place a grill pan over medium-high heat and when it's heated, add the oil. Cook the pork for 2 minutes on each side.

4. Remove the pork from the pan and keep warm. Pour the marinade into a skillet. Bring to a boil, reduce the heat to low, and add the pork. Cook on each side for another 2 minutes.

5. Remove the pork from the pan, pour the sauce over the pork, and serve while warm with cilantro or parsley.

Italian Sausages and Sweet Peppers

This dish can be made in a skillet if you don't have a grill pan.
You won't get the grill lines, but the flavor will be just as good.

INGREDIENTS | **SERVES 2**

2 sweet Italian sausage links
1 small onion, thickly sliced
½ red bell pepper, sliced
½ green bell pepper, sliced
1 tablespoon olive oil
1 teaspoon dried basil
1 teaspoon dried oregano
¼ cup chicken stock

1. Place a grill pan over medium heat and when it's heated, place the sausages at one end. Place the vegetables, oil, basil, and oregano in a bowl and toss to combine. Spread the onions over the rest of the grill pan.

2. Cook the sausages for 4 minutes on each side. Toss the vegetables every few minutes. Reduce the heat to low, cover the pan, and steam the sausages in the liquid created by the vegetables. Stir the vegetables every few minutes. Cook each side for another 8 minutes.

3. Remove the sausages and vegetables from the skillet and keep warm. Increase the heat to medium-high. Pour the chicken stock in the pan so it coats the surface. Scrape any stuck-on bits. Simmer for 4 minutes. Pour the liquid over the vegetables and sausages and serve.

Steak Sandwiches

If you prefer not to cook this on a stovetop, you can set a rack in your oven 8" from the broiler and cook for 5–7 minutes on each side.

INGREDIENTS | SERVES 6

1½ pounds flank or skirt steak

1 teaspoon plus 1 tablespoon olive oil

1 teaspoon plus 1 pinch salt

½ teaspoon ground black pepper

2 large Spanish onions, thinly sliced

8 ounces tomato sauce

¼ cup brown sugar

2 tablespoons Worcestershire sauce

2 French baguettes

1. Trim any fat or silver skin from the steak. Rub 1 teaspoon of olive oil over the steak and season on all sides with salt and pepper.

2. Place a grill pan over medium-high heat. Once it's heated, cook the beef on each side for 6–8 minutes. Once the steak is cooked through, place it on a plate and keep it warm for 10 minutes.

3. At the same time, place a skillet over medium heat. Add 1 tablespoon olive oil and the onions. Add a pinch of salt. Cook for 12–15 minutes, or until they've softened but aren't turning brown.

4. Stir the tomato sauce, sugar, and Worcestershire sauce into the skillet and cook for 5 minutes. The sauce should reduce slightly. Slice the meat on a deep angle and add it to the skillet, along with any juices on the cutting board.

5. Cut the baguettes into sections and slice the bread horizontally to make a sandwich. Fill each section with meat, onions, and sauce. Serve while warm.

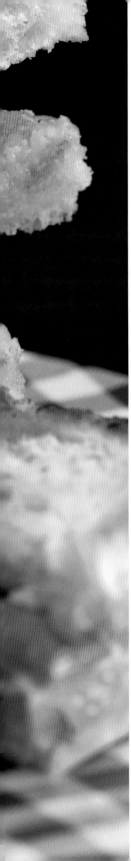

Chapter 12

Recipes for a Griddle

Blue Cheese Buttermilk Biscuits

You may like these even if you don't like the flavor of blue cheese.
The buttermilk cuts the sharp taste of the cheese that many people don't enjoy.

INGREDIENTS | **MAKES 12 BISCUITS**

2½ cups cake flour or all-purpose flour

2 teaspoons baking powder

¾ teaspoon kosher salt

½ teaspoon baking soda

⅔ cup chilled vegetable shortening, cut into cubes

1 cup blue cheese, crumbled

1 scallion, minced

1⅓ cups plus 1 tablespoon buttermilk

1. Preheat oven to 350°F and place griddle in the middle of the oven.

2. Whisk the dry ingredients together in a large bowl. Cut the shortening into the dry ingredients. Stir in the blue cheese and scallions.

3. Make a well in the center and pour in 1⅓ cup of buttermilk. Fold to combine. Divide the dough into twelve even balls and drop them on the hot griddle or skillet. Brush the surface of the biscuits with 1 tablespoon of buttermilk. Bake in the center of the oven for 20–25 minutes, or until they're golden brown. Serve with butter while warm.

Early American Johnnycakes

Historically these would have been fried in bacon fat.
But vegetable oil will work just fine.

INGREDIENTS | **SERVES 6–8**

1 cup cornmeal

1 teaspoon salt

1 teaspoon sugar

1½ cups boiling water

¼ cup vegetable oil or bacon drippings

1. Stir the dry ingredients in a bowl and whisk in the boiling water.

2. Place a griddle over medium-high heat. Once it's heated, add 2 tablespoons of the vegetable oil.

3. Drop the mixture onto the pan a few tablespoons at a time. Cook for 5 minutes before flipping and cooking the other side. Place them on a warmed plate until ready to serve with butter, maple syrup, or hot sauce.

Unleavened Bread

Baking powder and baking soda are the two most frequently used leaveners for dough. They create air pockets that give dough a lighter texture. But since baking soda wasn't common until the mid-1800s and baking powder wasn't invented until then, this recipe is probably very close to what would have been common fare before the Civil War.

Pancakes

Pancake-like sweets have been eaten for thousands of years.
The form we're used to became popular in Europe during medieval times.

INGREDIENTS | MAKES 8 4" PANCAKES

1½ cups flour
2 tablespoons sugar
2 teaspoons baking powder
½ teaspoon salt
1 large egg, beaten
1 cup milk
2 tablespoons vegetable oil

1. Stir together the flour, sugar, baking powder, and salt in a large bowl. Whisk together the egg, milk, and 1 tablespoon of oil in a small bowl.

2. Pour the liquid mixture into the dry ingredients. Stir together until all the flour is incorporated but the mixture is still lumpy.

3. Place a griddle over medium heat. Once it's heated through drizzle 1 teaspoon of oil over the pan and swirl to coat. Pour ¼ cup of batter for each pancake.

4. Cook until the bottom is golden brown and bubbles appear on the top surface. Flip and cook until the bottom is golden. Place on a plate and keep warm.

Almond Shortbread Cookies

Baking these cookies on a cast-iron griddle will make them crispier, and they'll cook more evenly.

INGREDIENTS | MAKES 2 DOZEN COOKIES

3 sticks unsalted butter, at room temperature
1 cup granulated sugar
1 teaspoon vanilla extract
1 teaspoon almond extract
3½ cups all-purpose flour
¼ teaspoon salt
1½ cups crushed almonds

1. Preheat oven to 350°F. Using the paddle attachment on a stand mixer or hand mixer, cream the butter and sugar together. Add the extracts and combine.

2. Sift the flour and salt together. Stir the almonds into the flour. Slowly add the flour to the butter while mixing slowly. When mixed, turn onto a floured surface and shape into a flat disk. Refrigerate for 1 hour.

3. Flour a surface and roll the dough until it is ½" thick. Cut into rounds or squares that are no larger than 2½" across. Place the cookies on a griddle, and bake in the middle of the oven for 20–25 minutes. The edges will turn brown. Cool to room temperature and serve.

Scones

These Scottish baked goods take their name from the Stone of Destiny, also called Scone, where Scottish kings were once crowned. The traditional triangular shape was believed to resemble the crown.

INGREDIENTS | **SERVES 8–10**

2 cups all-purpose flour

1 tablespoon baking powder

3 tablespoons sugar

¾ teaspoon salt

4 tablespoons butter, cold and cubed

½ cup dried fruit or nuts, chopped

¾ cup heavy cream

1 large egg, lightly beaten

1. Preheat oven to 400°F and place a griddle on a rack in the middle of the oven. Mix the flour, baking powder, sugar, and salt either in a food processor or by hand until well combined.

2. Add the butter and mix until it is coarse crumbs with a few larger chunks of butter, 12–14 pulses if using a food processor. Add the fruit or nuts and pulse quickly until combined.

3. Use a rubber spatula to stir in the cream and egg until a dough starts to form. Dump the mixture onto a floured surface and knead until it has come together but has a rough and sticky texture.

4. Pat the dough into a circle and use a sharp knife to cut it into eight triangular wedges. Place on the griddle and bake for 12–15 minutes. The tops should be golden brown when ready. Cool for 10 minutes before serving with butter, jam, or clotted cream.

Stuffed French Toast

*The good thing about this dish is that you can use just about any berry in the stuffing.
If your berries are large, like blackberries, cut them into halves or quarters.*

INGREDIENTS | SERVES 4

1 loaf Vienna Bread

6 ounces cream cheese

2 tablespoons honey

¼ teaspoon salt

1 pint strawberries, stemmed and sliced

1 tablespoon butter

4 eggs, beaten well

1. Cut the ends off the bread to get a rectangular loaf. Cut four 1½" thick slices from the bread. Cut the ends in half. Take a skinny knife and cut a pocket into the bread.

2. In a small bowl, mix the cream cheese, honey, and salt. Use a knife to spread one-quarter of the cream cheese in each bread pocket. Place several strawberry pieces in each pocket. Take one of the chunks cut from the end of the loaf and wedge it into the pocket opening.

3. Place griddle over medium heat and once it's heated melt the butter evenly across the surface of the griddle.

4. Carefully dunk each slice of bread into the egg, making sure all of the bread is coated. Carefully place the cut end of the bread on the griddle and cook for 2 minutes before laying the bread on its side. This seals the opening to prevent the cheese from leaking out. Repeat with each slice, cooking the bread for 3–4 minutes on each side until golden brown. Serve immediately.

Grilled Cheese with Tomato Sandwiches

Grilled cheese sandwiches are basic comfort food. Adding a slice of Cheddar cheese adds extra flavor and helps to hold the sliced tomato securely in place. You can also substitute pickle slices for the tomato.

INGREDIENTS | SERVES 2

2 tablespoons butter, softened

4 slices sandwich bread

2 slices American cheese

2 slices Cheddar cheese

2 slices of tomato

Gourmet Grilled Cheese

For an even more "grown up" version, you can substitute in dark rye bread, oat bread, or any other whole-grain bread. You can also spread a thin layer of Dijon mustard on the inside of the bread slice and layer on slices of Emmenthaler, Gouda, Gruyère, or even Brie cheeses.

1. Place a skillet over medium heat. While it warms up, spread ½ tablespoon of butter on one side of each slice of bread.

2. Place two slices of bread, butter side down, in the skillet. Add a layer of American cheese on top, then the slice of tomato, then the slice of Cheddar cheese, and then the final slice of bread, butter side up.

3. Use a spatula and press down lightly. Cook for 3 minutes, or until the bread has toasted and turned golden brown. Carefully turn the sandwiches over and cook for 3 minutes or until golden brown.

4. Let the sandwich rest for 30 seconds before cutting it in half and serving.

Pounded and Fried Plantains

Plantains are similar to bananas but are much starchier.
Choose plantains that are yellow-gold and firm.

INGREDIENTS | MAKES 18–24 PIECES

1 cup flour
½ teaspoon baking powder
¼ teaspoon salt
¾ cup cold water
1½ pounds plantains
6 tablespoons peanut oil for frying
Powdered sugar for sprinkling

1. Sift the flour, baking powder, and salt together. Add the cold water to the dry ingredients and stir until it is lump free. It should coat a spoon when dipped in the batter. Add a tablespoon of flour or water if necessary to get this texture.

2. Cut the ends off the plantains. Cut through the peel lengthwise several times and use the tip of a butter knife to pry off the peel. Cut the plantains in half and again in half lengthwise, and then cut each half into thirds. Use a rolling pin to flatten each plantain.

3. Place a griddle over medium-high heat. Once it is heated, pour 3 tablespoons of oil on the griddle and swirl so the surface is coated evenly. If the oil smokes, lower the heat until it stops smoking.

4. Dip each pounded strip into the batter and let the excess drain off. Place half of the slices of plantain on the griddle so they aren't touching. Fry each plantain for 1–2 minutes per side. They will darken more after they are removed from the oil. Add the rest of the oil and repeat with the rest of the plantains.

5. Sprinkle them with powdered sugar and eat while hot.

Panini Sandwiches

While salami, mortadella, or prosciutto are classic panini fillings,
just about any sliced meat, cheese, or other dry ingredient will work well.

INGREDIENTS | SERVES 1

1 crusty roll (a baguette or ciabatta)

2 slices prosciutto

4 slices mortadella

4 slices salami

2 slices provolone

Olive oil to taste

Two Skillets are Better Than One

This method of cooking works great when making grilled cheese sandwiches. Spread Dijon mustard on one slice of bread and mayonnaise on the other. Brush olive oil on the outside of each slice. Add a few teaspoons of shredded cheese. Place the sandwich in one heated skillet and place the other skillet directly on top. Cook for 4 minutes and serve.

1. Place a griddle and a skillet over medium heat.

2. Cut the bread open along one long side through the middle without cutting through the other long side. Open the bread slightly and insert the slices of meat and cheese. Make sure all the edges of the cheese are inside the bread. The meat can hang out slightly.

3. Brush the outside of the bread lightly with the olive oil. Place it in the middle of the griddle. Turn off the heat under the skillet and carefully balance the skillet on top of the sandwich. Press down lightly to make it stay in place. Cook for 4 minutes. Check to make sure the bottom of the sandwich has grill lines. Serve immediately.

Basic Grilled Vegetables

*These vegetables are delicious in their simplicity. But if you prefer
a little more tang, sprinkle them with a little flavored oil and vinegar.*

INGREDIENTS | SERVES 8–12

2 bunches asparagus

16 ounces button mushrooms

3 zucchinis

Salt to taste

6 cubanelle peppers

2 eggplants

¼ cup olive oil

Pepper to taste

1. Trim the bottoms off the asparagus. Cut thick stalks in half lengthwise. Slice the button mushrooms in half through the stem.

2. Cut the zucchini in half lengthwise, and then into ½" slices. Place on top of two layers of paper towels. Sprinkle lightly with salt. Let sit for 10 minutes. Flip over, sprinkle with salt and let sit for another 10 minutes.

3. Remove the stems and seeds from the peppers. Cut in half and make small cuts as needed in the bottom of the peppers so they will lie flat.

4. Cut the stems off the eggplants, then cut ½" slices along their length. Cut in half lengthwise if desired. Salt the same way as the zucchini, but let rest for 20 minutes on each side.

5. Place a griddle over medium-high heat on a stove top. Toss the asparagus and mushrooms in a tablespoon of olive oil separately. Sprinkle them lightly with salt and pepper. Brush the grill lightly with oil. Cook the asparagus for 2–4 minutes on each side. Place them on a warmed platter.

6. Cook the mushrooms for 2–4 minutes on each side and add them to the platter. Pat the eggplant and zucchini dry and place several slices on the pan. Cook for 4–6 minutes on each side. Place them on the platter.

7. Brush both sides of the peppers with oil. Place them on the pan skin side up. Grill for 2–4 minutes on each side. Sprinkle with salt and pepper and add to the platter. Keep the platter warm until ready to serve.

Chipotle Black Bean Quesadilla

If you have leftover black beans from the Stewed Black Beans (page 248), you can use those and omit the chipotle if desired.

INGREDIENTS | SERVES 4

1 15-ounce can black beans, drained and rinsed

2 tablespoons canned chipotle

1 cup diced tomato, seeded

8 flour or corn tortillas

1 cup shredded cheese

Perfect Cheese for Quesadilla

Any cheese that will melt is suitable for quesadillas. But some cheeses melt better and are less likely to clash with the black beans. If you don't have Mexican Chihuahua cheese at your grocery, use Monterey Jack or a mild Cheddar. These cheeses will melt easily without getting too greasy, and without clashing with the strong flavor of the beans.

1. Place the beans in a bowl and mash them with a fork. Stir in the chipotle and tomato.

2. Place a griddle over medium heat. Once it's heated place two or four tortillas on the griddle. Don't overlap them. Sprinkle ¼ cup of cheese on each tortilla. Spoon ¼ of the bean mixture on top of the cheese. Top with another tortilla and press down slightly.

3. Cook for 4–6 minutes on the first side, or until the tortilla is slightly browned. Press the top tortilla to make it stick to the cheese. Carefully flip the tortilla.

4. Cook on the second side for 4–6 minutes, or until the tortilla is slightly browned. Cut into wedges and serve with salsa and sour cream.

Spanish Griddle-Cooked Shrimp

This would be Gambas a la Plancha on a Tapas menu. Dishes cooked "a la plancha"
are common on Spanish menus and traditionally cooked on flat cast-iron pans.

INGREDIENTS | SERVES 4

3 medium tomatoes, seeded and chopped

3 green onions, thinly sliced

¼ cup chopped cilantro leaves

3 garlic cloves, minced

¼ cup spicy tomato salsa

1½ pounds large shrimp, peeled and deveined

Dash salt

Dash pepper

2 tablespoons oil

Juice from 1 lime

1 lime cut into wedges

1. Toss the tomatoes, green onion, cilantro, garlic, and salsa in a bowl and set aside. Toss the shrimp with the salt and pepper.

2. Place a griddle over medium-high heat. Once it's heated, pour 1 tablespoon of oil in the center of the pan and swirl to coat. Place half the shrimp on the pan so they aren't touching and cook for 1 minute. Remove the shrimp from the pan and place in a bowl. Repeat with 1 tablespoon of oil and the remaining shrimp.

3. Sprinkle the lime juice over the tomato mixture. Pour the mixture into the middle of the griddle and spread it out. Stir gently until the tomatoes are well-heated. Sprinkle the partially cooked shrimp on top of the mixture. Cook for 2 minutes or until they're cooked through and hot. Transfer to a large platter and serve with lime wedges.

Spicy Baked Fish

Red snapper can be hard to find. You may be able to substitute trout, grouper, or striped bass depending on what is available in your area.

INGREDIENTS | SERVES 4

1 whole 2–3-pound red snapper, cleaned

2 teaspoons salt

4 tablespoons Korean Spicy Red Pepper Paste (see below)

2 scallions, green part, minced

1 tablespoon toasted sesame oil

1 tablespoon rice wine vinegar

Korean Spicy Red Pepper Paste

Combine the following ingredients and store them in an airtight jar in the refrigerator for up to 2 months: 2 tablespoons red pepper flakes, ¼ teaspoon cayenne powder, 4 cloves minced garlic, 1 teaspoon minced fresh ginger, 1 tablespoon soy sauce, 1 tablespoon brown sugar, and the juice from 1 lemon.

1. Preheat oven to 375°F. Apply a thin layer of oil to the griddle if it isn't well seasoned. Place it in the middle of the oven.

2. Rinse the fish and pat it dry with paper towels. Make 3–4 slices through the skin and meat on each side of the fish, being careful not to cut through to the bones. Sprinkle the salt on the outside and inside of the fish evenly.

3. Combine all of the remaining ingredients in a bowl. Smear the sauce on the outside and inside of the fish, being sure to season the slits as well. Bake the fish on the griddle in the center of the oven for 10 minutes or until fish starts to firm up.

4. Increase the heat to 425°F. The skin should get very crispy. Cook for 3–5 minutes. Check to see if it's done by slicing into the thickest part of the fish; the meat should be opaque. Serve while warm with rice.

Whole Salt-Crusted Red Snapper

If you can't find red snapper, you can use any fish that is about 3–4 pounds.

INGREDIENTS | **SERVES 4–6**

1 whole 3–4-pound red snapper, cleaned

¼ cup thyme

1 lemon, sliced

¼ cup parsley, chopped

2 bay leaves

1 small yellow onion, thinly sliced

4 egg whites

1 cup coarse or kosher salt

1. Preheat oven to 350°F. Place a rack in the middle of the oven. Make sure that the fish is gutted and the scales, gills, and fins are removed by the butcher. Rinse the fish under cold water and pat dry.

2. Mix the thyme, lemon, parsley, bay leaves, and onion together in a large bowl. Stuff most of the mixture into the cavity of the fish. Put a few slices of onion on the griddle. Place the fish on top of the onions.

3. Place the egg whites in a bowl and use a hand-mixer to whip them to a stiff peak. Fold the salt into the egg whites to create a paste and smear over the fish. Place the griddle in the oven and cook for 35 minutes.

4. Crack the egg white shell and remove the large chunks. If the skin doesn't come off with the crust, peel it away. Use a long, skinny spatula to lift the top fillet off the skeleton. Carefully pull the skeleton off the fish and discard it. Separate the second fillet from the skin. Serve immediately.

Crispy Buffaloed Chicken Bites

This football-season classic gives you the feeling of having eaten fried wings without the mess or calories.

INGREDIENTS | **SERVES 6–8 AS AN APPETIZER**

1½ pounds boneless, skinless chicken breast

¼ cup butter, melted

¼ cup Tabasco sauce

1 tablespoon garlic powder

1 tablespoon apple cider vinegar

1 teaspoon salt

4 cups corn flakes, crushed

Bleu Cheese Dressing

Stir together ¾ cup sour cream, 1¼ cups mayonnaise, 1 teaspoon Worcestershire sauce, ½ teaspoon garlic powder, 1 teaspoon apple cider vinegar, ¼ teaspoon salt, and 4 ounces crumbled bleu cheese. Refrigerate for at least 1 hour before serving. If it's too thick, stir in a few tablespoons of milk.

1. Preheat oven to 375°F and place a large griddle pan on the middle rack. Rinse the chicken and pat dry. Cut the chicken into 1½" cubes.

2. Whisk the butter, Tabasco sauce, garlic powder, vinegar, and salt together in a wide, shallow bowl. Place the corn flakes into another wide, shallow bowl.

3. Dip a handful of chicken pieces into the liquid mixture. Shake off the excess and drop them into the cornflakes. Roll them until coated and set aside. Repeat with the rest of the chicken.

4. Once the oven and griddle are hot, place the chicken on the griddle, spreading them out evenly so they barely touch. Cook for 6 minutes on the first side. Flip them and cook for another 6 minutes.

5. Remove them from the oven and let them cool as you place them on a serving platter with celery sticks and bleu cheese dressing.

Basic Pizza Crust

Once the dough has risen, it can be placed in a sealable plastic bag and refrigerated for up to a week. Let it warm to room temperature for 20 minutes before rolling out.

INGREDIENTS | MAKES 2 PIZZA CRUSTS

1 package active dry yeast

1 tablespoon sugar

2 cups warm water

¼ cup and 1 tablespoon vegetable oil

4–6 cups all-purpose flour

1 jar prepared pizza sauce, as desired

1–2 cups shredded cheese, as desired

Pizza toppings, as desired

Cheese and Toppings

The most common cheese for pizza is mozzarella, but Monterey Jack and provolone will also work. A few tablespoons of Parmesan cheese will brown nicely. And don't limit your toppings to pepperoni and mushrooms. You can even substitute barbecue sauce for tomato sauce and add chunks of cooked chicken breast on top.

1. Combine the yeast, sugar, and water in the mixing bowl of a stand mixer, or in a large mixing bowl. Let sit for 10 minutes, or until the yeast becomes frothy.

2. Add ¼ cup of the vegetable oil and stir to combine. Using a dough hook on a low setting, or mixing with a fork by hand, stir in 4 cups of flour. Slowly add the flour in ½ cup increments until you get a firm ball of dough.

3. Flour a surface and knead the dough for a few minutes until it is smooth and elastic. Pour 1 tablespoon of oil into a clean bowl. Add the dough and roll it in the oil to coat. Cover and rest in a warm, draft-free area for 2 hours, until it has doubled in size.

4. Preheat oven to 475˚F. Punch the dough and let rest for 10 minutes before dividing it in half. Stretch or roll the dough into a round that matches the size of your griddle or skillet. Dock the dough all over with the tines of a fork to prevent it from rising too much while baking.

5. Top with prepared pizza sauce, toppings, and cheese as desired. Bake for 25–30 minutes, and serve warm.

Bacon and Sauerkraut Pancakes

The sauerkraut in this recipe can also be substituted with jarred kim chi
if you like. Or you can add a diced chili pepper to make it spicy.

INGREDIENTS | MAKES 4 MEDIUM-SIZED PANCAKES

1 cup sauerkraut
1¼ cups all-purpose flour
⅓ cup rice flour
1½ cups water
1 small potato, peeled and shredded
1 small onion, skinned and shredded
4 slices cooked bacon, crumbled
3 tablespoons vegetable oil
½ cup mustard or dipping sauce

Sour Cream Mustard Dipping Sauce

This sauce is great with these pancakes and can also be served with Oven-Braised Pork Roast (page 263). Combine 1 cup sour cream, 2 teaspoons Dijon mustard, 2 minced scallions, and ½ teaspoon Worcestershire sauce in a small bowl. Let it sit for at least 30 minutes and up to 24 hours before serving. Leftovers will keep for 1 week.

1. Place the sauerkraut in a small strainer and let it sit over a bowl for 30 minutes. Squeeze it regularly to remove as much of the moisture as possible. Combine the flours in a medium bowl. Slowly stir in the water until it is thoroughly mixed. Add the drained sauerkraut, potato, onion, and bacon to the batter. Stir until it is combined.

2. Place the griddle over medium-high heat. Add half of the oil to the pan and swirl so it is evenly coated.

3. Pour one-quarter of the batter slowly onto the griddle. Cook for 3 minutes, or until the bottom is golden and bubbles have risen to the top. Flip it over, press against the pancake with the back of your spatula, and cook for 3 minutes. Press firmly. If batter comes through on the top, flip and cook for 1 minute before pressing to make sure the center is cooked. Repeat with the rest of the batter.

4. Transfer to a serving platter and serve with mustard or Sour Cream Mustard Dipping Sauce.

Teriyaki Pork

"Teri" means "shiny" and "yaki" means "grill" or "broil." Anything that is cooked by a direct flame that becomes shiny is teriyaki. If you prefer, you can pound chicken thighs thin and use them in this dish instead of pork.

INGREDIENTS | **SERVES 3–4**

1 garlic clove, minced
1 tablespoon freshly grated ginger
¼ cup soy sauce
1 cup plus ¼ cup cold water
3 tablespoons brown sugar
2 tablespoons cornstarch
1 pound pork loin

1. Place the garlic and ginger in a small saucepan over medium heat with the soy sauce, 1 cup water, and brown sugar. Bring to a boil.

2. Dissolve the cornstarch in ¼ cup cold water and stir until there are no lumps. Slowly add the cornstarch mixture to the saucepan, whisking continuously. Bring back to a boil and thicken slightly. Remove from the heat and cool to room temperature.

3. Slice the pork loin into ½" slices. Pound them lightly with a meat tenderizer. Place in a bowl and add the marinade. Refrigerate for 30 minutes.

4. Preheat broiler. Place griddle pan over medium-low heat. Lay the pork slices on the pan and cook on each side for 2 minutes. Use a brush to baste each side of the pork.

5. Place the pan 4" from the broiler and cook each side for 2 minutes. The center of the meat should no longer be pink. The sugars in the marinade will become shiny and caramelized.

Welshcakes

These cakes are a traditional treat served on March 1st, St. David's Day.
They are a cross between a scone, a pancake, and a cookie.
They can be flavored with cinnamon, honey, or dried fruit.

INGREDIENTS | MAKES 20 CAKES

½ cup cold butter, diced

1⅔ cups self-rising cake flour

¼ cup sugar, plus 2 tablespoons

¼ teaspoon allspice

¼ teaspoon cinnamon

1 large egg, beaten

1 tablespoon butter or vegetable oil

1. Cut the butter into the flour until it's a crumbly mix. Stir in ¼ cup of sugar and spices. Add the egg to make a dough that is soft, but not sticky. If the dough is sticky add a tablespoon or two of flour.

2. Shape the dough into a disc, cover it with plastic wrap, and refrigerate for at least 30 minutes.

3. Flour a surface and roll the dough until it is ¼" thick. Use a biscuit cutter to make small cakes. Re-roll the scrap and cut more biscuits until you have used all the dough.

4. Place a griddle over medium heat. Once it's heated, grease the pan lightly. Add a few of the cakes and cook on each side for 3 minutes until golden brown. Keep them warm and sprinkle them with the remaining sugar. Serve while warm.

Chapter 13

Recipes for a Chicken Fryer or Fryer Kit

Hush Puppies

Even though food historians can't agree, hush puppies are believed to have been excess batter that was deep-fried and then fed to dogs to make them hush. But they're tasty for humans, too.

INGREDIENTS | **MAKES 16 HUSH PUPPIES**

2 cups yellow corn meal

1 cup all-purpose flour

2 teaspoons brown sugar

¾ teaspoon salt

½ teaspoon black pepper

1 teaspoon baking powder

¾ teaspoon baking soda

2 eggs

1 cup milk

2 tablespoons bacon fat

¾ cup frozen corn

4 cups peanut oil

1. Combine the dry ingredients in a large bowl. Whisk the eggs, milk, bacon fat, and corn in a small bowl. Make a well in the center of the dry ingredients and pour in the wet. Fold the dry into the wet to get a sticky dough.

2. Place a Dutch oven or chicken fryer over medium-high heat. There should be 2" of oil in the pan. Once the oil is hot, drop tablespoons of the dough into the oil. Cook until they are brown on the first side and flip over. They should float when they're done. Place them on paper towels to drain and sprinkle with salt. Serve warm.

Fried Ravioli Appetizer

This recipe works best with ravioli that are about 1½" to 2" across. Larger ravioli won't cook through and smaller ravioli will break up in the fryer.

INGREDIENTS | **SERVES 8–10**

1 large egg

½ cup panko or bread crumbs

1 teaspoon dried oregano

1 teaspoon garlic powder

¼ teaspoon black pepper

½ teaspoon salt

2 tablespoons shredded Parmesan cheese

1 package frozen ravioli, thawed

2 cups vegetable oil

1 cup marinara sauce, warmed

1. Whisk the egg in a small bowl. In a separate bowl combine the panko, spices, and cheese.

2. Dip each ravioli in the egg with one hand. Dip the ravioli in the panko mixture with the other hand.

3. Place a Dutch oven over medium heat and fill it with vegetable oil. Drop the ravioli in the oil and cook for 2 minutes on each side till they're lightly golden.

4. Remove them from the skillet and drain on paper towels. Serve with a bowl of warmed marinara sauce for dipping.

Deep-Fried Tuna with Spicy Garlic Sauce

Cooking tuna this way creates a crispy edge on the fish, cooked evenly on all sides. Because the fish seals quickly as it cooks, it doesn't soak up oil and get greasy.

INGREDIENTS | SERVES 4 AS AN APPETIZER, 2 AS A MEAL

2 tablespoons soy sauce
2 garlic cloves, minced
½ teaspoon fresh ginger, grated
½ teaspoon ground black pepper
¼ cup sake
1 tablespoon fish sauce
½ teaspoon chili sauce
1 tablespoon cornstarch
4 4-ounce tuna fillets
Pinch salt
Pinch pepper
1 quart vegetable oil

1. Combine the soy sauce, garlic, ginger, pepper, sake, fish sauce, and chili sauce in a small bowl. Refrigerate overnight.

2. Just before cooking the tuna, stir cornstarch into the cold sauce. Warm the sauce in a microwave or a small sauce pan, stirring frequently to thicken. Sprinkle the tuna with salt and pepper lightly.

3. Place a fryer over medium heat. Once the oil is heated, add two pieces of tuna and cook for 1 minute. Remove them from the oil and pat dry with paper towels. Repeat with the remaining tuna. Slice the tuna into ½" slices and pour the sauce over them. Serve while hot.

Battered Catfish

When purchasing catfish fillets, look for pieces that weigh 3–5 ounces each. The smaller pieces have less fatty tissue, which reduces the fishy taste. Remove any black membranes from the fish before cooking.

INGREDIENTS | SERVES 4–6

2 pounds catfish fillets
½ cup yellow cornmeal
¼ cup all-purpose flour
1½ teaspoons salt
¼ teaspoon ground black pepper
Pinch cayenne
2 eggs, beaten
1 12-ounce beer, lager-style
3 cups vegetable oil

1. Rinse the fillets and cut them into 2"-thick slices. Combine the cornmeal, flour, salt, pepper, and cayenne in a wide, shallow bowl. In a separate wide, shallow bowl whisk together the egg and the beer.

2. Dredge the catfish in the flour, then the beer mixture, and then in the flour again. Place on a wire rack and rest for 10 minutes.

3. Place a fryer over medium heat and add the oil. Once the oil is heated, carefully slide 3–4 pieces of fish into the oil. Cook until lightly browned. Flip halfway through. Dry on a wire rack with paper towels underneath. Serve with tartar sauce, remoulade, or garlicky mayo.

Deep-Fried Calamari

This dish is often served with Cocktail Sauce (page 230) but can also be served with a spicy or garlicky mayonnaise or a remoulade sauce.

INGREDIENTS | SERVES 2–3

1 pound frozen calamari, cleaned
¼ cup fine cornmeal
2 tablespoons cornstarch
2 teaspoons Old Bay seasoning
½ teaspoon salt
1 quart canola or safflower oil

1. Thaw the calamari. Slice off the tentacles. Slice the tubes into ½"-wide rings. Pat dry with paper towels. Combine the cornmeal, cornstarch, Old Bay seasoning, and the salt in a plastic bag. Add the calamari to the bag and shake till coated evenly.

2. Preheat oven to 175°F. Place a wire rack over a baking sheet in the middle of the oven. Place the oil in a fryer over medium-high heat. Once the oil is heated, carefully add a handful of calamari pieces. Cook for 2–3 minutes or until they're lightly golden brown.

3. Remove the cooked calamari with a fryer basket or wire skimmer and place on the wire rack to drain.

Onion Rings

To get truly tasty onion rings, use large sweet onions. Look for the brand name, Vidalia, or Spanish onions. If you don't have beer, substitute with water mixed with 1 tablespoon apple cider vinegar.

INGREDIENTS | SERVES 6

1 cup flour
1 egg
1 tablespoon butter, melted
1 teaspoon salt
½ cup beer
1 large Spanish or Vidalia onion
1 quart vegetable oil

1. Combine the flour, egg, butter, salt, and beer in a blender until it is smooth. Cover and refrigerate for at least 4 hours. Preheat oven to 200°F. Place a wire rack over a baking tray.

2. Slice the onion into ¾" slices. Separate the rings. Place a fryer over medium heat. Add the oil.

3. Once the oil is heated, dip a few rings into the batter, then lower into the hot oil. Cook for 5–6 minutes, turning halfway through, or until golden on each side.

4. Remove from the oil and place on the rack in the oven. Repeat with the remaining rings. Serve with ketchup or other dipping sauces.

Malassadas

These fried doughnuts are Portuguese in origin but are very popular in Massachusetts and Hawaii where large Portuguese populations settled. They can be filled or left plain. Use new, clean oil for frying.

INGREDIENTS | MAKES 5 DOZEN

1 package fast-acting yeast

1⅔ cups warm water

1 teaspoon plus ⅓ cup sugar

6–7 cups flour

1 teaspoon salt

1⅓ cups cream or milk

⅓ cup melted butter

8 eggs, beaten

1 quart vegetable oil

1. Place the yeast, ⅓ cup warm water, and 1 teaspoon sugar in a bowl and let the yeast dissolve and become frothy. Stir the flour, salt, and ⅓ cup sugar in a large bowl. Mix the cream and 1⅓ cup water in a small bowl. Add to the flour mixture.

2. Stir the butter and eggs into the flour mixture. Add the yeast mixture and mix until the dough is soft and cannot be stirred. Knead lightly on a surface until smooth.

3. Place 1 teaspoon oil into a large clean bowl. Add the ball of dough and turn until coated. Cover the bowl with a towel and place in a warm, draft-free area for 1–2 hours, or until doubled. Punch down and divide into 4 even balls. Use your hands to roll the 4 portions into tubes.

4 Place the fryer over medium-high heat. Add the oil. Once it's hot, pinch off portions of dough that are 2" square. Cook on each side for 1–2 minutes until they're lightly golden brown and soft but not raw in the middle. Drain on a wire rack over paper towels and sprinkle with sugar. Serve hot or warm.

French Fries

Frying the potatoes twice seems like a lot of work, but they'll be crispier and puffier if you do. Frying with used oil will ensure good color on the fries.

INGREDIENTS | **SERVES 4–6**

4 large russet potatoes, peeled

Water, as needed

1 quart peanut oil

Salt to taste

Pepper to taste

1. Cut the potatoes into ¼" slices. Cut those slices into ¼" strips. To remove the starch, rinse the potatoes in cold water until the water runs clear. Put the potatoes in a bowl and cover with ice water. Refrigerate for 1 hour. Drain and pat dry.

2. Place a fryer over medium to medium-high heat and add the oil. Make sure there is at least 3" of room between the top of the oil and the top of the pan. The oil should maintain 360°F.

3. Add a handful of potatoes to the oil, being careful not to splash your hand. Use a skimmer or a slotted spoon to keep the potatoes from sticking to each other. Cook until they're a very light blond. Remove from the oil and drain on paper towels. Let rest for 10 minutes. Repeat with the rest of the potatoes. Preheat oven to 275°F.

4. Once all of the potatoes have been fried once, adjust the heat to 350°F. Return the potatoes to the fryer and cook for 1 minute, or until they're golden brown and slightly puffed. They will darken slightly as they cool. Place on a wire rack over a cookie sheet in the middle of the oven to stay warm and crisp. Season with salt and pepper. Serve warm.

Plantain Empanadas

Almost every culture has a dish that consists of dough with filling that is baked, boiled, steamed, or fried. Mexico has empanadas, which are usually made from dough similar to pie crust dough.

INGREDIENTS | MAKES 1 DOZEN EMPANADAS

2 large yellow-ripe plantains
¾ tablespoon salt
1 large garlic clove
1 cup all-purpose flour
Water, as needed
1½ cups queso fresco or other cheese
Vegetable oil, as needed

What Is a Plantain?

Plantains look like very large bananas. They're from the same plant family, but plantains are much starchier and very rarely eaten raw. They can be eaten at any stage if they're cooked, but it isn't until the skin has turned completely black and the fruit inside is very soft and fragrant that they're edible raw.

1. Preheat oven to 350°F. Cut the ends off the unpeeled plantains and then cut them in half lengthwise. Cook on a baking sheet for 40 minutes until very soft. Allow them to cool and remove the peel. Place the soft plantain into a food processor with the salt and garlic. Pulse several times until smooth. Add half the flour and pulse. Add the remainder of the flour and pulse until all of the flour is incorporated. Scrape down the sides of the bowl to get an even dough.

2. Prepare your work area by filling half a medium bowl with cold water. Tear three square sheets of wax paper. Set one of them aside for holding the empanadas before they're fried. Keep your hands wet at all times. Dip your palms into the water and divide the dough into twelve equal portions. Lightly wet one side of each piece of wax paper.

3. Place one of the dough balls onto the wet side of one piece of wax paper. Place the wet side of the other sheet on top. Lightly press down on the ball until you get a circle slightly larger than your palm. Carefully peel off the top piece of wax paper. Place a tablespoon of crumbled cheese into the center of the circle. Hold the wax paper in your hand and fold it to get even sides. Carefully peel the paper away from the empanada and use the tines of a fork to press the edges together. Set the empanada aside and repeat.

4. Place your fryer over medium-high heat. The oil should be 350°F. Fry two empanadas at a time. They should be golden-brown after 1 minute on each side. Place on a rack to drain over paper towels. Sprinkle with coarse salt. Serve warm with salsa.

Deep-Fried Shrimp and Oysters

This breading works and tastes great on shellfish, including clams and scallops.

INGREDIENTS | SERVES 6–8

2 quarts safflower or canola oil

1 cup all-purpose flour

2 teaspoons salt

1 teaspoon Old Bay seasoning

3 eggs, beaten

1½ cups fine bread crumbs or panko

12 ounces shucked oysters, drained and cooled

1 pound medium shrimp, peeled and deveined

Cocktail Sauce

To make your own cocktail sauce combine 1 cup ketchup, 1 teaspoon prepared horseradish, juice from 1 lemon, 1 minced garlic clove, and ¼ teaspoon Tabasco sauce. This easy sauce is great for most fried seafood and any leftover sauce can be stored for 2 weeks.

1. Place a fryer or Dutch oven over medium to medium-high heat and add the oil. Make sure the temperature is 375°F. Combine the flour, salt, and Old Bay in a wide, shallow bowl. Beat the eggs in another wide, shallow bowl. Add the bread crumbs to a third wide, shallow bowl. Preheat the oven to its lowest setting. Place a wire rack on a cookie sheet in the middle of the oven.

2. Pat the oysters and shrimp dry. Dredge them in the flour mixture with one hand. Dip them in the egg with the other hand. Dredge them in the bread crumbs with the first hand and set on a clean, dry plate.

3. Once you have one layer breaded, slide them into the oil and cook for 2 minutes, or until they're a light, golden brown. Place on the wire rack and sprinkle lightly with salt or more Old Bay. Serve warm with cocktail sauce.

Deep-Fried Soft-Shell Crab Sandwiches

Crabs have shells to protect themselves from predators.
But as they grow they molt to remove an old shell and permit a new shell to grow.
Once their shell is gone, the entire crab is edible.

INGREDIENTS | SERVES 4

4 soft-shell crabs

¼ cup cornstarch or arrowroot starch

1 quart vegetable oil

4 hamburger buns

4 tomato slices

4 lettuce leaves

4 tablespoons spicy mayonnaise

1. If the crabs aren't cleaned, you'll have to trim a few things before you cook them. Hold the body in one hand and use kitchen shears to cut off ½" of the front of the crab to get rid of the eyes and mouth. Flip the apron, or tail-like piece up and remove. Scrape out the innards. Lift up each side of the shell and remove the finger-like pieces of gill.

2. Place the crabs on a plate. Put the cornstarch in a small mesh strainer. Tap the strainer lightly to coat both sides of the crabs. Shake the crabs lightly to remove any extra starch.

3. Place the oil in a fryer over medium heat. Once the oil is heated, slide the crabs into the oil and cook for 4–5 minutes, turning the crabs halfway through. Remove the crab from the oil and let drain for a few minutes before assembling the sandwiches. Serve on hamburger buns with tomato, lettuce, and spicy mayonnaise.

Salt Cod Fritters

Salt cod is often found sealed in plastic and may be called bacalao or bacalhau.
It is a regular cod fillet that has been salted and dried to preserve it.
It tends to have a strong smell.

INGREDIENTS | MAKES 20 FRITTERS

1 pound salt cod, bones removed

Water, as needed

2 small russet potatoes, peeled and cubed

1 tablespoon butter

3 garlic cloves, minced

¼ cup all-purpose flour

½ cup milk

¼ teaspoon cayenne powder

3 tablespoons olive oil

1 large egg, beaten

¼ teaspoon baking powder

¼ teaspoon salt

¼ teaspoon pepper

4 cups vegetable oil

1 lemon cut into wedges

Garlic Mayonnaise (see below)

Easy Garlic Mayonnaise

It's best to make this a day before you plan to serve it. Mince 2 garlic cloves finely and sprinkle with salt. Use the back of a spoon to mash them into a paste. Stir the garlic and ¼ teaspoon of pepper into ½ cup of mayonnaise. Cover and refrigerate. Leftovers can be saved for 2 weeks if stored in a tightly sealed container.

1. Place the cod in a bowl of cold water. Cover and refrigerate for 12 hours. Refresh the water and soak for 12–18 hours more. Drain. Place the salt cod and potato in a saucepan. Cover with water by 2" and place over medium-high heat. Bring to a boil and then reduce to a simmer for 20 minutes. Drain.

2. Place a small skillet over medium heat. Add the butter. Once it has frothed, add the garlic and cook for 1 minute. Whisk in the flour and cook for 1 minute. Whisk in the milk and cayenne pepper slowly, stirring constantly. The sauce should be thickened and smooth. Set aside to cool.

3. Put the potatoes in a large bowl. Mash with a fork or other tool. Place the cod on a plate or cutting board. Use a fork to flake the fish apart and add to the potatoes. Stir in the warm sauce, olive oil, egg, baking powder, salt, and pepper until you get a thick mashed-potato like consistency. Let rest for 30 minutes

4. Place a Dutch oven over medium-high heat. Add 2" of oil. Divide the mixture in half. Use a large spoon to form the dough into ping-pong-sized balls, and drop into the oil. Stir them frequently to cook evenly. After 6 minutes remove them to paper towels and place in a warm oven. Repeat until all the balls are fried. Serve with lemon wedges and Garlic Mayonnaise.

Egg Rolls

Once the egg rolls are wrapped, they can be tightly sealed and frozen for up to 2 months. Or you can fry them all, freeze the cooked egg rolls, and bake them in a 350°F oven for 15 minutes when ready to serve. You can also serve them with the Sweet Chili Sauce (page 150).

INGREDIENTS | MAKES 20–25 EGG ROLLS

1 tablespoon peanut or vegetable oil

½ cabbage head, shredded

5 carrots, shredded

¼ pound shiitake mushrooms, thinly sliced

3 tablespoons soy sauce

½ teaspoon honey

3 garlic cloves, minced

1" piece fresh ginger, peeled and shredded

1 tablespoon rice wine vinegar

1 teaspoon sesame oil

1 package egg roll wrappers

1 tablespoon cornstarch

¼ cup cold water

Peanut oil, as needed

Sweet and Sour Dipping Sauce

Whisk together 2 tablespoons ketchup, ¼ cup apple cider or white wine vinegar, 2 tablespoons of any fruit jam or jelly, and ¼ cup honey. Heat in a microwave. Whisk in 1 tablespoon of cornstarch. If it doesn't thicken right away, heat a bit longer. Taste and add more jam or salt as needed. Refrigerate until ready for use.

1. Place a large skillet over medium-high heat. Once it's heated add 1 tablespoon oil, cabbage, and carrots. Stir to combine. Cover and cook for 5 minutes, stirring every minute. Add the mushrooms, soy sauce, honey, garlic, ginger, vinegar, and sesame oil. Stir continually until the liquid has evaporated. Place in a colander. Cool for 15 minutes.

2. Remove the egg roll wrappers from the package and cover with a towel to prevent them from drying out. Whisk the cornstarch and cold water together until there are no lumps.

3. Place 1 wrapper as a diamond in front of you. Place 1 heaping tablespoon of the mixture 2" from the point nearest you. Fold the point over the filling and make one complete roll away from you. Tightly fold the right edge toward the middle, being careful not to tear the wrapper, but leaving no air between the wrapper and the right edge of the filling. Repeat with the left edge. Roll away from you until the point is sticking out. Dip your fingertips in the cornstarch mixture and rub along the outer edges. Roll to seal and place on a platter with the seam-side down. Refrigerate wrapped egg rolls for at least 4 hours.

4. Place a Dutch oven over medium heat. Add 2" of oil. Place as many egg rolls as you can in the pan without crowding. Cook for 1½–2 minutes. They'll darken after they come out. Serve hot with a sweet and spicy sauce.

Crispy Fried Chicken

The double-dredge in this recipe is what makes the chicken so crispy.
The trick is to make the first flour coating very thin.

INGREDIENTS | SERVES 4–6

3½–4 pounds chicken pieces
1 quart buttermilk
½ of a head of garlic, minced
3 bay leaves
1 tablespoon chili powder
¼ cup sugar
¼ cup salt
2 tablespoons ground black pepper
4 cups all-purpose flour
1 large egg
1 teaspoon baking powder
½ teaspoon baking soda
1 cup whole milk
3 cups peanut or corn oil for frying

Avoiding Dough Hands

If you keep one hand reserved for the flour and vow to not get it wet, and keep the other hand reserved for the batter and vow to not let it touch flour, you should be able to coat the chicken without letting the dough coat your fingers. Letting the chicken rest to drip off excess batter and flour will result in a thinner and crispier coat with less waste floating in the oil.

1. Rinse all of the chicken pieces and trim off any extra pieces of fat or skin. In a gallon-size, sealable plastic bag combine the buttermilk, garlic, bay leaves, chili powder, sugar, salt, and pepper. Pat the pieces dry and nestle them into the bag. Remove any excess air and refrigerate overnight or for at least 3 hours.

2. Place a wire rack over a baking sheet and place the chicken pieces on the rack. Drain for 30 minutes. Put the flour in a shallow bowl. In a second bowl, whisk the egg, baking powder, and baking soda. Once combined, add the milk.

3. Place the chicken pieces, one at a time, in the flour and toss to coat. Shake off any excess and roll the pieces in the egg mixture with the other hand. Drain to remove any excess and place back in the flour. Toss to coat. Place pieces on the rack.

4. Heat the oil in a chicken fryer over medium-high heat to 360°F. Add a piece of chicken to the pan, skin side down. Add in two more pieces of chicken, waiting 1 minute between each. Cover and cook for 4 minutes, or until the bottom of the first piece is a deep golden brown. Turn over. Turn over the other pieces after waiting for intervals of 1 minute. Cook the second side of each for 6–7 minutes.

5. Remove the cooked chicken from the pan and place on a paper-towel lined plate. Wait for 4–5 minutes, or until the oil has come back up to 375°F, before repeating Step 4 with the next batch of chicken. Serve warm or cold.

Coconut Milk Fried Chicken

If you can't find ground spices, you can use whole spices and grind them in a food processor.

INGREDIENTS | SERVES 4–6

1 tablespoon ground cinnamon

1 tablespoon chili powder

1 tablespoon ground coriander

1 teaspoon ground cumin

1 teaspoon black pepper

2 teaspoons ground turmeric

2 teaspoons sugar

1 teaspoon salt

5 shallots, coarsely chopped

1 can coconut milk

3 pounds chicken parts

2–3 cups peanut oil for frying

Sweet and Spicy Dipping Sauce

Combine 2 tablespoons Worcestershire sauce, the juice from 2 limes, 1 teaspoon soy sauce, 2 teaspoons brown sugar, and 1 serrano pepper that has been sliced into rings. Place it in a covered glass bowl and refrigerate overnight.

1. Combine the spices, sugar, salt, and shallots in a food processor and pulse until the mixture resembles creamy mashed potatoes. Add the coconut milk and pulse till combined. Rinse the chicken pieces and trim any fat. Place the chicken into a glass bowl and cover with the coconut milk mixture. Cover and refrigerate for 3 hours or overnight.

2. Remove the chicken pieces from the milk mixture and pat dry. Cover and let sit at room temperature for 30 minutes. Place 1" of oil in a chicken fryer or Dutch oven on medium or medium-high heat. The oil should measure 375°F but shouldn't smoke.

3. Place two to three pieces of the chicken in the oil at a time. Fry for 10 minutes on each side. Larger pieces of dark meat may need to be fried up to 12 minutes on each side. Serve warm.

Korean Hot Wings

Because of the small bones and ratio of skin to meat in chicken wings, they make great chicken stock. Store the wing tips in a gallon-sized sealable bag in your freezer and turn into chicken stock.

INGREDIENTS | SERVES 4

3 tablespoons soy sauce

1 tablespoon water

1 teaspoon brown sugar

1 tablespoon white wine

Juice from 1 lemon

1 tablespoon chili paste

2 tablespoons honey

2 serrano peppers, thinly sliced

2 pounds chicken wings, split at joint, without tips

1 teaspoon salt

½ teaspoon ground pepper

2 tablespoons cornstarch

2 cups and 1 tablespoon canola, corn, or peanut oil

2 garlic cloves, sliced

1 thumb-sized piece fresh ginger, peeled and matchsticked

1. Combine the soy sauce, water, brown sugar, and white wine in a small bowl. Heat in the microwave until the sugar is dissolved. Add the lemon juice, chili paste, honey, and serrano slices and let rest at room temperature for 1 hour or in the refrigerator for 3 days.

2. Rinse the chicken wings and pat dry. Place in a bowl and sprinkle with salt, pepper, and cornstarch to coat. Let set for 5 minutes. Place a wire rack over a baking sheet. Place 2 cups oil in a chicken fryer over medium heat. The oil is hot when a sprinkle of cornstarch causes the oil to bubble instantly.

3. Use tongs to slip four pieces of chicken into the pan. Cook on the first side for 2 minutes and the second for 1 minute. Place the wings on the wire rack and repeat. Bring the oil back to temperature between batches. Drain the oil, filter, and cool.

4. Add 1 tablespoon oil to a skillet over medium low-heat. Add the garlic and ginger and cook for 30 seconds. Add the sauce and stir continually for 30 seconds. Add the chicken wings to the pan and stir for 3 minutes until heated through and evenly coated. Serve warm.

Scotch Eggs

It's important to get a thin coat of sausage on the egg. If the layer is too thick, the sausage won't cook through before it browns. If this happens, preheat an oven to 350°F and bake the eggs for 10 minutes, or until they're done.

INGREDIENTS | SERVES 4

1 pound loose pork sausage

1 teaspoon Worcestershire sauce

½ teaspoon ground mustard

1 tablespoon fresh thyme

2 tablespoons grated onion

¼ teaspoon ground cinnamon

Pinch ground nutmeg

1 cup vegetable oil

4 hard boiled eggs, shelled

¾ cup fine, dry bread crumbs

The Scotch Egg Is Really British

Even though they're called Scotch eggs, they were invented in a London Department store named Fortnum & Mason in the 1850s. The store had an elegant picnic take-out they offered that included these eggs with tomato sauce for dipping. The recipe was published in *High Class Cookery* in 1893 by the National Training School for Cookery.

1. Combine the sausage, Worcestershire sauce, mustard, thyme, onion, cinnamon, and nutmeg in a bowl until well-blended. Divide the mixture into six even portions.

2. Place a fryer over medium heat. Add the oil. While the oil comes to temperature, flatten the sausage into a patty. Use your fingers to stretch the sausage so it covers the egg. Roll each sausage-covered egg in bread crumbs and set it aside. Repeat with the remaining eggs.

3. Place two eggs in the oil. Cook for 6–8 minutes until the sausage is cooked and the bread crumbs are browned. Place the eggs on a rack over paper towels to drain. Repeat with the remaining eggs and serve hot or cold.

Shanghai Red Chicken

This dish's brick red color comes from the Chinese dark soy sauce traditionally used. If you can't find it, use Japanese tamari soy sauce. If you can't find Sichuan peppercorns, use red or black peppercorns.

INGREDIENTS | SERVES 4

4 pounds bone-in, skin-on chicken breasts, halved

2 tablespoons vegetable oil

2½ tablespoons grated fresh ginger

8 garlic cloves, minced

1 teaspoon Sichuan peppercorns

½ teaspoon ground anise, or 3 whole stars

½ cup chicken broth, low-sodium

½ cup dark soy sauce

¼ cup dry sherry or rice wine

3 tablespoons sesame oil

1½ tablespoons molasses

4 hard-boiled eggs, peeled

Rice-Sending Dishes

In Shanghai and other southern parts of China, it is common to eat mostly rice and vegetables. Meat is considering a secondary dietary addition, not the main portion of the dish. But dishes like this are believed to encourage one to eat more rice and are known as "Sha Fan," which translates to "rice sending" or "induce one to eat more rice."

1. Rinse the chicken and pat dry. Place a large Dutch oven over medium-high heat. Once it's heated add the vegetable oil and half the chicken. Brown on each side for 6 minutes. Remove the chicken to a plate and repeat with the remaining chicken.

2. Pour off all but 1 tablespoon of the fat. Add the ginger, garlic, peppercorns, and anise and cook for 30 seconds until very fragrant. Stir in the chicken broth, soy sauce, sherry, sesame oil, and molasses. Stir to combine and scrape the bottom of the pan.

3. Place the eggs and the chicken in the pan in one layer. Reduce the heat to low, cover, and simmer for 10 minutes. Turn everything over and cook for another 10–15 minutes. The chicken breast should register 160°F.

4. Place the chicken and eggs on a serving platter and tent with foil to keep warm. Remove the star anise and discard. Separate the fat from the sauce and pour it over the chicken and eggs. Serve with rice.

Chapter 14

Recipes for a Dutch Oven

Boston Baked Beans

*The molasses in this recipe has made this dish a Boston specialty
since the colonial days, when the city was part of the rum trade.*

INGREDIENTS | SERVES 6–8

1 pound small white or pink beans

Water, as needed, plus 9 cups

4 ounces salt pork, rind removed and cut into ½" cubes

3 slices of bacon, cut into matchsticks

1 medium onion, finely chopped

½ cup molasses

2 tablespoons stone-ground or brown mustard

1 tablespoon apple cider vinegar

Pinch salt

Pinch pepper

1. Rinse the beans and remove any bad beans or debris. Cover the beans with 3" of water and soak overnight. Place the salt pork in water in the refrigerator.

2. Preheat oven to 300˚F. Place the salt pork and bacon in a Dutch oven over medium-high heat. Cook for 7–9 minutes until the bacon is crispy. Drain off almost all pork fat. Add the onion and cook for 7–8 minutes.

3. Stir in the molasses, mustard, drained beans, and 9 cups water. Turn the heat to high and boil. Stir, cover, and cook in the middle of the oven for 3 hours.

4. Remove the lid and stir. Cook for another 1–1½ hours. The liquid should thicken to a syrup consistency. Stir in the vinegar, salt, and pepper. Serve hot or warm.

Onion Marmalade

*Even though this dish makes quite a bit of food, it stores well. You can keep it in your refrigerator
in a tightly sealed glass jar for up to 2 months. Or you can freeze it for up to 4 months.*

INGREDIENTS | CREATES 1 PINT

2 tablespoons olive oil

2 large white or yellow onions, thinly sliced

½ teaspoon salt

1 bay leaf

¼ cup sherry, brandy, or a sweet white wine

1. Place a Dutch oven over low heat. Once it's warm add the olive oil and stir in the onions with the salt and bay leaf. Cover and cook for 15 minutes.

2. Stir it a few times to prevent sticking. Once the onions are translucent, remove the lid. Add the sherry and stir. Let the liquid evaporate and stir every few minutes.

3. Replace the lid and cook for 1–1½ hours. If more liquid accumulates, remove the lid and let the liquid evaporate. Once there is no liquid in the pan and the onions are a light golden color, remove the bay leaf, and the marmalade is ready to serve.

Baked Barley Risotto with Mushrooms, Onions, and Carrots

Most risotto is made using a starchy, short-grain Italian rice. Even though this dish takes longer to cook than traditional risotto, it requires less hands-on time.

INGREDIENTS | SERVES 6–8

1 tablespoon olive oil

3 carrots, chopped

1 medium yellow onion, chopped

8 ounces white mushrooms, sliced

½ cup white wine or vermouth

1½ teaspoons dried thyme

2 cups barley

4 cups chicken or vegetable broth

3 tablespoons fresh parsley

½ cup grated Parmesan cheese

Salt to taste

Pepper to taste

Barley Should Not Be Ignored

Barley has been cultivated for thousands of years. Half of the barley grown in the United States is used for animal feed, and most of the rest is used for making beer xor whiskey. It contains all 8 essential amino acids, is able to maintain blood sugar levels for up to 10 hours, and has a fairly high concentration of fiber and protein.

1. Preheat oven to 350°F. Place a Dutch oven over medium heat and add the oil, carrots, and onion once heated. Stir frequently and cook until the onion is brown and the carrots are soft. Add the mushrooms and sauté for 10 minutes.

2. Increase the heat slightly and add the wine, thyme, and barley. Stir continually until the wine is evaporated, 3–4 minutes. Add the broth and boil.

3. Turn off the heat and cover. Cook in the middle of the oven for 50–60 minutes. Stir frequently until the liquid is absorbed and the barley is tender. Stir in the parsley and cheese. Taste before adding salt and pepper.

Basic Risotto

You can add vegetables or meat to this dish as you see fit.
About 2 cups of meat or vegetables should be the right balance.

INGREDIENTS | SERVES 6

8 cups chicken or vegetable stock
2 tablespoons olive oil or butter
1 medium onion, finely chopped
2 cups Arborio rice
½ cup dry white wine
¼ cup shredded Parmesan cheese
Salt to taste
Pepper to taste

Always Better at Home

Most restaurants don't make risotto individually as ordered. Generally they will start making the dish, and then set it aside. When an order is placed they'll take the half-cooked risotto and finish cooking it. But this means the texture is never as good as if you make it at home.

1. Pour the stock into a saucepan and place over medium-low heat. Place a Dutch oven over medium-high heat. Once it is heated through, add the oil and onion. Sauté for 5 minutes, or until the onion is translucent but not brown.

2. Add the rice to the Dutch oven and stir constantly until the rice loses its chalky appearance and has just a small white dot in the center of each grain. Add the wine, stirring continually for 2 minutes.

3. Add the stock to the Dutch oven 1 cup at a time and stir almost continually until the stock has been soaked up by the rice. After you've added 6 cups of stock to the pan, taste it to determine if it is done. Add stock ½ cup at a time until the rice is tender but not pasty. Stir in the cheese and taste before adding salt and pepper. Serve warm.

Pardner-Pleasing Beans

These Texas-style beans are a great alternative to Boston Baked Beans (page 242).

INGREDIENTS | SERVES 6–8

8 ounces dried pinto beans

Water, as needed

3 tablespoons olive oil

1 large onion, diced

1 large bell pepper, seeded and diced

6 garlic cloves, minced

2 jalapeño peppers, seeded and diced

3 15-ounce cans whole tomatoes, chopped

1½ teaspoons cinnamon

½ cup ketchup

½ cup yellow mustard

½ cup brown sugar

1 tablespoon red wine vinegar

Pinch salt

Pinch pepper

1. Rinse and sort the beans, removing any bad beans or debris. Rinse and drain.

2. Pour beans into a large saucepan and add enough water to cover by 2". Bring to a boil over high heat and cook for 1 minute, then remove from heat and let soak for 1 hour. Test for doneness and drain.

3. Preheat oven to 300°F. Place a Dutch oven over medium-high heat. Once it is heated through, add the oil, onion, and the bell pepper. Cook for 10 minutes. Add the garlic and stir continually for 1 minute. Add the jalapeño and stir to combine.

4. Add the drained beans, tomatoes, cinnamon, ketchup, mustard, brown sugar, and vinegar. Cover and cook in the center of the oven for 1 hour.

5. Stir the contents every 30 minutes for the next 2 hours. Keep the pan covered while it cooks. Remove the lid and cook for 30 more minutes. Add salt and pepper to taste. Serve with cornbread.

Cajun Red Beans and Rice

Andouille sausage provides the best flavor for this dish but can be hard to find in most of the country. You can substitute a smoked sausage like kielbasa.

INGREDIENTS | SERVES 8

1 pound dried red kidney beans, sorted

Water, as needed

2 tablespoons olive oil

1 large onion, chopped

1 red bell pepper, chopped

5 garlic cloves, minced

1 teaspoon dried thyme

1 teaspoon dried oregano

1 teaspoon dried basil

½ teaspoon dried black pepper

¼ teaspoon cayenne pepper

½ teaspoon celery salt

2 tablespoons sweet or Hungarian paprika

2 bay leaves

1 teaspoon Worcestershire sauce

1 quart vegetable broth

1 pound andouille sausage

1 ham bone or a smoked turkey leg

6 cups cooked rice

Salt to taste

Pickled Red Onions (page 262)

Tabasco sauce

1. Place the beans in a large bowl and cover them with cold water by 3". Cover and place over high heat. Bring to a boil for 10 minutes and remove from the heat. Cover and let sit for at least 8 hours. Drain the water, rinse the beans and set aside.

2. Place a Dutch oven over medium-high heat. Add the olive oil and vegetables. Stir frequently and sauté for 8–10 minutes. Add the garlic to the skillet and stir continually for 1 minute. Add the herbs and spices to the skillet. Add the Worcestershire sauce and the broth. Slice the sausage into thick rings and add it to the pot. Add the ham bone and beans to the pot.

3. Turn the heat to high and bring to a boil. Cover and reduce the heat to low. Simmer for 3–4 hours. Stir frequently to keep the beans from sticking. The beans are done when they start to fall apart and the dish becomes creamy. If the beans are soft but don't fall apart, take a potato masher to some of the beans. Taste and season as needed. Serve in a bowl over rice with salt, pickled onions, and Tabasco sauce.

Monday Is Laundry Day

Sundays in New Orleans were traditionally a day when a large meal was made, and a ham was common. Monday was traditionally reserved for doing laundry, which took all day, so adding the ham bone to a pot of beans created a dish that required very little work from the cook.

Refried Beans

*Canned refried beans aren't bad, but this version is much more flavorful.
If you make a large batch and freeze it in portions, you will have beans
for months and save money, too.*

INGREDIENTS | **MAKES 3 QUARTS**

1 pound dried pinto beans
Water, as needed
2 cups light beer or chicken broth
1½ teaspoons salt
2 tablespoons olive oil
1 medium onion, finely chopped
2 jalapeño chilies, seeded
1 teaspoon ground cumin
4 garlic cloves, minced
¼ cup chopped cilantro
Juice from 2 limes

Non-Vegetarian Refried Beans

It's common to fry beans in bacon drippings. If you wish to make beans that way, chop 6 slices of bacon into matchsticks. Cook until crispy and then add the onion, jalapeño, cumin, and garlic to the pan. The smoky and salty bacon flavor will add a level of flavor that the vegetarian version doesn't have.

1. Rinse and sort the beans. Place in a large bowl or pot and cover with water by several inches. Soak overnight. Drain off the water and place over a medium-low flame and cook for 4–5 hours, or until they're tender. Drain.

2. Place a few cups of the beans, some of the broth, and some of the salt in a food processor and purée it until smooth. Scrape down the sides of the bowl. Pour into a container and pulse another batch. Repeat until you have just a few cups of beans left. Pulse them slightly so they're chunky. Stir all the beans together.

3. Place a large skillet over medium heat. Add the oil, onion, jalapeño, and cumin to the skillet and cook for 5–7 minutes. Stir in the garlic and cook for 1 minute. Stir the beans into the skillet and simmer until reduced, thick, and creamy. Remove the beans from the heat and stir in the cilantro and lime juice. Taste and season with salt.

Stewed Black Beans

It is easier to sort beans if you pour them onto a white surface. The contrast makes it easier to see anything that isn't a bean, or any beans that look inedible. Black beans are hard to sort since they're smaller and dark.

INGREDIENTS | **SERVES 8-10**

8 ounces black beans

Water, as needed

¼ cup olive oil

2 yellow onions

2 red or yellow bell peppers

4 garlic cloves

1½ tablespoons ground cumin

¼ teaspoon baking soda

1 dried chipotle pepper, stemmed and seeded

1 tablespoon dried oregano

3 bay leaves

1 teaspoon ground coriander

2 teaspoons salt

¼ cup orange juice

Juice from 1 lime

2 tablespoons apple cider vinegar

Chopped cilantro to taste

1. Sort and rinse the beans. Cover them with a couple of inches of water in a large container and soak overnight.

2. Place a Dutch oven over medium heat. Add the oil, onion, and bell pepper. Sauté until the pepper starts to turn soft. Stir in the garlic and cumin.

3. Drain the beans and add them to the pot with enough water to cover them by 2". Add in the baking soda, dried pepper, oregano, bay leaves, and the coriander. Bring to a boil. Reduce the heat to a simmer, cover, and cook until they're soft, but not mushy, for 1–1½ hours.

4. Remove and reserve the water so there is just ½" of water above the beans. Simmer for 1 hour, uncovered, until the beans have soaked up the remaining water. Stir occasionally. Remove the dried pepper and bay leaves.

5. Add the salt, orange juice, lime juice, and vinegar. Taste and add more salt or more hot sauce if desired. Garnish with chopped cilantro and serve with rice or tortillas.

Down-Home Mac 'n' Cheese

This recipe can be made in any baking dish, but by making the cheese sauce in a cast-iron pan, you're likely to get a nice crust that contrasts well with the creamy noodles and sauce.

INGREDIENTS | **SERVES 6–8**

1 pound macaroni noodles or shells

5 ounces American cheese

8 ounces extra-sharp Cheddar cheese

3 ounces Monterey Jack cheese

4 tablespoons butter

5 tablespoons flour

3 cans evaporated milk

2 teaspoons salt

1 teaspoon paprika

½ teaspoon dried mustard

1 pinch nutmeg

½ cup bread crumbs or crumbled potato chips

¼ cup grated Parmesan cheese

Seaweed Is the Secret

Getting tasty and creamy mac 'n' cheese can be difficult. The carrageenan in evaporated milk, derived from seaweed, helps combine the flour with the cheese and the milk. The three cheeses each add something as well: Cheddar adds flavor, American won't separate like Cheddar, and Monterey Jack has a lot of body, texture, and gooeyness.

1. Preheat oven to 375°F. Cook the pasta according to the package directions until slightly underdone. Drain and rinse in cool water to stop it from cooking. Reserve ½ cup of the pasta water. Shred the cheese.

2. Place a large Dutch oven over medium heat. Once it's heated through add the butter and the flour. Stir continually for 2 minutes until the butter has melted and the flour has thickened. Very slowly pour in one can of milk. If it begins to get lumpy, stop pouring, and whisk until the mixture is smooth.

3. Add in the two remaining cans of milk with the dried spices. Whisk the ingredients into the sauce and stir it continually for 4 minutes. It should begin to thicken.

4. Turn off the heat and stir in the pasta water. Stir in the cheese 1 handful at a time to melt evenly. Stir in the pasta in two batches, coating evenly.

5. Sprinkle the bread crumbs and Parmesan cheese across the top and bake in the middle of the oven for 25–30 minutes. Cool for 3 minutes before serving.

Cioppino

This is a distinctly San Francisco dish believed to have been created by Italian fishermen as a way to use each day's catch. It goes perfectly with sourdough bread.

INGREDIENTS | **SERVES 8–10**

¼ cup butter or olive oil

2 medium onions, chopped

4 garlic cloves, minced

¼ cup parsley leaves

¼ cup oregano leaves

2 28-ounce cans whole tomatoes, peel removed

2 10-ounce cans of clams

2 bay leaves

2 tablespoons dried basil leaves

2 cups dry white wine

16 fresh clams

16 mussels

1½ pounds salmon cut into bite-sized chunks

1 pound fresh crabmeat or imitation crab stick, cut into chunks

1½ pounds small bay scallops

Salt to taste

Pepper to taste

1. Place a large Dutch oven over medium heat. Once it's heated through add the butter and onion. Cook for 10–12 minutes. Add the garlic and stir continually for 1 minute. Stir in the parsley and oregano.

2. Add the juice from the tomatoes to the pan. Squeeze each tomato in your hand to break apart. Add to the pan and press each tomato against the side to break it into smaller pieces. Pour the clam juice into the pan and refrigerate the clams for later. Stir in the dried herbs and wine.

3. Cover with a lid, reduce the heat to low, and simmer for 2 hours. (If necessary, you can complete this part up to 2 days ahead and refrigerate. Return it to the pan and bring to a boil before turning the flame to medium-low.)

4. Scrub the clams and mussels with a bristle-brush. Remove the beards from the mussels. Soak in cold water for 20 minutes. Gently lift the shellfish and reserved clams into the pan. Stir them into the sauce. Stir in the salmon, then the crabmeat. Stir in the scallops. Cover and steam for 5–8 minutes until the clams and mussels have opened.

5. Remove the bay leaves from the pan. Taste and season with salt and pepper if necessary. Serve directly from the pan while hot.

Moroccan Chicken Tagine

A traditionally shaped tagine looks like an upside-down cone on top of a casserole dish. But a chicken fryer holds the same amount, and slowly bastes the food as it cooks.

INGREDIENTS | SERVES 4

6 garlic cloves, minced and divided

1½ teaspoons sweet paprika

½ teaspoon cumin

½ teaspoon coriander

½ teaspoon cinnamon

¼ teaspoon ground ginger

⅛ teaspoon cayenne pepper

1 teaspoon minced lemon zest

4 pounds chicken thighs

Salt to taste

Pepper to taste

2 tablespoons olive oil

1 large onion cut into ¼" wedges

2 large carrots, peeled and cut into ½" rounds

2 cups chicken broth

1 tablespoon honey

1 cup pitted green olives

3 tablespoons chopped cilantro

Juice from 2 lemons

1. Combine half of the garlic with the spices and set aside. Combine the other half of the garlic with half of the lemon zest and set aside. Pat the chicken dry and season with salt and pepper.

2. Place the pan over medium-high heat. Add the oil and chicken. Brown on each side for 6 minutes. Cook the chicken in batches if necessary to prevent the chicken from touching. Remove the chicken and set aside.

3. Pour off all but 1 tablespoon of the fat and add the onion and lemon zest. Reduce the heat to medium and cook while stirring occasionally for 5–7 minutes. Add the garlic and spices and cook for 1 minute, stirring continually. Stir in the carrots, broth, and honey and scrape the bottom of the pan. Return the chicken to the pan, keeping everything on a single layer. Cover, reduce the heat to medium-low, and simmer 1 hour.

4. Transfer the chicken to a serving platter and tent with foil. Skim off the fat from the sauce, add the olives, and increase the heat to medium. Boil for 5–7 minutes. The sauce should thicken slightly, the carrots should be tender, and the olives warm. Stir in the garlic and lemon mixture, the cilantro, the lemon juice, and return the chicken to the pan, coating it in sauce. Serve with couscous or rice.

Chicken Paprikash

Cooking the chicken with the bones and the skin in this dish will make it more flavorful. And it's best to use a mix of white and dark meat to get a rich flavor.

INGREDIENTS | **SERVES 4**

4 pounds chicken pieces, bone-in, skin-on

Pinch salt

Pinch pepper

1 tablespoon vegetable oil

1 large onion, halved and thinly sliced

2 bell peppers, stemmed, seeded, sliced

1 tablespoon all-purpose flour

¼ cup sweet paprika

1 15-ounce can diced tomatoes

½ cup dry white wine

1 teaspoon dried oregano

½ cup sour cream

Peasant Food

This is a term used to describe food that doesn't require a long list of hard-to-find ingredients or highly skilled techniques, but is flavorful and delicious. This Hungarian dish uses items that most people have easy access to. If you like this dish, you may like other Hungarian dishes.

1. Rinse the chicken pieces, pat dry, and season with salt and pepper. Place a skillet over medium-high heat. Add the oil and half the chicken. Cook for 6–8 minutes on each side till browned. Transfer the chicken to a plate and repeat.

2. Reduce the heat to medium. Keep 1 tablespoon of fat and add the onion, stirring occasionally for 5–7 minutes. Stir in the pepper and cook for 4–5 minutes.

3. Sprinkle in the flour and 3 tablespoons of the paprika. Stir to combine and cook for 1 minute. Stir in the tomatoes, wine, and oregano. Scrape the bottom of the pan. Place the dark chicken in the pan in a single layer. Reduce the heat to medium-low, cover, and simmer for 35 minutes. Add the breast and cook for 20–25 minutes.

4. Place the chicken on a serving dish and cover loosely with foil. Skim off the fat. Stir the rest of the paprika and the sour cream into the skillet. Place on medium-low and cook for 1–2 minutes. As soon as the mixture simmers, remove from the heat. Season with salt and pepper as needed. Serve with egg noodles or mashed potatoes.

Coq Au Vin

This classic French dish, like so many others, was created to get the most out of the ingredients a farm kitchen was likely to have on hand. The long, slow cooking time is a great way to get a tasty dish out of what was probably an old rooster.

INGREDIENTS | SERVES 4–5

4 slices bacon

1 fryer chicken, or 3–4 pounds of chicken thighs

½ cup flour

1 teaspoon salt

¼ teaspoon ground pepper

1 cup chicken broth

2 cups dry red wine

2 tablespoons Dijon mustard

2 garlic cloves, minced

3–4 stalks fresh thyme

3 bay leaves

2 celery stalks

2 carrots

1 medium onion

2–3 tablespoons flour

1. Preheat oven to 325°F. Place a Dutch oven over medium heat. Cut the bacon into 1" pieces and add to the pot. Cook until they start to turn crispy and remove. Drain all but 1 tablespoon of the drippings.

2. Rinse the chicken under cold water and pat the pieces dry. Combine the flour, salt, and pepper in a wide, shallow bowl. Dredge the pieces through the flour and place them skin side down in the skillet. Cook for 3–4 minutes on each side, or until they're lightly honey-colored. Cook in batches if necessary.

3. Remove the chicken once it's cooked, and add the broth, wine, mustard, and garlic. Turn off the heat and place the chicken back in the Dutch oven. Tuck the thyme and bay leaves amongst the chicken. Sprinkle the celery, carrots, and onion on top of the chicken. Cover and put in the oven. Cook for 2–2½ hours.

4. Remove the chicken and vegetables to a large bowl and cover to keep warm. Discard the thyme and bay leaves. Place the Dutch oven over medium-high heat and let most of the liquid evaporate. Stir in a tablespoon of flour and whisk quickly to keep from getting lumps. Once you have thick gravy, pour it over the chicken pieces in the bowl and serve warm.

Senegalese Chicken

Senegal is a large country on the Atlantic Ocean in West Africa. Many dishes from this area have inspired American soul food dishes.

INGREDIENTS | SERVES 6–8

½ cup peanut oil

4 medium onions, roughly sliced

2 lemons, juiced

4 limes, juiced

½ cup apple cider vinegar

2 bay leaves

4 garlic cloves, chopped

2 tablespoons prepared mustard

1 serrano pepper, cleaned and diced

1 teaspoon salt

½ teaspoon black pepper

1 stewing chicken, 5–6 pounds, cut into individual pieces

2 tablespoons peanut oil

½ cabbage, cut into chunks

3 carrots, peeled and chunked

1. Mix everything but the chicken, 2 tablespoons of oil, cabbage, and carrots in a gallon-size sealable plastic bag. Add the chicken and toss to combine. Marinate for 4–24 hours.

2. Place a large skillet over medium-high heat. Once it's heated add 2 tablespoons of peanut oil. Place a few pieces of chicken in the skillet and cook for 4–5 minutes on each side until just browned. Remove the chicken to a dish. You may have to sauté the chicken in batches.

3. Once the chicken is sautéed, remove the onions from the marinade and cook for 10–12 minutes. Add the rest of the marinade and the vegetables to the skillet. Cover and boil for 10 minutes or until the carrots are not quite tender.

4. Place the chicken back in the pot, cover with a lid, and cook for 20 minutes. Stir occasionally. Serve over rice or couscous.

Basic Beef Roast

If you can't find an eye of round roast make sure to substitute with a cut that can handle low dry heat. Tougher cuts will need to be cooked for a long time in liquid in order to stay moist.

INGREDIENTS | SERVES 4

3–4 pounds eye of round roast

4 garlic cloves, cut into slivers

2 tablespoons vegetable oil

1 teaspoon salt

¼ teaspoon ground black pepper

½ teaspoon smoked paprika

½ teaspoon ground cumin

½ teaspoon onion powder

2 tablespoons brown sugar

1 cup beef or chicken broth

4 medium potatoes, cut in half

4 carrots, peeled and cut into large pieces

2 medium onions, peeled and quartered

1 tablespoon flour

1. Preheat oven to 325°F. Make several 1" deep cuts into the surface of the roast and slide a garlic sliver into each. Rub the oil over the surface of the roast. Combine the dried spices and brown sugar in a bowl. Rub them over the meat. Place the meat in a large sealable plastic bag and pour the broth into the bag. Refrigerate for 2–24 hours.

2. Place a skillet over medium-high heat. Once it is heated, add the roast and cook on each side for 3–4 minutes. Once the roast is seared on all sides, pour the liquid and spices from the bag over the roast and place in the oven. Cover and cook for 1 hour.

3. Place the vegetables around the sides of the roast in the skillet. Return the skillet to the oven and cook for 45–60 minutes or until a thermometer measures 120°F for medium rare, 130°F for medium, or 140°F for well done. Remove from the skillet and rest for 10 minutes.

4. Place the skillet over medium heat. Use a spoon to scrape the stuck-on bits from the bottom. If necessary, add ¼ cup of beef broth to the skillet. Simmer. Sprinkle in 1 tablespoon of flour and whisk constantly. Pour it into a dish to serve over the beef. Slice the beef thinly and serve with the vegetables.

Corned Beef Brisket

Making your own corned beef is cheaper and tastier and often more tender than corned beef you can buy. Brisket tends to be a tough cut of meat and the brining and curing process helps to tenderize it.

INGREDIENTS | **SERVES 6–8**

1 beef brisket, trimmed of fat

Water, as needed

1 cup kosher salt

½ cup brown sugar

2 tablespoons sodium nitrite, or meat cure

4 whole anise

1 teaspoon peppercorns

1 teaspoon mustard seeds

1 cinnamon stick, broken

8 whole cloves

3 bay leaves

6 allspice berries

1 teaspoon fennel seeds

2 pounds ice

1 large onion, quartered

4 large carrots, chopped

3 celery stalks, chopped

4 large potatoes

1. Place the brisket in a stockpot. Cover with water and stir in the salt, sugar, nitrite, anise, peppercorns, mustard seeds, cinnamon stick, cloves, bay leaves, allspice berries, and fennel seeds. Set on high heat and stir frequently until the sugar and salt are dissolved. Remove the pan from the heat and add ice.

2. Transfer the brine to 2-gallon sealable bag. Add the brisket to the bag, seal it, and place it inside another container. Place it in the refrigerator for 10 days. Stir the brine daily. After the brining period, remove the brisket from the brine and rinse.

3. Place the brisket in a large Dutch oven. Add the onion, carrots, and celery around the brisket. Cover with water by 1". Place over high heat and bring to a boil.

4. Place the pan over low heat, cover, and simmer for 4 hours. Add the potatoes and cook for 1 hour. Remove the meat from the liquid and slice it thinly against the grain. Serve while warm or cool.

Classic Corned Beef and Cabbage

Cabbage is often served with this dish. Once the corned beef is cooked, remove it and the vegetables from the pan and set aside to keep them warm. Increase the heat to high and add a head of cabbage that is cored and quartered. Cook for 10 minutes. Drain and serve.

Beef Short-Rib Cholent

This is a traditional Jewish stew that is simmered for 12 hours,
beginning before sundown on Friday so it is ready for eating on the Sabbath.

INGREDIENTS | **SERVES 6–8**

3 pounds bone-in beef short ribs

Salt to taste

½ cup dried kidney beans

½ cup dried chickpeas

Water, as needed

1 tablespoon vegetable oil

1 cup dry red wine

1 pound onions, coarsely chopped

1 garlic head, peeled

2 tablespoons brown sugar

1 tablespoon sweet paprika

¼ teaspoon ground cayenne pepper

1 teaspoon cumin seeds

½ teaspoon ground black pepper

1 pound baking potatoes, peeled and quartered

2 large carrots, peeled and cut into chunks

4 large eggs

Cholent Cookoff

Many Americans have heard of chili cookoffs, but there has been such a resurgence in cholent popularity that the cholent cookoff has been revived. Various synagogues around the country have annual cookoffs to see who has the best recipe. Just like chili, there are many variations on this basic recipe.

1. The night before cooking, trim the excess fat off the ribs and cut into sections of 3–4 ribs. Sprinkle with salt and refrigerate in a tightly sealed container. Sort the beans and chickpeas and place in a large bowl. Cover with water by 2–3". The day you're serving, place a rack in the middle of the oven and preheat to 200°F. Pat the meat dry with paper towels.

2. Place a 6–7 quart Dutch oven over medium heat. Add the vegetable oil and a few of the ribs. Sear each side for 4 minutes. Once all the meat is browned, place on a platter and pour off the fat.

3. Add the wine and scrape the bottom of the pan. Add the onions and cook for 5–7 minutes. Add the garlic cloves, brown sugar, paprika, cayenne pepper, cumin seeds, and pepper. Stir and cook for 2–3 minutes.

4. Drain the beans and chickpeas and spread over the onions. Lay the meat on top of the beans. Layer the potatoes on top and sprinkle the carrots on the potatoes. Nestle the eggs in the carrots. Add 4 cups of water gently so the layers don't move. Cover and place over medium-high heat. Bring to a boil.

5. Cook in the middle of the oven for 8 hours. Uncover the pan and skim off as much fat as possible. Place the layers around the edges of a platter and place the ribs in the center. Peel the eggs and cut in half. Use the braising liquid as a gravy and serve immediately.

Braised Country-Style Short Ribs

You can also cook these ribs in the Kansas City-Style Barbecue Sauce (page 57).
Simply follow this recipe and add in the sauce, skipping step 3.

INGREDIENTS | **SERVES 4**

4 pounds beef short ribs
2 tablespoons vegetable oil
1 medium yellow onion, thickly sliced
1 cup pomegranate juice
2 sprigs rosemary
1 15-ounce can chopped tomatoes
1 cup cider vinegar
1 cup beef broth
¼ cup molasses
1 tablespoon Worcestershire sauce
1 tablespoon prepared mustard

1. Preheat oven to 350°F. Place the Dutch oven over medium-high heat. Once it's heated, add the beef ribs in batches. Don't crowd them. Cook on each side for about 4 minutes. Remove from the pan and set aside.

2. Add the vegetable oil and onion. Cover and steam for several minutes, stirring frequently. When translucent, remove and place on top of the ribs.

3. Add the pomegranate juice and scrape to release the fond. Add the rosemary, tomatoes, vinegar, broth, molasses, Worcestershire sauce, and mustard. Stir till everything is well combined. Turn off the heat.

4. Stir the ribs and the onions back into the sauce. Cook in the middle of the oven for 2–2½ hours. Remove the meat to a plate and keep warm. Let the sauce rest for several minutes until the fat floats to the top.

5. Use a large spoon to scoop out as much fat as possible. If the sauce is runny, place it over a medium burner with the lid off and boil until it reduces. Place the ribs back into the sauce to warm and serve immediately.

Garlic and Lemon Fresh Ham

Fresh picnic ham is just the uncured portion of the back leg used for making ham.
The connective tissue breaks down during the slow-cooking to provide a great pork flavor.

INGREDIENTS | SERVES 8–14

1 fresh picnic ham, 8–10 pounds

1 cup olive oil

4 tablespoons chopped fresh rosemary

2 tablespoons chopped fresh sage

2 tablespoons fennel seeds

6 garlic cloves, minced

Zest from 3 lemons

½ cup kosher salt

1 tablespoon ground black pepper

2 pounds red potatoes, scrubbed and chopped

Water, as needed

Italian Ballpark Food

When Americans go to a ball game or a racetrack they indulge in pretzels, hot dogs, and caramel corn. But slow-roasted whole pig is fairly common at racetracks as well as other sporting events. This slow-roasted picnic ham is similar to something you might find at a "rosticcerie" in Italy.

1. Preheat oven to 325°F. Use a sharp knife to score through the skin and fat in a diamond pattern. Make the cuts about 1" apart from each other. Combine the remaining ingredients except potatoes in a large jar. Rub at least half of the mixture on the ham and place it in large Dutch oven. Add 1" of water in the bottom of the pan.

2. Cook in the middle of the oven for 2½–3 hours. It should cook for 20 minutes per pound. Be sure the meat near the center of the bone is 160°F. Remove it from the pan, cover with foil, and let rest for 20 minutes.

3. Use a wooden spoon to mix up the contents at the bottom of the pan. Add the potatoes and enough water to cover the potatoes halfway. Place the pan over medium-high heat and cook for 20 minutes, stirring occasionally. Remove the lid, decrease the heat to medium-low, and stir frequently while the potatoes cook for another 10 minutes. Slice the pork and serve with the potatoes.

Cassoulet

This French dish is named for the earthenware pot that this dish was originally made in.
But a Dutch oven has a similar shape and cooking tendency.
This dish is also made with goose and mutton.

INGREDIENTS | SERVES 6-8

1 pound cannellini beans
Water, as needed
4 duck legs
1 pound garlicky, non-spicy sausage
1 pound lamb shoulder, cubed
½ pound bacon, cut into strips
2 ham hocks
1 large onion, roughly chopped
2 large carrots, roughly chopped
2 celery stalks, roughly chopped
7 garlic cloves, minced
2 quarts chicken broth
2 tablespoons tomato paste
2 bay leaves
2 tablespoons fresh thyme, or
2 teaspoons dried
1 tablespoon sweet or smoked paprika
Salt to taste
2 cups bread crumbs
6 tablespoons chopped parsley
2 tablespoons melted butter

1. Sort the cannellini beans and remove any debris. Cover with water by several inches in a large bowl and soak overnight.

2. Place a large Dutch oven over medium-high heat. Place the duck legs skin side down in the pan and cook each side for 3–4 minutes. Remove and add the sausage, browning each side. Remove and add the lamb. Cook for 8–10 minutes until browned on each side. Remove and add the bacon. Cook until it starts to render its fat. Add the ham hocks and cook until browned on all sides. Remove the hocks.

3. Add the onion, carrot, and celery to the bacon. Cook for 10 minutes, or until the vegetables have softened and the bacon is crispy. Add 5 minced garlic cloves and cook for 1 minute.

4. Add the broth, tomato paste, bay leaves, and thyme. Stir till blended. Increase heat and bring to a boil. Add the beans and meat. Cover and reduce the heat to low. Simmer for 3–4 hours. Turn off the heat.

5. Remove the meat from the pan. Cut the sausage into chunks and set aside. Remove the ham and duck meat from the bones and set aside. Skim the fat from the stew and add the paprika. Taste and add salt as necessary. Return the meat to the pan.

6. Turn on the broiler and set an oven rack on almost the lowest setting. Combine the bread crumbs, parsley, and remaining garlic and spread over the pan. Drizzle butter on top. Place the pan under the broiler and cook until browned. Serve warm.

Pulled Pork

To create the shredded texture, use a fork in each hand to pull the pork apart.
If it has cooked long enough it will fall apart easily.

INGREDIENTS | **SERVES 12–14**

3–4 pounds pork butt
½ cup brown sugar
1 tablespoon paprika
1 tablespoon garlic powder
1 tablespoon onion powder
1 tablespoon ground cumin
1 tablespoon chili powder
1 tablespoon ground marjoram
1 teaspoon black pepper

Pickled Red Onions

Pickled onions provide a great crunch to complement the pulled pork sandwich. Thinly slice a large red onion and separate the rings. Place them into a large glass jar. Pour in ½ cup water, ½ cup white vinegar, ¼ cup sugar, and 2 bay leaves. Refrigerate for at least 2 days before serving.

1. Rinse the pork butt and pat dry with paper towels. Trim off any large pieces of fat. Combine all of the remaining ingredients and stir together. Sprinkle some of the mixture on each side of the pork butt and rub to make it stick. Place it on a plate and cover tightly with plastic wrap. Refrigerate for up to 24 hours, or let it sit unrefrigerated for 2 hours.

2. Place a large Dutch oven in the middle of your oven and preheat to 350°F. Once it has come to temperature, place the pork in the middle of the pan and cover tightly with a lid. Place it back in the oven and cook for 3 hours without opening it. The steam will help keep the meat juicy.

3. Once the meat has cooked, remove it from the pan and let it rest for 10–15 minutes. Use 2 forks to pull the meat apart. Once the meat is shredded, serve with the barbecue sauce of your choice on hamburger buns or rolls. You can also serve with pickled red onions.

Oven-Braised Pork Roast

This typical German roast is served on New Year's Day with sauerkraut, crusty bread, potatoes, and apples. Pork butt roast, from the shoulder, is perfect for this dish, but don't use tenderloin.

INGREDIENTS | SERVES 8–10

1 4-pound pork roast

1 large onion, cut into thick rings

2 celery stalks, cut into 1" pieces

1 14-ounce can of chicken or vegetable broth

2 garlic cloves, smashed

7 whole peppercorns

2 tablespoons salt

1 whole allspice

1 12-ounce dark ale

1. Place a Dutch oven over medium-high heat. Place the fat side of the roast down in the pan. Cook for 4 minutes on each of its four sides. Remove it to a plate and let sit.

2. Place the onions and celery in the pan and cook for a few minutes before adding the broth. Stir to remove the fond from the bottom of the pan.

3. Add the garlic, peppercorns, salt, and allspice and stir to combine. Stir in the ale. Reduce the heat to low. Return the roast to the center of the pan. Cover and simmer for 3–3½ hours. The roast should be tender and easy to cut.

4. Remove the roast to a pan to keep warm. Use a stick blender to purée the vegetables left in the pan. Follow the directions for Chicken Gravy (page 55) to create a gravy from the contents of the pan if you wish. Serve with mashed potatoes.

Chapter 15

Soups and Stews

Healthy Clam Chowder

This version doesn't have any cream in it, which can dilute the flavor of the clams. If you prefer a traditional creamy chowder, stir in 1 cup of heavy cream just before removing it from the heat.

INGREDIENTS | **SERVES 4**

1 Spanish onion, chopped

2 cups fresh or frozen shelled clams

3 cups fish stock or clam juice

1 bay leaf

1 teaspoon dried thyme

1 celery stalk, finely chopped

1 carrot, finely chopped

1 large baking potato, peeled and cubed

1 garlic clove, minced

Pinch salt

Pinch pepper

Fresh parsley, chopped, to taste

1. Place a Dutch oven over medium heat. Add the onion, clams, fish stock, bay leaf, and thyme. Boil before covering the pan and reducing the heat to low. Simmer for 45 minutes.

2. Add the celery and carrots and continue cooking on low for 30 minutes. Add the potato and garlic and cook for 20 minutes.

3. Remove the bay leaf. Taste before adding salt and pepper. Serve while warm with a sprinkle of fresh parsley on top.

White Bean Chili

If you like the idea of making this dish but don't have 4–5 hours, substitute 3 15-ounce cans of white beans for the dried, and cook for 20 minutes on medium low.

INGREDIENTS | **SERVES 4–6**

1 pound cannellini or Great Northern beans

Water, as needed

1 tablespoon olive oil

1 medium onion, finely chopped

2 garlic cloves, minced

1 teaspoon ground cumin

1 smoked turkey leg, meat removed and chopped

6 cups vegetable stock

1 teaspoon cayenne powder

½ teaspoon chili powder

1. Sort the beans and remove any debris. Place them in a large bowl and cover them with water by several inches and soak overnight. Drain and rinse the beans.

2. Place a Dutch oven over medium-high heat. Once it's heated through, add the oil and the onion. Cook the onions for 8–10 minutes.

3. Lower the heat to medium and stir in the garlic and the cumin. Cook for 1 minute before adding the turkey meat and the stock.

4. Bring to a simmer before adding the beans, cayenne powder, and chili powder. Reduce the heat to low and simmer for 4–5 hours, or until the beans are tender.

Swiss Chard and Lentil Soup

*Swiss chard is a hearty green leaf vegetable. If it is hard to find in your area,
you can substitute spinach or any type of greens.*

INGREDIENTS | **SERVES 4**

2 14-ounce cans vegetable or chicken broth

Water, as needed

1 cup lentils

4 cups packed Swiss chard leaves

2 shiitake mushrooms, chopped in tiny pieces

¼ teaspoon ground ginger

1 teaspoon garlic powder

2 teaspoons dried coriander

Salt to taste

Pepper to taste

1. Place a Dutch oven over medium heat. Add the broth and 2 cans of water. Sort the lentils and remove any debris. Once the liquid boils, add the lentils, cover, and boil again. Reduce the heat to low and cook for 20 minutes. Bite into a lentil; if the outside is soft, but the inside is still dense or crunchy, they're ready.

2. Rinse the chard well to remove any sand or dirt. Cut the stem out of the leaf and discard. Tear the leaves into 3" pieces. Once the lentils seem almost done, add the chard, mushroom, ginger, garlic powder, and coriander. Cover, return to a simmer and cook for 5–10 minutes more, or until the lentils are no longer crunchy in the center. Add salt and pepper to taste.

Tom Ka Kai

*This name translates as coconut soup with chicken. It's commonly served as street food because the
longer it simmers, the more flavorful it gets. The lemongrass and ginger should not be eaten.*

INGREDIENTS | **SERVES 2**

1 lemongrass stalk

1 15-ounce can coconut milk

1 15-ounce can chicken broth

Zest from 2 limes

1" piece of ginger, peeled and sliced

½ pound chicken breast, cut into bite-sized slices

4 ounces button mushrooms, sliced

½ cup fish broth or sauce

Juice from 3 limes

1 teaspoon honey

2 serrano or Thai chili peppers, stemmed and thickly sliced

¼ cup chopped cilantro

1. Remove the outer leaves from the lemongrass stalk. Cut off the base end and the top dried portion. Cut the stalk in half lengthwise and then into 1" chunks.

2. Place a Dutch oven over medium heat. Add the coconut milk, chicken broth, lemongrass, lime zest, and ginger. Cover and bring to a boil.

3. Add the chicken breast, mushrooms, fish broth, lime juice, honey, and chili peppers. Cover and bring to a boil again. Taste and add salt if necessary.

4. Remove the lemongrass, ginger, and chili. Dish and sprinkle with chopped cilantro and serve while warm.

Fresh-Roasted Tomato Soup

Roasting the tomatoes takes the most work in this recipe. If you don't have fresh, in-season tomatoes, use a 28-ounce can of whole tomatoes. Serve with Grilled Cheese Sandwiches (page 209) or the Croque Madame (page 22).

INGREDIENTS | SERVES 3-4

10 plum tomatoes, halved and seeded

6 garlic cloves, smashed

¼ cup olive oil

Pinch salt

Pinch pepper

1 medium onion, diced

1 large leek, cleaned and thinly sliced

3 cups vegetable stock

1 tablespoon balsamic vinegar

1 tablespoon fresh basil or thyme (or 1 teaspoon dried)

1 cup heavy cream

1. Preheat oven to 325°F. Place the tomato halves in a large skillet. Add the garlic cloves and drizzle half the oil on top. Season liberally with salt and pepper. Place the pan in the oven and bake for 30 minutes.

2. Place a Dutch oven over medium-high heat. Add the rest of the oil, onions, and leeks. Cook 10 minutes. Stir the tomatoes, garlic, and juices into the pan. Stir in the stock, vinegar, and herbs. Use a spoon to crush the tomatoes while they cook. Cook for 20 minutes. Use a stick blender to purée the tomato mixture, or let the soup cool slightly before adding to a stand mixer.

3. Boil again and let any unwanted liquid boil off. Turn off heat and stir in cream. Cover for 5 minutes before serving.

Italian Meatball Soup

Resist the urge to make larger meatballs for this soup. They'll be more likely to fall apart and will take longer to cook. Serve with crusty bread.

INGREDIENTS | SERVES 4

6 cups beef or chicken broth

12 ounces lean ground pork

4 large eggs

⅓ cup freshly grated Parmesan cheese

2 garlic cloves, minced

1 tablespoon parsley, chopped

Pinch ground nutmeg

1½ teaspoons salt

10 ounces fresh ricotta cheese

4 tablespoons unseasoned bread crumbs

1. Add the broth to a large Dutch oven over medium heat. Cover the pan and bring to a boil. Mix the ground pork in a bowl with 1 egg, cheese, garlic, parsley, nutmeg, and ½ teaspoon salt in a large bowl.

2. Once the broth comes to a boil, remove the lid. Use a teaspoon to measure the pork mixture. Roll them lightly between your palms to create a ball shape. Add to the broth. Cover and cook for 10 minutes, or until the meatballs are cooked through.

3. Whisk together 3 eggs, ricotta, bread crumbs, and 1 teaspoon salt. Slowly pour the egg mixture into the broth while stirring briskly to cook in strands. Serve hot.

French Onion Soup

To make your soup even more flavorful, cook the onions for more than 1 hour.

INGREDIENTS | SERVES 6

2 tablespoons olive oil

1 tablespoon butter

3 pounds yellow onions, thinly sliced

1 teaspoon salt

5 cups water

4 cups chicken or beef broth

Thumb size bundle of thyme

1 bay leaf

¼ cup red wine

Pepper to taste

6 slices baguette, cut 1" thick

8 ounces Gruyère or other soft cheese, shredded

1. Place a Dutch oven over medium heat. Add the oil and butter. Once the butter has melted add the onions and salt. Stir to coat. Cover and steam for 10 minutes.

2. Uncover and cook for 20–30 minutes or until the oil has evaporated and the onions are translucent. Reduce the heat to low and cook, stirring frequently, for 1 hour until the onions are brown and there is a crust on the bottom of the pan.

3. Preheat oven to 350°F. Stir in ¼ cup of water and scrape the crust off the bottom of the pan. Cook until the water has evaporated. Scrape the bottom of the pan as you add the remaining water, broth, thyme, and bay leaf. Simmer for 10 minutes. Add the wine and simmer for 10 minutes. Remove from the heat and discard the herbs. Taste before seasoning with salt and pepper.

4. Once the oven has warmed to temperature, place the bread slices on the oven rack and toast for 7–10 minutes. Remove and set the oven to broil.

5. Place six broiler-safe dishes on a baking sheet. Fill each about two-thirds with the soup. Place a bread slice on top and sprinkle the cheese on the dishes evenly. Broil for 5–7 minutes, or until the cheese is brown and bubbly. Cool for 5 minutes before serving.

Garlic Soup

In France this dish is called "aigo bouido," which translates as "boiled water."
It is a classic peasant dish because the ingredients are so basic and inexpensive.

INGREDIENTS | SERVES 4

2 tablespoons olive oil

3 small yellow onions, peeled and thinly sliced

2 large heads garlic, peeled and smashed

2 quarts water

2 teaspoons salt

Large pinch pepper

2 whole cloves

1 bay leaf

1 teaspoon ground sage

1 teaspoon dried thyme

1 teaspoon ground marjoram

4 slices stale bread

Plump Up Your Soup

If you prefer a heartier soup, you can use this as a soup base and add a number of items after the soup has been puréed: 2 cups cooked rice, 2 cups chopped potatoes, ½ cup oatmeal or barley, 1 cup dried pasta, 1 pound chopped white fish, ½ cup shredded Parmesan cheese, 4 poached eggs, 1 cup cooked and shredded chicken or turkey, a strip of crumbled bacon, or a package of baked tofu cut into cubes.

1. Preheat oven to 350°F. Place a Dutch oven over medium heat. Once it's warmed, add the olive oil and onions. Stir frequently. If the onions start to stick, add more oil, and if they start to brown, reduce the heat.

2. Add the garlic to the pot. Stir to combine and cook for 3 minutes. Once you start to smell a warm garlic aroma, and before the garlic browns, turn off the heat.

3. Add the water and dried spices to the pot. Stir to combine. Cover and place in the middle of the oven. Cook for 2 hours.

4. Remove the bay leaf and cloves from the pot and either use an immersion blender or carefully pour the soup into a heat-safe blender and purée. Taste and season accordingly. Toast the bread and then add one slice to each dish. Ladle soup over the bread to serve.

Colcannon Soup

Colcannon is an Anglicization of the Gaelic word for cabbage. This inexpensive soup was traditionally served on Halloween with prizes or coins concealed in it.

INGREDIENTS | SERVES 6

3 slices bacon, cut into matchsticks

2 tablespoons butter

2 cups shredded cabbage

1½ pounds boiling potatoes, peeled and cubed

1 pound leeks, washed and chopped

2 garlic cloves, minced

1 tablespoon flour

4 cups chicken broth

¾ cup heavy cream

¼ teaspoon ground nutmeg

Salt to taste

Pepper to taste

Make Potato Soup Healthier

This is a pretty basic potato soup with leek and cabbage added for texture, flavor, and to provide some vitamins and minerals. But if you'd like to add fiber and more vitamins, you can do so easily by adding kale. Take 1 pound of kale and cut the stem out. Chop it fairly small and add when you add the chicken broth.

1. Place a Dutch oven over medium heat. Once it's heated add the bacon and cook for 4–6 minutes until crispy. Remove the bacon, leaving the fat. Add the butter. Scrape the bottom of the pan as it melts.

2. Reduce the heat to medium-low. Stir in the cabbage, potatoes, and leeks and toss in the butter. Cover and cook for 10 minutes, stirring a few times to prevent sticking. Stir in the garlic and flour and cook for 1 minute.

3. Stir in the chicken broth and bring to a boil. Reduce the heat to low, cover, and simmer until the potatoes are very soft, about 15–20 minutes.

4. Remove the pan from the heat and stir in the cream and nutmeg. Use a potato masher or an immersion blender to break up the potatoes. Taste and season with salt and pepper. Sprinkle with the reserved bacon and serve while warm.

Hearty Gourmet Mushroom Soup

Mushroom varieties can be hard to come by. Regular button mushrooms will work, but if you have other types available, choose a handful of each to add to this recipe. To sauté the mushrooms, refer to Sautéed Mushrooms (page 27).

INGREDIENTS | SERVES 4–6

6 tablespoons olive oil

5 tablespoons butter

1 large red onion, chopped

2 garlic cloves, minced

1 quart veggie or chicken stock

1½ pounds mushrooms, cleaned and sliced

Pinch salt

Pinch pepper

1 quart water

2 tablespoons miso paste

1 tablespoon toasted sesame oil

Soy sauce to taste

1. Place a Dutch oven over medium heat. Add 1 tablespoon of oil, 1 tablespoon of butter, and the onion. Cook for 5 minutes until it is softened but not yet starting to brown. Add garlic and cook for 1 minute, stirring continually. Stir in the stock.

2. Place a skillet over medium heat. Once it is heated, add 1 tablespoon of oil, 1 tablespoon of butter, and a handful of the sliced mushrooms. Sprinkle lightly with salt and pepper. Cook until they've reduced in size and are slightly browned. Remove from the skillet, transfer to the Dutch oven, and repeat with another batch of mushrooms.

3. Add the water to the skillet and scrape the bottom of the pan. Pour the water into the Dutch oven. Add the miso paste and stir well until combined. Once the Dutch oven starts to simmer, reduce the heat to low and simmer uncovered for 15 minutes. Add the sesame oil. Taste and add soy sauce or salt and pepper to taste.

Sweet Potato and Peanut Soup

In the United States sweet potatoes are often a side dish, but in many West African countries they're a main dish. Peanuts are used in many savory dishes and go well with sweet potatoes.

INGREDIENTS | **SERVES 4–6**

1 tablespoon olive oil

1 large white onion, chopped

6 cloves garlic, minced

3 carrots, chopped

2 large sweet potatoes, peeled and cubed

1 teaspoon salt

1 teaspoon cumin

1 teaspoon thyme

1 teaspoon smoked paprika

½ teaspoon turmeric

¼ teaspoon cinnamon

½–1 teaspoon hot sauce

Ground black pepper to taste

1 15-ounce can diced tomatoes

6 cups vegetable or chicken broth

½ cup peanut butter

1 scallion, diced

1. Place a large pot over medium heat. Once it is warmed, add the oil and the onions. Cook for 5–7 minutes. Add the garlic and cook for 1 minute. Add the carrots, sweet potatoes, and the spices and stir thoroughly. Cook for 5 minutes and add a little broth if necessary to keep the vegetables from sticking.

2. Increase the heat to medium-high and add the can of tomatoes and the broth. Stir the bottom of the pan. Bring to a boil. Reduce the heat to low and let the vegetables simmer for 25–30 minutes. Use an immersion blender or potato masher to break up the potato chunks and make smooth.

3. Increase the heat to medium and stir in the peanut butter. Cook for 5 minutes until the peanut butter is thoroughly combined and warmed. Serve over rice with a sprinkle of scallion for garnish.

Sardinian Minestrone Stew

Until the 1900s, Italy was divided into regions and people from each area ate different foods, or ate the same foods differently. The contents of minestrone vary by region, but there are some similarities. They all tend to have chunky vegetables, beans, and a rich broth.

INGREDIENTS | **SERVES 4–6**

2 tablespoons olive oil, plus more as needed

1 celery stalk, chopped

1 carrot, chopped

1 medium white onion, chopped

2 quarts vegetable or chicken stock

2 16-ounce cans chickpeas, rinsed and drained

1 15-ounce can chopped tomatoes, chopped

½ pound arugula, washed and chopped roughly

1 head of endive, sliced in long, thin strips

8 ounces small pasta

Salt to taste

Pepper to taste

1. Place a Dutch oven over medium-high heat. Once the pan is heated, add 2 tablespoons olive oil and chopped vegetables. Cook for 10 minutes. Add a cup of stock and scrape the bottom of the pan.

2. Add the rest of the stock, the chickpeas, the tomato, and the greens and stir to combine.

3. Reduce the heat to low and cover. Cook for 1 hour. Add the pasta and cook for 10 minutes. Taste and add salt and pepper as needed. Once the pasta is al dente, serve it in large bowls with a drizzle of olive oil floating on top.

Crawfish Maque Choux

This Cajun dish (pronounced MOCKshoe) can also be served as a side dish.
It's best made with the sweetest fresh corn you can find.

INGREDIENTS | SERVES 4

2 12-ounce packages frozen crawfish tails, or 2 pounds medium shrimp

½ cup dry white wine

Juice from 1 lemon

½ teaspoon salt

8 ears white corn on the cob

3 tablespoons bacon drippings or olive oil

1 green bell pepper, finely chopped

1 large white onion, finely chopped

¼ cup butter

2 tablespoons heavy cream or whole milk

2 cups chicken stock

1 15-ounce can diced tomatoes, drained

1 teaspoon ground black pepper

½ teaspoon Tabasco sauce

2 tablespoons chopped parsley

1. Place the crawfish or peeled shrimp in a large glass bowl. Add the wine, lemon juice, and salt and toss to combine. Let it marinate for 20 minutes. Stand each ear of corn on end and cut the kernels off. Then run the back of the knife down the cobs to get the corn milk and corn germ out of the cob.

2. Place a large skillet over medium heat. Add the bacon drippings and bell pepper and cook for 2 minutes, stirring frequently. Add the chopped onion and cook until it is translucent and just starting to brown. Remove the vegetables to another bowl.

3. Add the corn, butter, cream, and stock. Stir continuously for 10 minutes until some of the stock has evaporated. Add the tomatoes and cook for 5 minutes.

4. Discard the marinade from the shellfish and add the meat to the skillet. Cook while stirring frequently for 5 minutes. If the mixture seems a bit dry, add some more stock or water. Add the black pepper and the reserved vegetables. Taste before adding Tabasco sauce and salt if necessary. Garnish with parsley. Serve in bowls immediately.

Chicken and Dumplings

This classic American dish isn't health food, but is fairly low-fat. To increase the health benefits, add some chopped vegetables just before you top the stock with biscuits.

INGREDIENTS | SERVES 6–8

2 tablespoons vegetable oil

1 roasting hen, cut into 8 pieces

5 celery stalks, chopped

3 carrots, chopped

1 large onion, chopped

1 garlic clove

1½ teaspoons salt

¼ teaspoon ground black pepper

1 bay leaf

3 quarts water

2 cups all-purpose flour

1 tablespoon baking powder

1 teaspoon salt

1½ cups milk

2 tablespoons melted butter

1. Place a Dutch oven over medium-high heat. Once it's heated, add the oil and one layer of chicken. Cook each side for 3–4 minutes. Repeat with the remaining pieces. Set aside.

2. Add the celery, carrot, and onion and cook for 10–12 minutes. Add the garlic and cook for 1 minute, stirring constantly.

3. Add the salt, pepper, and bay leaf. Place the chicken on top of the vegetables and add enough water to cover the chicken by 3". Bring to a boil. Reduce the heat to low, cover, and cook for 1 hour.

4. Cook, uncovered, for 1 hour. Remove the chicken and set aside. Strain the stock to remove the vegetables and discard. Return the stock to the pan and place over medium heat.

5. Combine the flour, baking powder, and salt in a large bowl. Add the milk and melted butter, stirring to combine. Roll the dough and cut it into biscuits, or leave the dough loose to create drop-biscuits.

6. When the chicken is cool, remove the meat from the bones in bite-size pieces and add to the pan. Once the stock is boiling, drop balls of dough onto the liquid. Reduce the heat to medium-low and simmer, uncovered, for 20–25 minutes. The stock should thicken significantly. Ladle into bowls and serve hot.

Smoked Turkey Chili

New Mexico chilies are often used fresh when they're green and once they ripen and turn red, they're dried and hung in clusters. They provide a rich taste, but not a lot of heat.

INGREDIENTS | SERVES 6–8

1 pound of cannellini or Great Northern beans

Water, as needed

6 dried New Mexico chilies, stemmed, seeded, cut in strips

1 medium yellow onion, chopped

1 tablespoon olive oil

2 garlic cloves, minced

2 teaspoons ground cumin

1 smoked turkey leg

4–6 cups vegetable stock

Salt to taste

Pepper to taste

1. Sort beans and remove any debris. Place the beans in a large pot and cover with cold water by 3". Cover the pan and place it over high heat and bring to a boil. Boil for 10 minutes and remove from the heat. Cover and let soak for at least 8 hours. Drain, rinse the beans, and set aside.

2. Put the pepper strips in a bowl and cover with hot water. Soak for 30 minutes. Transfer the peppers to a blender and add 1 cup of the soaking water. Purée to get a fine texture. Discard the rest of the water.

3. Preheat oven to 325°F. Place a Dutch oven over medium heat and add the onion and oil. Cook for 7–10 minutes, stirring frequently. Add the garlic and cumin. Stir continually for 1 minute, add the pepper purée, and stir to combine.

4. Cut the meat off the turkey leg and chop into small pieces. Stir it into the pot. Add the soaked beans and 4 cups vegetable stock. Cover and bring the beans to a boil. Turn off the heat and place in the oven.

5. Cook for 3–4 hours. If the beans start to dry out, add more broth. Stir the beans every 45 minutes. If the beans seem soupy, remove the lid after 2 hours of cooking to let the liquid evaporate.

Gumbo

The Cajun Roux (page 50) makes the right amount of roux for this dish. If you can't find andouille sausage, a spicy Italian sausage would also work.

INGREDIENTS | SERVES 6–8

2 teaspoons paprika

1 teaspoon garlic powder

½ teaspoon dried oregano

½ teaspoon black pepper

½ teaspoon dried thyme

½ teaspoon onion powder

¼ teaspoon cayenne powder

1 teaspoon salt

1 small frying chicken, cut into 10 pieces

1 pound andouille sausage

2 bay leaves

3 garlic cloves, chopped

2 quarts chicken stock

½ pound okra, cut into ½" rounds

1 pound shelled shrimp

8 ounces crabmeat

½ cup cooked long-grain rice per person

½ cup fresh parsley, chopped

Gumbo: Variety and Myth

Some gumbo recipes only use seafood, some focus more on poultry, others are heavy with sausage. All gumbo is thickened and served over rice. Because there is no original recipe, it's hard to determine where it was invented. It may be a descendent of a French seafood soup called bouillabaisse, but it is also similar to West African stews.

1. Preheat oven to 350°F. Mix all the spices together and rub over the pieces of chicken. Place in a Dutch oven. Cut the sausage at an angle into ¼" thick slices. Sprinkle the sausage over the chicken. Cook in the oven for 40 minutes. Pour off all the fat.

2. Save the sausage on a platter. Lay the chicken pieces out to cool. Once it is cool to the touch, remove all the meat from the bones and set the bones and skin aside for making stock.

3. Place the chicken meat and sausage back in the Dutch oven. Add the bay leaves and any leftover seasoning mix to the pan. Tuck the garlic cloves around the meat with the bay leaves. Cover with chicken stock by 2". Turn the heat to medium-high, cover, and boil. Lower the heat to a simmer and cook for 45 minutes. Stir to prevent sticking.

4. Add the okra and cook for 30 minutes. Sprinkle the shrimp on top, cut up the crabmeat and add to the pan. Cook for 6–8 minutes. Taste and salt if necessary. Ladle the gumbo over rice in a bowl. Garnish with parsley. Serve with Tabasco and crusty bread.

Indonesian Chicken Soup

Indonesia is one of the Spice Islands where many of the spices we use daily were discovered. Most of their dishes use a flavorful spice paste for seasoning.

INGREDIENTS | SERVES 6–8

1 3–3½-pound chicken

2 quarts water

2 stalks lemongrass

Zest from 1 lime

1 teaspoon salt

2 jalapeño peppers or 1 serrano pepper

1 teaspoon ground coriander

1 teaspoon ground cumin

3 shallots, peeled

3 garlic cloves

1 teaspoon ground turmeric

2" piece ginger, peeled

1 package glass noodles

Juice from 1 lime

¼ cup chopped cilantro

1. Place a large Dutch oven over medium-high heat. Rinse the chicken and place breast down in the pan. Add the water. Cut off the base and the tips of the lemongrass and cut the stalk into 4" pieces. Tuck around the chicken. Sprinkle the zest in the water. Bring to a boil and skim the foam off the surface.

2. Once it boils, reduce the heat to low and cover the pan with a lid. Cook for 45 minutes and skim the foam off the top. Meanwhile, combine all of the remaining ingredients except noodles, lime, and cilantro in a food processor. Pulse for several minutes to create a creamy paste.

3. Once the chicken is cooked so the legs are loose, remove the chicken to a platter or bowl. Increase the heat to medium and stir in the flavoring paste.

4. Remove the skin from the chicken and discard. Cut off the chicken in large chunks and discard the bones. Return the chicken to the pot and cook for 10 minutes. Cook the glass noodles according to package directions and serve in bowls topped with the soup, with lime juice and cilantro as garnish.

Beef Goulash

This dish has been made for hundreds of years. Originally, beef was dried in the sun and then rehydrated in water. When it was rehydrated in a lot of water, a stew similar to this would be made.

INGREDIENTS | SERVES 6

3 pounds boneless chuck roast cut into 1" cubes

Salt to taste, plus 1 teaspoon

Pepper to taste

3 tablespoons vegetable oil

3 large white onions, chopped

5 garlic cloves, minced

6 tablespoons sweet paprika

¼ cup all-purpose flour

3 tablespoons tomato paste

3½ cups chicken broth

2 bay leaves

1 teaspoon dried oregano

2 large yellow or red bell peppers, seeded and roughly chopped

½ cup sour cream

Tempering Is Nothing to Get Angry about

A cold sauce (like sour cream, or anything containing eggs) will curdle if poured directly into a hot liquid. Tempering is the solution. Instead of adding cold to hot, add a little hot to the cold and stir quickly to combine. Pour the mixed sauce into the hot liquid and you won't get curdled milk, cooked eggs, or a separated sauce.

1. Preheat oven to 325°F. Place a rack in the middle of the oven. Pat the beef dry and season liberally with salt and pepper.

2. Place a large Dutch oven over medium-high heat. Add 1 tablespoon oil and half of the meat. Cook each side for 2 minutes. After 8–10 minutes the meat should be well browned. Remove it, add 1 tablespoon of oil, and repeat with the remaining beef.

3. Add the remainder of the oil with the onions. Sprinkle in 1 teaspoon of salt. Cook for 8–10 minutes, stirring frequently. Add garlic and stir continually for 1 minute. Stir in the paprika, flour, and tomato paste until everything is well mixed.

4. Whisk in the broth slowly to prevent lumps, and scrape the bottom of the pan. Once the broth is incorporated, return the meat and any juices to the pan. Add the bay leaves and oregano. Cook, covered, in the middle of the oven for 1 hour.

5. Stir the peppers into the pot and cook for 1 hour. Remove the pot from the oven and let rest for 10 minutes covered. Skim the excess fat off the top of the pan. Discard the bay leaves. Temper the sour cream with ½ cup of the pan sauce before stirring it into the pan. Serve over mashed potatoes or boiled egg noodles.

Solyanka

This rich and salty stew is one of the more popular dishes in Russia. A bowl with a large piece of crusty pumpernickel rye bread should be enough to warm up anyone on a cold day.

INGREDIENTS | SERVES 4–6

1 pound cucumbers, diced

2 tablespoons salt

2 tablespoons vegetable oil

12 ounces stew meat chunks, diced

8 ounces bacon, sliced into 1" pieces

4 smoked pork sausages

1 large onion, quartered and sliced

6 cups water

2 tablespoons tomato paste

1 cup black olives

3 bay leaves

¼ cup capers

1 cup sour cream

1 lemon, thinly sliced

1 bunch fresh dill, chopped

1. Place the cucumbers in a colander or strainer. Sprinkle salt over the cucumbers and toss till coated. Let them sit in the colander for at least 20 minutes.

2. Preheat oven to 350°F. Place a Dutch oven over medium heat. Add the oil and beef. Cook for 6 minutes. Turn so all the beef is browned.

3. Remove the beef from the pan and add the bacon. Cook until it is brown but not crispy. Add the sausages and onion and cook for 10–12 minutes.

4. Once the sausages are browned return the reserved meat and add 6 cups of water. Bring it to a boil and reduce the heat to low. Simmer for 10 minutes.

5. Stir in the cucumbers, tomato paste, olives, bay leaves, and capers. Place in the middle of the oven and cook for 30 minutes. Remove when the sausages are cooked through. Stir in the sour cream. Ladle into bowls and serve while warm with lemon slices and chopped dill as garnish.

Basic Beef Stew

The vegetables recommended here are just a suggestion. You could use sweet potato, parsnip, rutabaga, or even celery root for a different flavor.

INGREDIENTS | **SERVES 6–8**

2–4 tablespoons vegetable oil

2½ pounds beef chuck, cut into 2" cubes

Pinch salt, plus 2 teaspoons

Pinch pepper

2 tablespoons butter

2 medium onions, peeled and quartered

5 garlic cloves, crushed

2 tablespoons tomato paste

⅓ cup all-purpose flour

10 cups beef or chicken broth

1 tablespoon dried thyme

2 bay leaves

4 medium red potatoes, cut into large cubes

4 carrots, peeled and cut into 2" pieces

2 celery stalks, cut into 2" pieces

1 can whole, peeled tomatoes

3 tablespoons red wine or balsamic vinegar

Beef Stew Meat Isn't the Best for Stew

Meat labeled "beef stew meat" tends to be small, odd-shaped pieces from different cuts. They're apt to have fat and sinew that requires trimming, and will not cook uniformly. Chuck comes from the shoulder of the cow. It is a flavorful but tough cut that is best when braised, as in stew.

1. Place a large Dutch oven over medium-high heat. Once it's heated, add 1 tablespoon of oil. Season the meat with a pinch of salt and pepper and add one layer to the pan. Cook for about 8 minutes turning so all of the beef is browned. Remove and set aside. Repeat with the rest of the beef, adding more oil as necessary.

2. Add the butter. Once it has melted, add the onion and stir frequently for 5 minutes. Add garlic and cook for 1 minute. Add the tomato paste and cook for 1 minute.

3. Return the beef to the pan and stir until it is coated evenly. Sprinkle the flour over the beef. Stir and cook for 4 minutes.

4. Add the broth and simmer. Add the thyme, bay leaves, and 2 teaspoons of salt. Reduce the heat to low, cover, and simmer for 1½ hours. Add the potatoes, carrots, celery, and tomatoes. Cook for 1 hour. Discard the bay leaves and thyme sprigs. Stir in the vinegar. Taste and season with salt and pepper as needed. Serve warm.

Chapter 16

Recipes for Bakeware and Desserts

Moist Turkey Meatloaf

Ground turkey isn't as flavorful as ground beef and is leaner, so it dries out more easily.
Adding the shredded zucchini keeps it moist and adds flavor.

INGREDIENTS | SERVES 6

1½ pounds ground turkey

½ cup shredded zucchini

¾ cup cooked rice or bread crumbs

1 large egg, beaten

¼ cup ketchup

1 tablespoon soy sauce

1 tablespoon Worcestershire sauce

1 teaspoon dried mustard powder

½ small onion, grated

½ cup chopped green pepper

½ teaspoon ground pepper

1. Preheat oven to 350°F. Place a loaf pan on a rack in the middle of the oven.

2. Break up the ground turkey into slightly smaller pieces in a large bowl. Add the remaining ingredients to the bowl and mix thoroughly with your hands.

3. Remove the loaf pan from the oven and carefully add the ground meat mixture. Drizzle some ketchup across the top, and place it in the oven. Bake for 1¼ hours. Drain the fat and turn onto a cutting board. Let rest for 10 minutes. Slice and serve.

Bread Pudding

Because of the eggs and sugar, it's necessary to use a well-seasoned pan
or a pan that has had the sides greased with butter to keep this dish from sticking.

INGREDIENTS | MAKES 1 LOAF OR 12 MUFFINS

2 tablespoons butter, melted

¼ cup packed brown sugar

1 teaspoon vanilla extract

1 teaspoon ground cinnamon

½ cup whole milk

3 eggs

6 slices of bread, cubed

1. Preheat oven to 350°F. Place loaf pan or muffin pans on the middle rack.

2. Add the melted butter to a large mixing bowl. Whisk in the brown sugar, vanilla extract, ground cinnamon, milk, and eggs. Add the bread to the bowl and press lightly till they have soaked up all of the liquid.

3. Pour the contents into a loaf pan and use a spoon to spread out. Bake for 40 minutes. Or fill the muffin cups about two-thirds with the mix and bake for 30 minutes.

4. Let the pans rest for 10 minutes before running a knife along the outside edge to help dislodge the contents.

Cheddar and Jalapeño Corn Sticks

If you like the jalapeño flavor but don't want the crunchy texture in your sticks, heat the milk till it is not quite boiling and then add jalapeño rings to the milk. Refrigerate overnight and discard the jalapeño before cooking.

INGREDIENTS | MAKES 14 STICKS

1 cup yellow cornmeal

1 teaspoon sugar

½ teaspoon baking soda

½ teaspoon salt

1 cup milk

1 egg

1 cup shredded Cheddar cheese

2 scallions, finely chopped

2 jalapeños, seeded and minced

2 tablespoons melted butter

1. Preheat oven to 425°F. Place the corn stick pans on the middle rack.

2. Combine the dry ingredients in a large bowl. Whisk the milk and egg together. Add the milk mixture, cheese, scallions, and the jalapeños to the dry mixture and stir gently until everything is combined.

3. Remove the pans from the oven and use a brush to apply the melted butter. Pour the batter into the pans, being careful not to get any batter on the outside of the pans.

4. Bake for 12–15 minutes, or until golden brown. Remove the sticks from the pan and let them cool for 5 minutes.

Oatmeal Muffins

If you wish to make a traditional muffin recipe in a cast-iron muffin pan, reduce the oven temperature by 25°F to prevent the outside from cooking before the center does.

INGREDIENTS | SERVES 12–18 MUFFINS

2 cups rolled oats

1½ cups buttermilk

½ cup sugar

2 large eggs

4 tablespoons shortening or butter, small cubes

1 cup all-purpose flour

1 teaspoon baking soda

½ teaspoon salt

1. Place the oats and the buttermilk in a covered bowl and refrigerate for 6–24 hours. Preheat oven to 400°F. Stir the sugar, eggs, and 2 tablespoons of shortening into the oat mixture. Combine the flour, baking soda, and salt, and then fold into the oat mixture.

2. Use the remaining shortening to thoroughly grease each muffin pan cup. Fill the cups two-thirds full with batter. Bake for 20–25 minutes, until an inserted toothpick comes out clean.

3. Once the muffins are cooked through, turn them out of the pan immediately and let cool slightly before serving.

Cherry Almond Cake

When baking bread in a loaf pan that isn't well seasoned, butter the inside of the pan
and cut a piece of wax or parchment paper so it covers the inside of the pan.
When it's finished cooking, grab the paper to lift the bread out.

INGREDIENTS | **MAKES 1 LOAF CAKE**

1 cup fresh cherries

¼ cup all-purpose flour

1 cup butter, softened

½ cup and 1 tablespoon sugar

3 large eggs, beaten

¼ teaspoon almond extract

1⅔ cups self-rising cake flour

½ cup finely chopped almonds

⅓ cup milk

1. Preheat oven to 325°F. Pit the cherries and cut in half. Place them on a plate and sprinkle with all-purpose flour. Toss to coat them evenly and shake to remove the excess.

2. Place the butter and sugar in a mixer bowl and beat until light and fluffy. Add the eggs gradually until well blended. Add the almond extract and combine.

3. Combine the cake flour and almonds. Sprinkle the flour mixture over the wet ingredients and fold in the flour gently. Fold in the cherries and milk.

4. Once the liquid is combined, pour into the loaf pan and bake for 45–60 minutes, or until an inserted toothpick comes out clean.

Indian Vegetable Loaf

This is like a savory cake baked in the oven. But it is also like a vegetarian meatloaf-style dish that can be served as a main-dish or as a side.

INGREDIENTS | SERVES 4–6

4 eggs

1 jalapeño, seeded and diced

1½ teaspoons salt

¼ teaspoon pepper

2 tablespoons vegetable oil or butter

1 medium onion, chopped

½ red bell pepper, chopped

½ cup crumbled fresh cheese or Parmesan cheese

1 zucchini, grated

1 large carrot, peeled and grated

1 cup frozen corn

⅓ cup flour

½ teaspoon baking powder

1. Preheat oven to 350°F. Grease a loaf pan. Beat the eggs with the jalapeño, salt, and pepper in a bowl and set aside.

2. Place a skillet over medium-high heat. Add the oil, onion, and bell pepper. Cook for 5–7 minutes, stirring frequently. Add to the egg mixture. Stir the cheese, zucchini, carrot, and corn into the egg mixture.

3. Mix the flour and baking powder together in a large bowl. Stir in the egg mixture until combined but not smooth. Pour the mixture into the loaf pan and bake in the center of the oven for 25–30 minutes. Cool for 5 minutes before slicing and serving.

Banana Bread

This recipe makes two loaves of bread. If you only want one, cut the recipe in half.
But the second loaf can be frozen for up to 3 months if tightly sealed.

INGREDIENTS | MAKES 2 LOAVES

1 cup butter or shortening, softened
2 cups sugar
1 tablespoon vanilla
2 eggs
½ cup milk
6 overripe bananas, mashed
½ teaspoon salt
4 cups flour
2 teaspoons baking powder
1 teaspoon cinnamon
½ teaspoon nutmeg
½ teaspoon ginger
1 teaspoon ground cardamom

1. Preheat oven to 325°F. Mix the butter, sugar, and vanilla with a hand-mixer until smooth. Beat the eggs in one at a time until the yolk is incorporated. Stir in the milk and bananas until combined.

2. In a smaller bowl combine the salt, flour, baking powder, and spices. Pour the dry ingredients into the wet ingredients and stir until just combined.

3. Pour the mix into two loaf pans. Bake for 45–60 minutes, or until a toothpick inserted in the middle of the loaf comes out clean.

4. Remove from the pan immediately and cool for 5 minutes before slicing and serving.

Mediterranean Olive Bread

Any type of olive can be used in this bread, but a mixture
of black and green olives that have pits will taste best.

INGREDIENTS | MAKES 1 LOAF

Butter, as needed
1½ cups all-purpose white flour
¾ cup whole-wheat flour
1½ teaspoons baking powder
½ teaspoon salt
¾ teaspoon dried rosemary or thyme
2 large eggs
1 cup milk
¼ cup olive oil
½ cup olives, pitted and coarsely chopped

1. Preheat oven to 350°F. Place a rack in the lower third of the oven. Grease a 6-cup loaf pan with butter.

2. In a medium bowl, whisk together the flours, baking powder, and salt. Coarsely grind the dried herbs. Stir it into the flour mixture. In a large bowl, whisk eggs, milk, and oil until the yolks are incorporated. Add the flour mixture and the olives to the liquid mixture. Fold together until the dry ingredients are barely moistened.

3. The thick batter should be scraped into the pan and spread evenly with a spatula. Bake for 40–45 minutes or until a toothpick inserted comes out clean. Cool for 5 minutes before slicing. Serve warm or cold.

Garbanzo Bean Brownies

This recipe makes fudgy brownies. But if you prefer cake-like brownies,
divide the mixture into 2 skillets and bake for 45 minutes.

INGREDIENTS | **SERVES 6–10**

4 eggs

1 can garbanzo beans, drained

1½ cups chocolate chips

1¼ cups sugar

1 tablespoon vanilla

¼ cup chickpea flour

¾ teaspoon baking powder

1. Place a skillet in the middle of the oven and preheat to 350°F. Place eggs in a food processor with garbanzo beans. Purée until very smooth. It should have air bubbles, but stop before it starts to look like a meringue.

2. Melt the chocolate chips in a double-boiler or microwave. Add a few tablespoons of chocolate to the processor and pulse. Then slowly pour in the rest of the chocolate. Scrape down the sides as necessary.

3. Once the mixture is a uniform color, add sugar and vanilla. Purée 1 minute. Add flour and baking powder. Purée until incorporated. Pour mixture into a skillet and bake 1 hour. Cool 5 minutes before turning out and cutting.

Popovers

Cast-iron muffin or popover pans are best for this recipe because you can heat them
before adding the batter. This makes the rising process quicker.

INGREDIENTS | **MAKES 6–8 POPOVERS**

Butter, as needed

2 eggs, room temperature

1 cup milk, room temperature

1 tablespoon vegetable oil

1 cup flour

½ teaspoon salt

1. Preheat oven to 400°F. Grease each cup of the pan generously with butter or solid vegetable shortening. Place the pan in the oven and bring to temperature.

2. Combine remaining ingredients in a blender and blend for slightly less than 1 minute. Scrape down the sides several times. When the pan is heated through, remove it from the oven and fill the cups halfway with batter.

3. Bake for 35–40 minutes. Popovers should be puffed and golden. To prevent them from collapsing, do not open the oven for 35 minutes. If they seem wet after 40 minutes, pierce with a butter knife, turn off the heat, and return them to the oven for 5 minutes.

Ebelskiver

This Scandinavian pancake was traditionally made with apple slices, but can be made with any filling, or served plain with powdered sugar or syrup on top.

INGREDIENTS | SERVES 4–6

3 eggs
2 tablespoons sugar
3 tablespoons melted butter
1½ cups buttermilk
½ cup milk
½ teaspoon salt
1 teaspoon vanilla extract
2 cups flour
1 teaspoon baking soda
1 teaspoon baking powder
2 tablespoons canola or vegetable oil
¼ cup fruit syrup, or ½ cup cooked fruit chunks

Savory Ebelskivers

If you want to make something more suitable for dinner, leave out the sugar and the vanilla extract. You can add 1 tablespoon of dried herbs, 2 tablespoons of minced fresh herbs, drop a small piece of soft cheese in the middle of each depression while cooking, mix in 2 cloves of minced garlic, or even stir in ½ cup of grated Parmesan cheese.

1. Separate the egg whites from the yolks and place into two bowls. Whip the whites to a stiff peak. Beat the yolks with the sugar, butter, milks, salt, and vanilla. Sift the flour, baking soda, and baking powder together. Stir it into the egg yolk mixture. Fold in the egg whites.

2. Place the ebelskiver pan over medium heat and let it warm for several minutes. Use a basting brush to brush the depressions with oil. Once the pan is hot, fill the depressions half way with batter. Place ½ teaspoon syrup in the center of the depression and cover with more batter if necessary. Cook for 1–2 minutes on the first side or until there are visible bubbles and the surface starts to look dry.

3. Use a skewer or a crochet hook to lightly pierce the cooked edge of the batter and flip it upside down. Repeat in the same order the depressions were filled. Cook for 1 minute before removing. Oil the depressions again and repeat until all the batter has been used. Serve warm.

Fresh Fig Muffins

You can often find fresh figs in grocery stores during the fall.
They are also available frozen or dried.

INGREDIENTS | **MAKES 12 MUFFINS**

8 fresh figs

¼ cup dry sherry

1⅔ cup flour

½ cup almond slivers

1 teaspoon salt

1 teaspoon baking soda

1 teaspoon cinnamon

1 teaspoon nutmeg

1½ cup sugar

½ cup vegetable oil

2 eggs

Rehydrating Dried Figs

Dried figs are easier to find than other types. Place 2 cups of apple juice or water in a small sauce pan and bring it to a boil. Place the figs into the liquid and let them sit for 2–4 hours. The figs will be ready for this recipe.

1. Preheat oven 350°F. Remove the stems and cut the figs into ¼" slices and then into ¼" cubes. Place them in a small bowl and add the sherry. Let sit for about 15 minutes.

2. In a medium-sized bowl, combine the flour, almonds, salt, baking soda, cinnamon, and nutmeg. In a separate and larger mixing bowl beat the sugar, oil, and eggs. Reduce the mixer speed to low and slowly add the flour mixture.

3. Fold the figs and sherry in by hand, being careful not to over-stir. Pour the batter into a well-greased muffin pan. Bake for 1 hour and 15 minutes.

4. When the top has browned and a muffin feels slightly firm, remove them from the oven. Let them sit in the pan for 10–15 minutes. An inserted toothpick should come out clean. Turn onto a rack to cool further.

Corn Sticks

Most people love the crunchy edges of cornbread. Using corn stick pans permits everyone to enjoy the crunchy exterior and soft interior.

INGREDIENTS | **MAKES 2 TRAYS OF CORN STICKS**

Vegetable oil, as needed, plus 2 tablespoons

⅓ cup flour, sifted

1 teaspoon sugar

1 teaspoon baking powder

½ teaspoon baking soda

½ teaspoon salt

1⅓ cups yellow cornmeal

1 egg, beaten

1 cup sour cream

¾ cup milk

1. Preheat oven to 400°F. Use a basting brush to thoroughly apply vegetable oil to the corn stick pans. Place the pans in the middle of the oven.

2. In a medium bowl combine the flour, sugar, baking powder, baking soda, salt, and cornmeal. In a large bowl whisk the egg, sour cream, milk, and 2 tablespoons vegetable oil. Once it is thoroughly combined and the egg is completely incorporated, pour the dry ingredients into the wet ingredients. Stir until the dry ingredients are moistened but not smooth.

4. Remove one of the pans. Use a small cup or spoon to fill the pan about two-thirds with batter. Place the first tray in the oven and repeat with the second. The pans should sizzle when you add the mix.

5. Bake the sticks for about 25 minutes, or until golden brown. Carefully remove from the pan immediately. Serve while hot with butter and honey.

Cherry Pudding Cake

This is a modification of the traditional French recipe known as Cherry Clafouti.

INGREDIENTS | SERVES 4–6

1 pound cherries, pitted

1 tablespoon butter

1 cup sugar

4 eggs

½ teaspoon vanilla extract

1 tablespoon brandy or amaretto liqueur

1 cup all-purpose flour

1½ cups milk

Powdered sugar, optional

Cherries Are the Pits

It's hard to remove pits from cherries without a cherry pitter, but it isn't impossible. If you don't have one, you can put an icing piping tip base-down on a plate or shallow bowl and press the cherry over the tip. You can also open a paperclip and use it to cut and scoop out the pit.

1. Place a rack in the center of the oven and preheat to 425°F. Wash the cherries. Remove the stems and pits.

2. Place a skillet over medium heat. Once it's heated, stir the cherries, butter, and ¼ cup of the sugar in the skillet. Cook for 5–7 minutes. Once the butter and sugar have melted and started to caramelize turn off the heat.

3. Combine the remaining ingredients except the powdered sugar in a blender and pulse for 60 seconds. Scrape down the sides of the carafe. Pour 1 cup of the batter in the skillet and cook in the oven for 5 minutes.

4. Pour the rest of the batter into the skillet and return it to the oven for 15–20 minutes or until an inserted toothpick comes out clean. Slide the cake out of the skillet and let it rest for 10 minutes before slicing. Sprinkle with powdered sugar and serve.

Cornbread

Sweet cornbread is common in the South. If you prefer your cornbread savory, just eliminate the sugar. You can also mince two jalapeños and add them to the mix if you like it spicy.

INGREDIENTS | SERVES 6–8

2 cups yellow cornmeal

1 teaspoon kosher salt

¼ cup sugar

2 teaspoons baking powder

½ teaspoon baking soda

1½ cups buttermilk

2 eggs

2 tablespoons vegetable oil

1. Place a skillet in the middle of the oven and preheat to 425°F. In a bowl combine the cornmeal, salt, sugar, baking powder, and baking soda. Whisk together until well combined.

2. In a large bowl whisk together the buttermilk and eggs. Once the yolks are completely incorporated, pour the dry ingredients into the wet ingredients. Stir gently to combine. Add more buttermilk if necessary to get a pourable consistency.

3. Add the vegetable oil to the skillet and swirl to coat the bottom and sides. Pour the batter into the skillet. You should hear the batter sizzle.

4. Bake for 20 minutes. If you press gently in the middle of the cornbread it should spring back. Let it cool in the skillet for 10 minutes before serving.

Buttered Rum Pineapple

This is similar to the caramelized glaze on the Pineapple Upside-Down Cake (page 298). The addition of rum deepens the flavors.

INGREDIENTS | SERVES 4

½ cup brown sugar

¼ cup dark rum

3 tablespoons butter

1 pineapple, cored and cut into ½" slices

1. Place a skillet over medium heat. Once it is heated through, add the brown sugar, rum, and butter and stir until the butter is melted and bubbling.

2. Place the pineapple slices in the skillet one at a time and cook for 3 minutes or until they're warmed through. Serve while hot.

Dutch Apple Baby

The "Dutch" in this name actually refers to the German-American immigrants known as Pennsylvania Deutsch.

INGREDIENTS | **SERVES 4**

2 Golden Delicious or Granny Smith apples

¼ cup unsalted butter

¼ cup sugar

2 tablespoons ground cinnamon

3 tablespoons sugar

¾ cup all-purpose flour

¼ teaspoon salt

¾ cup whole milk

4 large eggs

1 teaspoon vanilla extract

Confectioner's sugar or whipped cream for garnish

1. Preheat oven to 425°F. Core the apples and cut into ¼" thick slices. Place a skillet over medium heat and once it's heated, add the butter and apples. Sauté in the melted butter for 3–4 minutes. Stir in the sugar and cinnamon and cook for 3–4 minutes. Spread the apple slices evenly over the bottom of the pan.

2. Mix the dry ingredients in a large bowl. Mix the wet ingredients in a smaller bowl. Once the eggs are whipped and combined, pour into the dry ingredients and stir to combine. Pour the batter mixture over the apple slices, being careful not to move the apples. Bake for 15–20 minutes. The mixture will puff up considerably and the top will brown. A toothpick inserted should come out clean.

3. Remove from the oven and slide a knife along the outside of the skillet to loosen the edges. Place a plate on top of the skillet, and flip the pan upside down to transfer it to the plate. Let it cool for 10 minutes before sifting with confectioner's sugar or serving with whipped cream.

Pineapple Upside-Down Cake

This cake is the perfect dessert to make in a cast-iron skillet. Making the caramel in the pan and then pouring the cake batter on top makes the caramel become part of the cake.

INGREDIENTS | SERVES 7

1 18-ounce can pineapple rings
4 tablespoons butter
½ cup brown sugar
7 maraschino cherries
4 tablespoons cold butter
1 cup brown sugar
2 large eggs
½ cup milk
½ cup sour cream
1½ teaspoons vanilla extract
1½ cups all-purpose flour
1½ teaspoons baking powder
½ teaspoon salt

The Flip Side of the Pineapple Upside-Down Cake

In 1925, the Hawaiian Pineapple Company ran ads looking for creative pineapple recipes. They received 1,500 recipes for the pineapple upside-down cake. The winning entry came from Mrs. Robert Davis of Norfolk, Virginia, and was published in their cookbook.

1. Preheat oven to 350°F. Place a skillet over medium-high heat. Drain the juice from the can of pineapple into the skillet. Add 4 tablespoons butter and ½ cup of brown sugar. Stir with a wooden spoon as everything melts. Boil to a thick caramel-like consistency. Turn off the heat, lay 6 pineapple rings around the outside and 1 in the center of the skillet with a maraschino cherry in the center of each ring. Place in the oven to preheat the pan while you prepare the cake.

2. Combine the cold butter and sugar in a mixing bowl until it is light and creamy. Beat in the eggs one at a time. Make sure the first egg is completely incorporated before mixing in the second. Add the milk, sour cream, and vanilla. Stop mixing once it is combined but not smooth.

3. Sift together the flour, baking powder, and salt. Use a spatula or spoon to fold in the wet ingredients. Remove the skillet from the oven and pour the batter in. Gently shake the skillet back and forth to even out the batter. Bake for 45–50 minutes.

4. Let sit for 5–10 minutes. Place a large plate upside down on top of the skillet. Turn the skillet upside down. If any caramel or fruit sticks, remove with a spatula and place it back on the cake. Let the cake cool for 10 minutes before serving.

Irish Soda Bread

*The acid in the buttermilk is what causes the loaf to rise and make air bubbles.
If you don't have buttermilk, substitute plain yogurt that has half a lemon squeezed into it.*

INGREDIENTS | MAKES 1 LOAF

3 cups all-purpose flour

1 cup cake flour

2 tablespoons sugar

1½ teaspoons baking soda

1½ teaspoons cream of tartar

2 teaspoons salt

3 tablespoons butter, softened

1½ cups buttermilk

1. Place a rack in the upper third of the oven and preheat to 400°F. Place a Dutch oven on the rack. Whisk together the flours, sugar, baking soda, cream of tartar, and salt. Cut 2 tablespoons of the butter into small bits and use forks or a pastry knife to work the butter into the flour mixture until it's crumbly and coarse.

2. Add the buttermilk and stir with a fork until the dough has just come together. Sprinkle some flour onto a surface and knead the dough until everything sticks together and it is still bumpy.

3. Pat the dough into a circle the size of your pan and no more than 2" thick. Cut an X into the top of the dough.

4. Place the dough in the Dutch oven, cover, and bake for 20 minutes. Bake, uncovered, for another 20–25 minutes. Rub the remaining butter on top of the crust and let the loaf sit for 30 minutes or until it has cooled.

Upside-Down Apple Pie

If you prefer, you can substitute vegetable shortening for the butter when making the crust. Peeled apples will give a better texture, and soak up more caramel.

INGREDIENTS | SERVES 8

2¼ cups all-purpose flour

¼ cup confectioner's sugar

¾ teaspoon salt

6 tablespoons butter, cold and cubed

1 egg, lightly beaten

2 tablespoons cold water (if needed)

6 tablespoons butter

⅔ cup granulated sugar

¼ teaspoon nutmeg

1 teaspoon cinnamon

½ teaspoon ground cardamom

3 pounds Fuji or Granny Smith apples, cored, peeled, sliced

1. Add the flour, sugar, and salt to a food processor. Pulse a few times. Add the cold butter and pulse till it resembles coarse cornmeal. Pour the mixture into a bowl. Stir in the egg until chunks form. If necessary, add a little cold water to get this consistency. Press the chunks together into a disk and wrap in plastic wrap. Refrigerate for at least 1 hour.

2. Place a rack in the middle of the oven and preheat to 375°F. Place a skillet over medium-heat. Add the butter and when melted add the sugar. Cook for 5 minutes. Stir in the spices and cook for 1 minute more. Turn off the heat.

3. Layer the apple slices around the outside of the pan so the tips are touching the skillet wall and the thin edge of each slice is under the thicker edge of the slice next to it. Fill in the center with apple slices. Cook over high heat for 12 minutes or until the caramel mixture is very dark and the apples have soaked up most of it. Tilt the pan to cover the apple slices with juice. Cook for 5 minutes. Turn off the heat.

4. Meanwhile, roll the dough between 2 sheets of parchment paper into a 14" circle. Place the dough on the skillet. Tuck the dough edges under so they touch the skillet but are not visible. Cut four 1" slits in the center of the pie.

5. Bake for 20–25 minutes or until the crust is golden brown. Let cool for 20 minutes. Loosen the edges of the crust with a knife. Place a plate on top of the skillet and invert. Scrape out any apples that stick and rearrange them on top.

Not-So-Fancy Apple Foldover

Apples and Cheddar cheese are good together if you like salty and sweet.
These flavors meld together in a baked pie.

INGREDIENTS | SERVES 8

2½ cups all-purpose flour
½ cup cornmeal
½ cup sugar
2 sticks cold butter, cubed
½ cup cold water in a spray bottle
2 tart apples, peeled, cored, thinly sliced
3 tablespoons cider vinegar
¼ teaspoon ground nutmeg
¼ teaspoon ground mace
2 tablespoons butter
½ cup shredded sharp Cheddar cheese
1 teaspoon flour
1 egg white

1. Place the flour, cornmeal, and 3 tablespoons sugar in a food processor and pulse several times. Add half of the butter and pulse 8–10 times to get even-sized lumps. Add the rest of the butter and repeat. Spray the top of the flour with water until it is evenly dampened. Pulse three times, wait 30 seconds, and pulse three more times. Press on the dough. It should come together. Repeat the spraying if it doesn't.

2. Pour the dough into a large sealable bag and mold into a disk. Refrigerate for 30 minutes.

3. Preheat oven to 400°F. Place a skillet over medium heat. When warm, add the apples and toss for 30 seconds. Add the vinegar. Stir for 30 seconds or until the vinegar evaporates. Add ¼ cup sugar and toss to combine. Cook for 2–3 minutes, or until the apples start to soften.

4. Remove the skillet from the heat and add the spices and 2 tablespoons butter. Stir until the butter has melted and coats the apple. Stir in the cheese. Cool apples in a bowl to room temperature. Clean the skillet.

5. Place the dough between two sheets of wax paper. Roll until it is about ¼" thick. Slide the dough into the skillet. Pile the apple mixture onto the center, leaving about 2" of crust on all sides. Sprinkle the apples with flour. Fold the extra crust toward the center and pinch where the edges meet.

6. Brush the top of the crust with the egg white and sprinkle with 1 tablespoon of sugar. Bake in the center of the oven for 30 minutes. The crust should be golden brown. Let the pie rest for about 20 minutes before serving.

Appendix

Online Resources

The Wagner and Griswold Society
www.wag-society.org
This organization promotes collecting cast-iron and aluminum cookware and can provide help with determining the origin of antique cookware.

The Pan Man
www.panman.com
David Smith has a collection of links, books, catalogs, and items for sale available on his personal website.

eBay
www.ebay.com
eBay is the most popular place to purchase used and collectible cast-iron cookware online. Prices and quality can vary so let the buyer beware.

International Dutch Oven Society
www.idos.org
This nonprofit organization seeks to preserve and continue the use of Dutch ovens in the United States. They have an annual conference and a World Championship Dutch Oven Cook-Off every year.

Arkansas Dutch Oven Society
www.arkdos.org
This website collects information about regional Dutch oven societies and gatherings throughout the United States.

Dutch Oven University
www.dutchovenuniversity.com
The Miklaszewiczs offer classes in Abbotsford, Wisconsin. A lot of information about using Dutch ovens over campfires is available on this website.

Lodge Cast-Iron
www.lodgemfg.com
This company has been making and selling cookware in the United States for more than 100 years. They offer information about their line of cookware, as well as information about using, caring for, and collecting cast-iron cookware.

What's Cooking America:
The Irreplaceable Cast-Iron Skillet
http://whatscookingamerica.net/Information/CastIronPans.htm
If you're looking for more information about how to revive a cast-iron pan that looks worse-for-wear, this site may be able to help you.

Cast-Iron Cookware Shop
www.castironcookwareshop.com
This website has the largest variety of cast-iron cookware available. They sell from a variety of manufacturers. They also have a thorough blog with more information about specific pans, cooking techniques, cleaning, general care, and history (*http://castironcookware.storeblogs.com*).

Black Iron Dude
http://blackirondude.blogspot.com
Greg has a list of articles with pictures of cleaning techniques, recipes, seasoning tips, and more.

Cooking In Cast-iron
www.cookingincastiron.com/page2/page2.html
This group blog has five writers who take turns writing about their adventures in cooking with cast-iron cookware.

Standard U.S./Metric Conversion Chart

VOLUME CONVERSIONS

U.S. Volume Measure	Metric Equivalent
⅛ teaspoon	0.5 milliliter
¼ teaspoon	1 milliliter
½ teaspoon	2 milliliters
1 teaspoon	5 milliliters
½ tablespoon	7 milliliters
1 tablespoon (3 teaspoons)	15 milliliters
2 tablespoons (1 fluid ounce)	30 milliliters
¼ cup (4 tablespoons)	60 milliliters
⅓ cup	90 milliliters
½ cup (4 fluid ounces)	125 milliliters
⅔ cup	160 milliliters
¾ cup (6 fluid ounces)	180 milliliters
1 cup (16 tablespoons)	250 milliliters
1 pint (2 cups)	500 milliliters
1 quart (4 cups)	1 liter (about)

WEIGHT CONVERSIONS

U.S. Weight Measure	Metric Equivalent
½ ounce	15 grams
1 ounce	30 grams
2 ounces	60 grams
3 ounces	85 grams
¼ pound (4 ounces)	115 grams
½ pound (8 ounces)	225 grams
¾ pound (12 ounces)	340 grams
1 pound (16 ounces)	454 grams

OVEN TEMPERATURE CONVERSIONS

Degrees Fahrenheit	Degrees Celsius
200 degrees F	95 degrees C
250 degrees F	120 degrees C
275 degrees F	135 degrees C
300 degrees F	150 degrees C
325 degrees F	160 degrees C
350 degrees F	180 degrees C
375 degrees F	190 degrees C
400 degrees F	205 degrees C
425 degrees F	220 degrees C
450 degrees F	230 degrees C

BAKING PAN SIZES

U.S.	Metric
8 × 1½ inch round baking pan	20 × 4 cm cake tin
9 × 1½ inch round baking pan	23 × 3.5 cm cake tin
11 × 7 × 1½ inch baking pan	28 × 18 × 4 cm baking tin
13 × 9 × 2 inch baking pan	30 × 20 × 5 cm baking tin
2 quart rectangular baking dish	30 × 20 × 3 cm baking tin
15 × 10 × 2 inch baking pan	30 × 25 × 2 cm baking tin (Swiss roll tin)
9 inch pie plate	22 × 4 or 23 × 4 cm pie plate
7 or 8 inch springform pan	18 or 20 cm springform or loose-bottom cake tin
9 × 5 × 3 inch loaf pan	23 × 13 × 7 cm or 2 lb narrow loaf or pâté tin
1½ quart casserole	1.5 liter casserole
2 quart casserole	2 liter casserole

Index

Note: Page numbers in **bold** indicate recipe category lists.

Image Credits